Arcturians:
How to Heal, Ascend, and Help Planet Earth

channeled through David K. Miller
with additional commentary by Gudrun Miller

Other Publications by
David K. Miller

Teachings from the Sacred Triangle, Vol. 1

Teachings from the Sacred Triangle, Vol. 2

Teachings from the Sacred Triangle, Vol. 3

New Spiritual Technology for the Fifth-Dimensional Earth

Connecting with the Arcturians

Raising the Spiritual Light Quotient

Kaballah and the Ascension

Biorelativity

Arcturians:
How to Heal, Ascend, and Help Planet Earth

channeled through David K. Miller

with additional commentary by Gudrun Miller

LIGHT Technology
PUBLISHING

ISBN-13: 978-1-62233-002-7

Published and printed in the United States of America by:

PO Box 3540
Flagstaff, AZ 86003
1-800-450-0985
1-928-526-1345
www.lighttechnology.com

This book is dedicated to Oliver Hauck, a Group of Forty member in Germany who is also the producer and director of the movie The Blue Jewel, *an award-winning documentary about planetary healers.*

Table of Contents

Introduction

This book is based on channelings and lectures that I gave during the years 2011 and 2012. Some of these channeled lectures were given in workshops in Spain and Australia. This book also contains lectures from Gudrun Miller, who was also a presenter in the seminars. Her lectures in this book cover a range of fascinating material related to starseeds, soul work on Earth, hypnotic regressions into past lives, and personal issues related to the ascension.

My channeling experiences began in 1994, when I received spiritual guidance from Juliano, an Arcturian guide and teacher. Through his guidance and instruction, I have developed and explored new spiritual concepts related to such subjects as planetary healing, personal ascension, and new spiritual tools for self-development. Some of the new planetary tools include: Biorelativity, shimmering, the Sacred Triangle, ascension (both personal and planetary), thought projection and remote healing energy, etheric crystals and how they relate to the new Earth meridians, and planetary cities of light. All of these concepts have been discussed in my earlier books, which are also now available through Light Technology Publishing. Further information and updates on all of these subjects will be explored in this new edition.

Familiarity with these concepts is not required for the first-time reader of this book. The articles and the explanations of these new spiritual technologies can stand on their own and will be understandable to all new readers. However, for those already familiar with my work, further explanations of these tools are offered here, along with newer ideas, updates, and perspectives.

The Earth crisis and the shifting of Earth changes continue to dramatically unfold. As I am writing this introduction in the beginning of 2013, the crisis in the biosphere still remains unresolved, and a new spiritual energy and perspective is desperately needed to help humanity develop the resources and perspective to properly resolve our planetary problems. It is always helpful to receive a new spiritual perspective from other higher-dimensional beings in our galaxy. Lectures in this new edition also are given by other ascended, higher-dimensional masters such as Sananda, Vwyamus, and the Native American ascended guide and teacher Chief White Eagle.

I have tried to promote these new spiritual teachings and perspectives through the development of an international planetary healing group called the Group of Forty. I have also tried to expand these teachings personally by traveling around the world, offering channeled workshops on these important subjects. This book offers a compilation of my most recent efforts in working toward the goals of extending the Arcturian perspective on healing planet Earth.

I would like to offer a special acknowledgment of gratitude to Magda Ferrer and David Arbiz, both of whom are Group of Forty members and coordinators in Sant Pere de Ribes, Spain. David and Magda oversaw and coordinated the transcriptions of these lectures. Thank you, Magda and David, for your devoted work and assistance. I also would like to acknowledge the assistance of my wife and devoted partner, Gudrun Miller. Finally, I would like to thank the over 1,200 Group of Forty members around Earth who are working with me to create a new Earth balance.

David K. Miller
Prescott, Arizona
January, 2013
www.groupofforty.com
davidmiller@groupofforty.com

BOOK I:

A Summary of New Spiritual
Technologies from the Sacred Triangle

BOOK 1
Part 1

Juliano, the Arcturians,
Archangel Metatron,
and Chief White Eagle

through David Miller
Turkey, May 2011

CHAPTER ONE

Introduction to Spiritual Light Technology

Juliano and the Arcturians

Greetings, I am Juliano. We are the Arcturians. We are interested in your spiritual evolution because Earth can become part of the galactic hierarchy. This means that there now is an opportunity to become part of a family. There are many things that are happening in this part of the galaxy where Earth is.

One of the things that is happening is a powerful alignment. This alignment has been called the 2012 alignment. This means that Earth is coming into a special relationship with the galactic center. The Native American peoples in Mexico, known as the Maya, have predicted this alignment. They have described this as a time of great changes and events that could be somewhat catastrophic. Events could become much more powerful and disruptive than even current Earth changes now. This means that a clearing or purification is going to happen to Earth. But this change will not mark the end of time or the end of the world calendar, as they say.

The Sides of the Sacred Triangle

What does it mean to have a special alignment with the center of the galaxy? It means that a special energy, a New Earth–type of vibrational energy, is coming to Earth. This new energy brings some new and powerful ideas. These new ideas and energy are based on the fifth-dimensional paradigm. I want to talk about this new paradigm. We have called this new paradigm the Sacred Triangle because it represents a new way of understanding reality. The old patterns that have been in place are not going to work. So a new idea and new techniques are needed. We

3

want to discuss the new spiritual technology. The old spiritual ideas are still good, but a new paradigm is necessary to describe what has to happen.

The new paradigm that we are working with is called the Sacred Triangle. It is the integration of three powerful energies on Earth. The first energy is called the *galactic spirituality*. Galactic spirituality is the spiritual thinking that includes other dimensions and planets besides Earth. We understand Earth's situation in relation to other planets. For example, we will look at a prophet like Jesus. Jesus was here on Earth but he also visits other planets. I must say that the other planets have been more receptive to him and have treated him very well — better than he was treated here on Earth.

On the subject of galactic spirituality, we will discuss the whole nature of the planet. Galactic spirituality will speak about a planet as a living spiritual being and also includes the study of different dimensions. The subject includes the archangels as fifth-dimensional beings, as well as other fifth-dimensional beings like us, the Arcturians. And galactic spirituality includes information about the ascension and an understanding that there is a technology and a teaching about how to ascend. We, in galactic spirituality, will study the natures of a planet and how a planet can ascend.

Let us look at the next side of the Sacred Triangle, which is the **White Brotherhood and Sisterhood**. This is a term that describes the family of the ascended masters from all religions. If you take all of the higher mystical thoughts of Christianity, Judaism, the Muslim religion, the Hindu and the Buddhist religions, as well as many of the other religions, you will find that the mystical sides of these religions are similar and they use similar language. We call this side the White Brotherhood and the White Sisterhood because the color white represents purity and integration of high energy. White refers to the pure energies of what these groups work with.

The third side of this triangle represents the *native energies* of the world. This originally was made for the Native Americans in America, but it changed to encompass all of the native peoples around the world. One of the reasons why the native energies are chosen is because the native peoples have a long history of being able to pray and interact with the energy of Earth.

Biorelativity
The ability of being able to relate to Earth as a spiritual being includes the concept of Biorelativity. Native peoples have a history of how to practice Biorelativity. The idea of the Sacred Triangle includes integrating all three: the native side, the

White Brotherhood and Sisterhood side, and the galactic spirituality side. We are saying that these three sides must be united and then a new healing paradigm comes. This new paradigm is going to be used for both personal healing and planetary healing.

The next new spiritual technology includes the concept of the planetary healer and planetary healing. In planetary healing, we are saying that people can work to heal Earth. Let me explain the word "healing" in terms of the planet. Healing Earth means helping to preserve the biosphere for humanity. This also assumes that Earth wants to hold and support humanity. This means that Earth is honored to have humans on her and that Earth wants to work with humankind to hold this special energy that is necessary. The planet can ascend. Yes, you can ascend and the planet can also ascend. We are also working on techniques and methods for planetary healing using the Sacred Triangle. I would like to give some instructions on becoming a planetary healer. Some of you came to Earth to be planetary healers.

The Spiritual Light Quotient

Now I will speak about the concept of the spiritual light quotient. The spiritual light quotient is a concept that includes the awareness of the relationship between spirituality and Earth. The spiritual light quotient is a measurement to determine how well people understand spiritual concepts. In my early teachings, I compared it to the intelligence quotient used by psychology, but your intelligence quotient often declines as you get older. However, the spiritual light quotient can increase as you get older. There are things you can do to raise your spiritual light quotient. You can go to spiritual workshops, you can go to spiritual places to connect with higher energy, you can meditate, you can read books, and you can also work with others to enhance and accelerate the spiritual energy you work with.

It is important that we raise the spiritual light quotient of cities and the entire planet. Remember, there is a relationship between the spiritual light quotient and the technology and spiritual wisdom of a planet. The spiritual wisdom can only increase if the spiritual light quotient goes up. We will encourage the activities for raising and holding the spiritual light quotient. To this purpose, we created the Group of Forty to participate in group practice that focuses on spirituality on Earth, and it gives you an opportunity to connect with other people who share similar ideas and feelings.

Shimmering

Another spiritual technique is called shimmering. Shimmering is a method used to help you practice being in the fifth dimension. In the shimmering practice, first you bring your aura or your energy body in the physical world to a high vibration and then you direct your spirit to leave or travel from your third-dimensional body to your fifth-dimensional body. You also need a focus area to direct your energies to the fifth dimension. This means that we help you by identifying a place where you can comfortably hold your fifth-dimensional body, and then you will make this comfortable place available so that you can shimmer yourself to the fifth-dimensional place. That place is called the Arcturian crystal lake or temple. Shimmering is the idea of accelerating your spiritual energy and light. In the shimmering process, you actually raise your vibration. Now I want to explain thought projection.

Thought Projection

Thought projection is the ability to direct your spiritual aura, your spirit, to another level and place, just by directing it, just by projecting yourself there through thought. This projection usually happens through a corridor. Corridors are gateways, hallways, to the fifth dimension. You can travel through the corridor by using your thoughts to project yourself. One of the important roles of the planetary healer is to create corridors from Earth to higher dimensions. The ascension is actually a point where the dimensions — that is, the third and fifth dimensions — intersect. At that point of intersection, there is a transfer of energy that can only occur when there is such an intersection. And this connection is increased by many different methods.

One of the methods of increasing the power of the connections between the two dimensions has to do with setting up corridors; another method has to do with using a special planetary crystal healing method. We call this planetary healing method the technique of the etheric crystals. In this technique, we designate places on Earth that are receptive as holders of fifth-dimensional energy, and with special group energy and participation, we download Arcturian etheric crystals in these special places. These places that receive the etheric crystals and hold the light and the energy become attractors of fifth-dimensional energy into Earth. There are now twelve etheric crystals on Earth. They are in different parts of the planet.

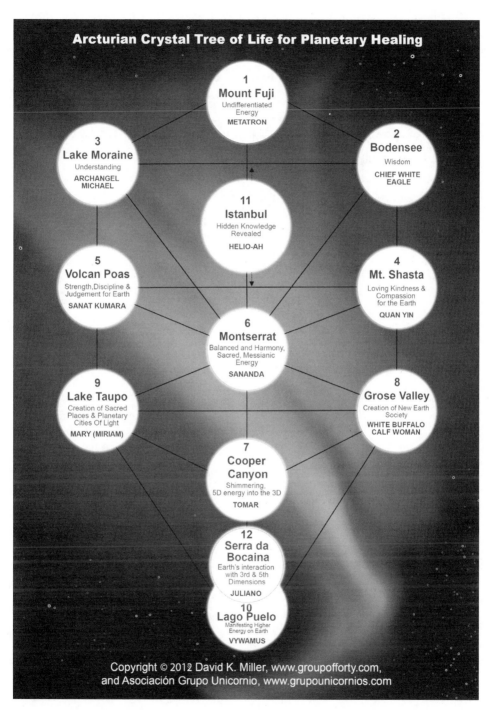

An update to the Tree of Life, which we call the Arcturian Planetary Tree of Life

For example, in 2009 we downloaded an Arcturian etheric crystal in Istanbul because we feel it is a very sacred area for the planet and this area can easily be an attractor of fifth-dimensional energy. We used starseed Group of Forty group participation when we did this downloading. The locations of the other etheric crystals are found in the map on the previous page.

Each one of these places has sacred and fifth-dimensional energy. We want to work with the energy of these etheric crystals, and we want to do more shimmering and thought-projection exercises using the crystals. We will also discuss how these areas can be used to increase the power of etheric healing. I am Juliano. We are the Arcturians.

CHAPTER TWO

The Planetary Tree of Life

Juliano and the Arcturians

Greetings, I am Juliano. We are the Arcturians. You have come to Earth for personal development and personal evolution, and many of you have also come to Earth for service to the planet. Now we want to spend some time looking at how a person can be of service to the planet.

Let us look at how to understand a planet. We were excited when the pictures of Earth were delivered to humans from the space shuttle and the space program. This was the first time that everyone on Earth had a picture of how the planet looks from space. This view from space helps in working on Earth's energy field. Earth has an energy field just as you do. Earth's energy field can also have problems; it can have holes in its aura. For example, nuclear bombs can cause holes in the aura and Earth's life-force energy can leak out.

Earth also has an energy field linked to the galaxy. As Earth moves through the galaxy, it comes across different particle waves. Remember that some Earth changes and things that affect Earth come from the position Earth is in at the time it is going around the Milky Way. We want people to consider their relationship to Earth and how each person can help to send healing to the planet. We call this activity being a planetary healer, and 2011 is the year of the planetary healer. You and others have awakened in consciousness to develop techniques and technology to heal Earth. For example, people like you can get together in groups and begin to visualize calmness in the atmosphere. You can visualize a peaceful vibration in Earth so that there are no earthquakes. These activities send thought waves to the spirit of Earth. Remember, thought waves are also vibrations.

Balance in Judgment and Compassion

We have shown you our update of the Tree of Life, which has been modified to be used as a tool for planetary healing. We call this the Arcturian Planetary Tree of Life. Planets go through different transitions and changes. Visualize the Planetary Tree of Life. For this discussion, I want you to consider that you have one row of spheres on the right and one row of spheres on the left. Using that image, we are going to talk about the energies of planets. Some planets have gone through the same crisis as Earth. The crisis involves the overuse of resources, the creation of destructive weapons, and the abuse of the planet's environment. Some of the other planets did not solve the problem, and they ended up destroying themselves. Such planetary destruction is a possibility on Earth — but Earth now has a lot of people who are willing to become planetary healers.

Let me talk about the spheres and how they can relate to a planet. It is said in the *Kaballah* that there were other planets, and this is true. There have been many other planets with other life forms that were human-like. Let us say that one sphere on the Planetary Tree of Life represents justice and another sphere represents planetary compassion.

When justice rules a planet, this also could mean that strong punishment is implemented for mistakes made. If you do something wrong, then you are immediately punished. If a planet has a lot of justice energy and there are many people on the planet making mistakes, before you know it, everyone is going to die due to severe punishment. Certainly, lower-consciousness people make mistakes.

On the other hand, let us look at a planet that has only compassion. People make mistakes and you have compassion for them. You might say, "Oh, they are trying the best they can. They are really good people." You will give them a break. There will be no punishment today, but you will give them a warning: "Do not do this again. We know you will listen and learn your lesson." On a planet, you need to have both a balance between justice and compassion. So you have justice on one side, and on the other side you have compassion. They go together and work together.

The energies of judgment and compassion are used to balance the energies of a planet. If the planet has judgment and no compassion, this becomes a big problem, as many things are destroyed through punishment. But if you have compassion without judgment, then there is too much compassion and this can become a problem. For example, to demonstrate how to understand balancing compassion with justice, imagine that you capture a terrorist, and you say to the terrorist compassionately, "I understand why you are killing people. There are many things that you think are wrong in the world, and you are trying to correct them. We will let you go because you are really trying to do something that is good." In this example, having too much compassion means that you would let the criminals go free. There has to be a balance between compassion and judgment.

Let us take those two ideas of compassion and justice and apply the principles from these energies to look at Earth. As a planet, Earth has a lot of compassion for humanity. Humanity has done many negative things to the environment. Humanity has used many nuclear bombs and there are too many people on the planet. Earth is working hard to help humankind live here, but Earth also has an energy in her that can be called judgment. Some people call this energy Earth changes or the energy of purification. If Earth goes too far out of balance and there is too much distortion and destruction to the planet, then Earth can react with judgment and deliver punishment.

An Energetic Balance Must Be Kept

Many people have difficulty understanding how a planet can use judgment. To understand this, I have to explain to you another new concept: the Earth feedback loop system. This system within Earth is working to keep a certain energetic balance for life. If there is too much rain on one part of the planet, then Earth balances it with more dryness on another. If there is too much blocking of Earth energy in rivers, perhaps from dams, Earth may decide to have some more volcanic eruptions. That could help to balance Earth using the feedback loop system.

There are certain animals and life forms that contribute to keeping a certain balance on Earth now. For example, the dolphins and the whales are playing a very important role in the balance. They are helping energetically to keep a balance in the ocean and for life on Earth. But people do not yet scientifically understand how a species such as the dolphin could play a central role in keeping a planetary balance. In other words, what does the dolphin do to keep the ocean alive? The truth is that the dolphin and the whale are necessary for life to survive in the ocean. There are still people in some countries killing dolphins and whales. In many parts of the world, the dolphins are committing suicide and are showing up on the beaches. This is not a good sign. This is one example of how humanity needs the help of other species to keep a planetary balance.

Right now we have to look at the planet as a whole system. We cannot give too much compassion to people who are destroying the dolphins and the whales, because if they continue to do that, then the ocean life is going to die. Maybe there needs to be more justice delivered to people whose negligence is destroying valuable animals in the ocean. The same thing applies to nuclear energy. The nuclear energy destroys key elements in the biosphere of the planet. There are many nuclear dumpsites on this planet where nuclear reactors reside and where bombs are being made. Sometimes compassion for this activity is not going to help. Earth knows how to correct an imbalance. Some of the methods that a planet will use to correct imbalances created by humans may not be very pleasant for humankind.

Let me give you another simple example of balancing compassion and justice that occurs in the Bible: Noah's flood. Here is a story of an Earth change and justice being demonstrated. In this example, because of humanity's evilness, God delivered a flood in order to purify the Earth. Do we want that kind of event now? No. We want to find ways that Earth can be brought into balance without catastrophes such as floods.

I want you to think again of the spheres in the Planetary Tree of Life: three spheres on the right and three spheres on the left. I want you to think about the idea of sacred places of holy energy. Sacred places are places where humans have agreed to protect the energy. There are many examples of sacred energy sites in the world. The Native Americans have many sacred mountains, and they protect them. If an oil company comes, they try to stop the development because they say the place is sacred and it cannot be developed. On one hand, there are people who want to use everything available on the planet, even if the resources needed are on sacred sites. The counterbalance to humanity's exploitation of the environment is that we need to create more sacred places. One of the things that planetary healers do is work to counterbalance all of the use and exploitation of the planet with creating more sacred spaces. At this time, there is a tremendous need for more sacred places.

Guided Meditation: Planetary City of Light Activation

This brings me to the next important subject in planetary healing: the planetary cities of light. The planetary cities of light are small cities that have starseeds living in them, and they are making the cities sacred. The starseeds say that they are creating a special energy boundary of higher light around the city. This means that only higher unified energy will be allowed to develop and come into the city. The method that we use for creating this is to use the starseeds to go around the city and to meditate and visualize a high-energy light field surrounding the city.

As an exercise to demonstrate this technique, I want you to look at the space you are in now, and I will demonstrate an exercise of a planetary city of light activation. Focus on the center of the room, and I will give you the instructions. I want you to understand that this type of exercise will be done for the activation of a city of light. Visualize a circle of white light around the room. I am bringing down a corridor of light into the center of the room. I want you to see that a large basket is above this building. It is an etheric spiritual energy basket. I, Juliano, bring the basket down into the room and underneath the whole room. So the whole room is now sitting on the basket.

Now we are going to lift the basket together. This means that we are lifting the room up into the corridor. Very slowly, with my help, together we raise the room up into the corridor, and we bring the basket up the corridor to a higher platform and into a garden that is in the fifth dimension. We all can feel this wonderful fifth-dimensional light. The whole room is activated with this beautiful energetic light. Great fifth-dimensional light is healing the room. Light from other fifth-dimensional sources is now also being downloaded into this beautiful room on the platform in the fifth dimension.

Now we are going to bring the room down in the basket and back into the third dimension. Very slowly, we drop the basket down the corridor and all the light and energy that we gathered is staying in the room, and the room is back in the third dimension as the basket is now back. This room is now highly activated with fifth-dimensional energy and light. People who come into this room will feel it. This will also mean that this room will help other people who need to receive this kind of energy. But lower-vibrational energy will just bounce away; it will not be able to come into the room.

I want you to imagine doing the same thing for a whole city. When we do this type of activation for a whole city, we place crystals around its boundaries. We have people go around the same city as much as possible at the same time. They will use the etheric basket to raise the city up. They will do this exercise periodically to maintain the energetic boundary of the city. We recommend that you work in a small neighborhood instead of a large city, because it would be too much to make a whole city a city of light. It is better at first to work in a section of a large city. Right now there are over fifty planetary cities of light that have received this kind of energy on the planet. This is creating a new balance. The planetary cities of light are balancing the overuse and the exploitation of the planet. Remember, the Planetary Tree of Life is showing the different balances versus imbalances. Humankind can influence and help create balances. These exercises are tools for planetary healing. I am Juliano. We are the Arcturians.

CHAPTER THREE

The Eleventh Etheric Crystal in Istanbul

Juliano and the Arcturians

Greetings, I am Juliano. We are the Arcturians. The twelve etheric crystals contain powerful fifth-dimensional magnetic energy. The energy in the etheric crystal is connected to the fifth dimension, and each etheric crystal has a particular vibration. This means that every place has a certain vibration. The Istanbul etheric crystal is related to the idea of hidden knowledge. Knowledge is hidden deep in the history of this area. We know that there have been many civilizations that have come through this area and that a lot of ancient knowledge from many civilizations has been preserved here. And now we must find ways of opening up the hidden knowledge to everyone. This hidden knowledge can mean something to you at a personal level because there is hidden knowledge about you that is available here. This means that there are secrets about you, about who you were in your past lives, and what your goal is here in Istanbul.

The hidden knowledge can come on both a personal level and on a planetary level. You know that crystals magnify and increase the power of a thought. There is a way for you to send your thoughts to a crystal so that the crystal will then take those thoughts and increase their power. It is like an amplifier that increases the power of a sound or a signal. Imagine that you send a thought to the etheric crystal. Then the thought that you have is magnified in power. It becomes stronger and stronger. This is an important concept in planetary healing because a small number of people with the right thought can increase the power of that thought so that it becomes more energetic. Basically, the Istanbul etheric crystal is right in

The etheric crystal of Istanbul lies a mile below these waters.

front of and below the famous Fatih Sultan Mehmet Bridge. This is a bridge across the Bosphorus waterway.

The crystal is in the water, and it is almost one mile deep. This crystal is now connected to the other eleven crystals around the world. I would like you to think about this question. The question is: "What hidden knowledge about yourself do you want to become known to you?" It could be anything about yourself that could be helpful. In the work of the etheric crystal techniques, we measure the power of the thought. Imagine that you have five watts of energy, but then you send the five watts into an amplifier and the amplifier sends back twenty-five watts — so five watts in and twenty-five watts out. In the Arcturian crystal vocabulary, we use the word "arcan" as the measurement of the power of a thought. By sending five arcans of thought energy into the crystal, you will amplify the thought to twenty-five arcans. This is a big increase. Imagine also that you say, "I want the hidden knowledge of the world to be revealed." Maybe there is hidden knowledge in how to better rule the world or how to clean our nuclear waste. That hidden knowledge can be opened up and revealed.

Exercise: Amplify Thought Energy

Now we will begin the exercise. Visualize the place of the eleventh etheric crystal that I have described in Istanbul. Focus your energy on the area in front of the Fatih Sultan Mehmet Bridge. I, Juliano, am using my powers to raise that beautiful crystal out of the water. You are there by the bridge and shore right now, and you

Send your thoughts to the etheric crystal and it will be transmitted all around Istanbul.

see very bright, beautiful sunlight coming up as the crystal is raised. This beautiful sunlight is radiating like a rainbow from that area.

Connect to your third eye now by projecting light from your third eye directly into that etheric crystal by the bridge. You are helping to strengthen this etheric crystal. Send the thought from your third eye to the crystal. Say: "I want to be able to receive hidden knowledge about myself." Or say: "I am receiving hidden knowledge now about myself." And send that thought to the crystal that is now above the water. The power of that thinking is now going to come back to you five times stronger than when you sent it in. Be open now, in the next twenty-four hours, to new thoughts that will come to you, new information that will come to you about this etheric crystal and about yourself. Even now it could be coming back to you at this moment. Special and hidden knowledge about you is coming because you are being activated. Be ready to receive new light. There is a bright light. You will see that people will immediately begin talking about how there is an unusual light in front of the bridge.

Now, in the second part of this exercise, I want you to think that hidden knowledge about planetary healing will be revealed around the world. Remember, you are sending the thought, "Hidden knowledge on healing Earth will be shown now." What I want you to do is send that thought to the crystal, and then it will be transmitted all around Istanbul. We will receive this energy from your thinking as you send it directly to the crystal that transmits it outward. And then it is going to be transmitted around the whole world.

Let the hidden knowledge on healing the planet be opened up now and transmitted around the world. Let the hidden knowledge about yourself now be opened up. Stay open now to any information that you can receive. There is much hidden knowledge that will be revealed. Now, return to yourself and your normal consciousness. The hidden knowledge is being revealed to you now. I am going to leave this etheric crystal above the water for the next three to four hours.

I have seen a shape of diamonds. Does this have a relation to the Arcturian crystal?
Yes. Keep open to the images and what you see now. You are opening up. You will get a lot of visions and information. Do not censor; do not limit.

Let the light of the hidden knowledge be activated and transmitted around the world. This is Juliano. We are the Arcturians.

CHAPTER FOUR

The Ascension Ladder
and Shimmering

Juliano and the Arcturians

Greetings, I am Juliano. We are the Arcturians. We would like to discuss now another new idea of fifth-dimensional spiritual technology. New spiritual technology means that there are new techniques to interact with the other dimensions. So there needs to be a shift in the mind and also a new understanding of what your energy field is like because everything is vibrating and you exist in an electromagnetic energy field. You are able to use certain techniques to project yourself. This method is called thought projection. Thought projection is based on thinking. Thinking and thought are the fastest energies in the universe. Thinking and thought are faster than the speed of light. The new spiritual technologies include thought projection, shimmering, and using the corridors for thought projection. We have new spiritual technology to aid the planet in its fifth-dimensional work. Some of the spiritual technology for healing the planet includes the ring of ascension, the twelve etheric crystals, the planetary cities of light, and the main technique of Biorelativity, of course.

The Arcturian Crystal Lake

Let us talk about the Arcturian crystal lake. The Arcturian crystal lake is a special place that we are maintaining and holding for you. It is in the fifth dimension. We know that sometimes it is difficult to travel through the fourth dimension to the fifth dimension. We believe that it is better to have your destination in the fifth dimension. The crystal lake provides you a fifth-dimensional destination so that you can direct yourself to this place.

This lake holds a beautiful crystal. The crystal itself is so big that the whole crystal is in the water, and the lake itself is one mile in diameter. The lake is helping to keep the power of the crystal lower because the energy from the crystal is so powerful that it can make you faint. We slowly and carefully can raise the crystal out of the water. In shimmering, we work with the Arcturian crystal lake and with the idea that your fifth-dimensional body has a multidimensional presence in the crystal lake area.

Multidimensional presence means that you are operating in two bodies at the same time. Remember, time is circular. You can think of daytime and nighttime. In daytime you are in waking consciousness, and at nighttime you are in a sleep state in which you are dreaming. You are in the dream state, the dream consciousness. If the line and time are circular, then time comes together. You can interact with your dreamtime and with your normal consciousness.

I use this example because I want you to think about the crystal lake the same way you think about dreamtime. You are in dreamtime in certain hours of the day, but you can interact with the dreamtime at any time. You can decide to take a nap and go into dreamtime during the day. You can go into the fifth-dimensional consciousness at any time. You have a fifth-dimensional presence and body at the crystal lake. And you can visit it any time you want to. You need to learn the technique of how to project your spirit to your fifth-dimensional body.

The Technique of Shimmering

We have developed and are teaching a special method called shimmering. In shimmering, we work with the shape and pulse of the aura. We begin to increase the pulse of the aura. For example, let us say that the aura has a certain pulse. You can think of the pulse of your aura based on the outline of the aura. The aura's pulse might sound like this — this would be a representation of the speed: [tones: *Ta-ta-ta*]. You notice that it is a little bit slow. In the shimmering, we want to speed up the pulsing, the speed. [Tones (more quickly): *Ta-ta-ta*.] Now we increase in speed again. At a certain point of increase in speed, you begin to shimmer.

I can give you a description of shimmering in two ways. The first way is to describe what it would look like if people were looking at you from outside and they were watching you shimmer. They would see you flicker like a candle in the wind, your body going in and out, in and out. Eventually you flicker so much that your spirit leaves your body and goes directly to your fifth-dimensional body. After you have left your body, your presence is in the fifth-dimensional body. But your physical body in Earth is still flickering in and out.

When your pulse reaches a certain level, I will have the channel say the word: "Shimmer, now." That means that you are going to be able to transport your spirit to your fifth-dimensional body. Then your spirit goes to your fifth-dimensional body on the crystal lake, and you will be there in a cross-legged yoga position, receiving your third-dimensional body. Then you will be in your fifth-dimensional body and you will receive the light and energy from the fifth dimension. After you are there for a while, you will have absorbed a lot of the fifth-dimensional energy, and then you shimmer back to your third-dimensional body. And I will say again, "Shimmer in your fifth-dimensional body." Then I will say, "Shimmer back to your third-dimensional body now." I will repeat the instructions again when we are doing the exercise. When I say, "Shimmer back," you are going from your fifth-dimensional body back to your third-dimensional body.

Is this astral travel?

Yes, it is very similar, but in astral traveling, you can go to places in the fourth dimension. This is only going to the fifth dimension. We bypass the fourth dimension in shimmering.

Exercise: Shimmering

We will now begin the exercise. Please try to put yourself in a comfortable position. Follow your breathing, listen to my voice, and become aware of your aura and the pulse of your aura. [Tones (speeding up): *Ta-ta-ta.*] Begin to shimmer. Shimmer, shimmer, shimmer. Shimmer to your fifth-dimensional body. Shimmer to your fifth-dimensional body, now!

You are now in your fifth-dimensional body. Absorb the fifth-dimensional energy into your body. You are in your fifth-dimensional body in the crystal lake. I, Juliano, am going to raise the crystal out of the water a little. The crystal is now a third of the way out of the water. You can feel the powerful crystal energy in your third eye. In your fifth-dimensional body, your third eye and your crown chakra are wide open.

Now I am going to leave the crystal one-third above the lake and we are going to go back into your third-dimensional body. When you return, you will bring the fifth-dimensional energy with you. So when I say, "Shimmer and then back," you will then bring your spirit body back into your third-dimensional body. Feel yourself still in your fifth-dimensional body. [Tones: *Ta-ta-ta.*] Shimmer. Shimmer. Shimmer. Shimmer. Shimmer from your fifth-dimensional body back to your third-dimensional body now. Shimmer back now. You are back in your third-dimensional body, but you have brought with you all of the energy that you could from the fifth dimension.

We will do another round of shimmering. Remember the shimmering is also a preparation for your ascension. Shimmer in your third-dimensional body to your fifth-dimensional body. Now you are back into your fifth-dimensional body again. The crystal is now one-third above the crystal lake. As we are here around the lake, we are receiving powerful energy from this crystal.

I, Juliano, am also connecting with the eleventh crystal in the Istanbul area. Remember that this crystal is by Anadolu Hisar almost in front of Sultan Mehmet Bridge. And this crystal is now rising up a little bit. And it is receiving an activation light from the crystal in the crystal lake.

Shimmer. Shimmer. Shimmer. Shimmer, shimmer, shimmer back to your third-dimensional body. Shimmer back to your third-dimensional body now. You are now back in your third-dimensional body. You are connected to the Arcturian crystal in the crystal lake.

You are shimmering, but you will stay in place now. Shimmer, shimmer, shimmer, shimmer, shimmer, shimmer. You have a deep connection now to the Arcturian crystal lake and to the crystal here in Istanbul. You can use this crystal to activate interaction with fifth-dimensional light. Shimmer. Your fifth-dimensional body is ready to work with you now at any time you wish. When you nap, you go into your dream body. Now when you close your eyes and meditate, you can go into your fifth-dimensional body.

The crystal in the crystal lake is also coming back into the water. You are comfortably experiencing this fifth-dimensional energy in your body. This completes our exercise on the shimmering. Do you have any questions or reports you wish to make about the exercise?

I have seen beautiful colors again: violet, purple, and dark blue. I felt this very concentrated energy.

The idea of the shimmering is that you also bring back this energy into your third-dimensional body. I am Juliano. We are the Arcturians. Good day.

CHAPTER FIVE

The Keys for Ascension

Archangel Metatron

Greetings, I am Archangel Metatron. I am working with the Arcturians for the ascension. I am a guardian for the stargate. The stargate is that place you will be able to go to after the ascension. Through this beautiful gate, you will be able to go on to other places of high energy. But I am also here to talk to you about the ascension, the keys of ascension, and the unlocking of the keys of ascension. You have the program to ascend within you. That means that your body knows how to ascend. This may sound unusual, but your body knows how to ascend and how to die. Maybe you do not know how to die as an ego state, but your body does know how to go through the dying process so that you can leave this plane. Also you, your mind, and your body have the information on how to ascend.

We speak about unlocking the codes of ascension. That means that there is a certain energy that is helping you open up to your own ascension. In the *Kaballah*, we say that the tones and sounds carry the energy. There is a special tone and a special energy sound that have a certain vibration for the ascension. Remember, the power of words is in the vibration of the tones of the words. I am going to sing the tone to activate the ascension energy within you. These tones and words are going to be in ancient Hebrew. The vibrations of these words are actually of a galactic origin. Some of the words and tones were actually brought from other parts of the galaxy. These tones and sounds are known in many parts of the galaxy. You just need to listen and let the tones and sounds do their work on you. They may even sound familiar to you.

[Tones and sounds: *Hebrew words.*]

Feel the tones and the vibrations of the tones activating your ascension energies. Now please return back into your body. Know that this activation has a great effect on preparing you for your ascension. When the opportunity for ascension begins, you will be receiving a sound. The nature of that sound is going to be the activation for your ascension. Blessings from the stargate. I am Archangel Metatron. Good day.

CHAPTER SIX

Chief White Eagle Talks in Istanbul

Chief White Eagle

Greetings, I am Chief White Eagle. It is wonderful to be here in Istanbul, home of the great crystal in the Bosphorus [a strait forming one of the boundaries between Europe and Asia] and a city of such wonderful history and so many different energies from all over the world. This is a true city of global energy.

I, Chief White Eagle, am happy to meet with you, and also happy that you are open to understanding the ways of the Native peoples. The Native peoples in North America are often very connected to Earth in their ancient ways. And now we are seeing that many of the white people are looking to us for spiritual guidance. Only 200 years ago — or even less — they thought we were primitive people. They thought we were very primitive and did not know anything.

Sacred Words about Earth

We knew from our prophecies that this time in the twenty-first century would come and that our knowledge and abilities would be important to Earth. We have been practicing Biorelativity for many, many moons. In many ways, Biorelativity is part of our culture. We talk to Earth, saying, "Oh, Mother Earth, please hear our words. We are here gathered as planetary healers, and we want to offer our open-heart energy to you, Mother Earth. We know that you can hear us and we also want to hear you. We want to know what it is that we can do to help you be more in balance."

I, Chief White Eagle, am here to be of service to Mother Earth. All my relations. Ho. We are gathered here in a talking circle, and I ask that you each say a word of prayer for Earth. We will now pass the stick around, and I am going to ask each of you to say something to or about Mother Earth. Please start by saying, "All my words are sacred," and then your name.

First participant: All my words are sacred. I am Gudrun, spirit painter. I want to praise you, Mother Earth, for all the beauty that I see in all the places that I visit. I am especially moved in Istanbul by the beautiful Bosphorus strait. I thank you for allowing us to place the crystal in the Bosphorus. All my relations. Ho.

Second participant: I am so happy to be here on Earth, experiencing this beautiful life, with the leaves on the trees and the sounds of birds, trees, and nature. Hopefully we will be able to protect all these beauties for the next generations. All my relations. Ho.

Third participant: I want to help protect all these beauties. I will do my best. I am thankful for everything in this Earth. Thank you. All my relations. Ho.

Fourth participant: I feel very connected with Chief White Eagle. I will try to enlighten everyone about Earth and the environment. I will try to explain the dynamics and warn everyone kindly. Whenever I touch food, I am thankful for it and for the people who helped it grow. I wish this Mother Earth would be a much prettier place. All my relations. Ho.

Fifth participant: I am thankful for everything. I have a question: What is the first caution that must be taken into account to help Mother Earth be in balance again?

Sixth participant: Everyone can do something for Earth. This is my thinking. I will do my best to protect Earth. All my relations. Ho.

Seventh participant: Earth is part of our life. Earth is part of us. We cannot live without Earth. We must heal Earth in order to heal ourselves. When we heal ourselves, we heal our Earth, our world. When we do something for Earth, we do something very powerful for ourselves. All my relations. Ho.

You are all speaking so beautifully to Earth. This is the first step in Biorelativity: Talk kindly to your mother. From our perspective, Earth is feminine; it is our mother. I want to ask each of you to think about this: How do I treat my mother?

How do I treat Earth? What can I do to be a planetary healer? I want you to think about the role of the planetary healer on Earth now. We also sing to Earth. We have special chants, because Earth has a vibrational energy field, as you do.

[Chants.]

Open your heart to Earth. Open yourself to your mission for Earth. You have something special to give Earth. Open yourself to the fifth dimension and receive from your guides instructions on what you can do for Earth. Find more sacred places in your country. There are many ancient spirits in your land. They will guide you to sacred land and sacred areas. We are all brothers and sisters. The time is right for White Buffalo Calf Woman to return. She represents the great feminine light that is coming to Earth. She will show us the way through the feminine wisdom. Here in Istanbul, you have the great representation of Saint Sofia. Divine wisdom is the feminine light. Agia Sofia is holding feminine energy and light for the world. White Buffalo Calf Woman is a great feminine healer. Ho.

Feminine Energy and Light

Now I would like to ask each of you to speak from your heart and tell me how you see the feminine energy and light, and how the powerful new feminine light can help Earth.

First participant: All my words are sacred. I am Gudrun, spirit painter. I see the powerful feminine light as a powerful regeneration and renewal, as the power of growth, compassion, and love in spite of all that has happened here on Mother Earth, and as the power of wisdom and forgiveness. All my relations. Ho.

Second participant: The feminine energy is mother energy; it is protective. It protects with affection and compassion. All my relations. Ho.

Third participant: The feminine energy is compassionate, just like a mother. It protects her children, just like a mother. All my relations. Ho.

Fourth participant: The feminine energy is creative and productive. Its power comes from compassion. All my relations. Ho.

Fifth participant: The feminine energy is reproductive; it expands and it never ends. All my relations. Ho.

Sixth participant:The feminine energy covers everything; it feeds energy, even male energy as well. It is increasing in the world, because feminine energy has much more compassion than any other energy. All my relations. Ho.

Seventh participant:The feminine energy pours affection to people. I believe that in the ancient times, women ruled society and there was more love at that time, because females are mothers. I hope that we will have a better society with feminine energy, full of love and without the cruelty we have now. All my relations. Ho.

Eighth participant: I think that the feminine energy is the energy of beauty. It emanates beauty around the world. All my relations. Ho.

Ninth participant:The feminine energy contains both female and male energy, because women give birth to men. All my relations. Ho.

Tenth participant:The feminine energy is protective like a mother, compassionate. It takes its power from love. All my relations. Ho.

Eleventh participant: We have a connection in our right brain to the Creator. We carry our feminine energy in this right hemisphere, so the feminine energy connects us to the Creator. All my relations. Ho.

You are all speaking from your hearts, and this is creating a wonderful energy to send to Earth. The fact that you are gathered in a circle is making your words more powerful.

Now I want to speak to you about the idea of miracles. I know that Juliano was talking to you about time. The time he was referring to was linear: past, present, and future. We agree and have the view that time is a circle. We honor our elders, the ancient ones who are still in our mountains and valleys in spirit. I am sure that in Turkey it is the same — you feel the ancient spirits. There are many ancient areas and beautiful sacred lands in this country.

The energy from the spirits of the ancient ones needs to be called on. We need to talk to the ancient spirits, because they are also guarding much of the beautiful sacred areas on the planet. We are connecting ourselves to the past, because the past is still alive in our ancient spirits and relatives. When we are speaking to the ancient ones, we are asking them to help as well.

We are also calling on all the spirit guides of the people here to be with us. Remember that I said we are going to talk about miracles. The word "miracle" implies something that is not logical; it transcends logic. Many of the problems we face on Earth now do require miracles. We need miracles to solve our problems, because they look like they are not going to be solved with normal thinking. The planetary healer is open to miracles. The planetary healer is open to working with ceremonies and talking to Earth. The planetary healer is interested in working with groups and building up energy to create the planetary cities of light.

[Chants.]

Projecting Energy for the Fifth-Dimensional Earth

Let us walk around the circle. The circle represents time — past, present, and future. Feel the connection to your past. Feel the connection to your present. Feel the connection to your future self. Feel the connection to Earth and her past. Feel the connection to Earth as you know her now. See Earth as a fifth-dimensional planet. Know that the fifth-dimensional planets are living in harmony with the population. Earth will be a fifth-dimensional planet. You will help to unlock the codes of ascension for Earth.

Let us project energy for the fifth-dimensional Earth. I will ask each of you to speak of the vision you may have about how the fifth-dimensional Earth will appear. We, the Native peoples, love to get visions. We love to speak and tell our visions to others. When we speak our vision, it gives power to the vision so that it may happen. Now I will ask you to speak of the vision you have about what a fifth-dimensional Earth looks like to you.

First participant: All my words are sacred. I am Gudrun, spirit painter. When I think of Earth in the fifth dimension, I visualize small communities living in harmony. I hear much laughter and joy. I see people living together as equals, doing their soul work and finding fulfillment. I see Earth as very beautiful, very green, and very fresh. All my relations. Ho.

Second participant: I feel the peace of being at home with no evil and no cruelty, only love and compassion. I had to go back there. It was a long journey. Now it is time to rest in peace. All my relations. Ho.

Third participant: I have seen a greener Earth and a flow of water in the middle of the green valleys. There were children. I thought it was the purity of reincarnation. All my relations. Ho.

Fourth participant: I have a vision for Mother Earth in the fifth dimension that I have just created. All people will hold hands all over the world. It all begins with a sound, and a huge energy emanates everywhere and everyone feels equal, without disconnection. We all live in love. All my relations. Ho.

Fifth participant: All my words are sacred. I dream of a world where there is no race and no religion, and there are no social status differences. People do not need to be rude. There is full equality. There is only love, and you are described as rich if you share the most. I see the fifth-dimensional world like this. All my relations. Ho.

Sixth participant: I have seen a world with no holes in its aura. All the water sources are clean. All people are happy and healthy, just like the world. All my relations. Ho.

Seventh participant: This is a place where there is finally peace and love. My world in the fifth dimension is a very beautiful world with green valleys, purple trees, and singing birds. There are blue rivers, and everyone is happy. It is very beautiful. All my relations. Ho.

Eighth participant: I think I am an eagle in this world, because I have seen a very beautiful land, but I was at the top of it. I have seen mountains, and I felt very secure. There was no reason for fear. Finally, I felt myself free. I was maybe flying or walking, but free. It was just great and beautiful. All my relations. Ho.

Again, you are all speaking from your hearts, but your visions are also important. Let those visions enter the center of the room, and then send them to Earth. There is a universal unconscious for Earth. The new images of the fifth dimension are important. You can send that light, idea, and vision into Earth. That will have a good effect on Mother Earth too. The Earth receives your images and beautiful thoughts.

The Planetary Cities of Light and the Just Society

I want to say something about sacred cities and the just society. The planetary cities of light are sacred cities activated by the starseeds. These cities can also create a new and better social justice system. This is what is going to come in the fifth-dimensional Earth: sacred areas and a just society. The galaxy will be in alignment with the central part of this solar system, your Sun. In other words, your Sun is going to come into alignment with the Central Sun of the galaxy. This Sun is sending out great spiritual energy and light.

The alignment means that there is going to be a new wave of energy coming from the fifth dimension to Earth. Some people will not understand it and will become more confused, but others will be able to use this new energy as a force to bring in the fifth-dimensional energy and make it work on Earth. People will realize that Earth does have a relationship to the galaxy. Earth needs humanity to help her ascend. I call on the energy from Mount Fuji, I call on the energy from Jerusalem, and I call on the energy of Sedona, Arizona.

There is a ladder of ascension in Sedona — a natural ladder that is opening up as a corridor to the fifth dimension. At the moment of ascension, you can go to the place where there is a ladder of ascension. There is also a ladder of ascension on the Dome of the Rock in Jerusalem. This is exactly the place where Mohamed ascended. And now there is a fifth-dimensional corridor over the Dome of the Rock.

When the ascension occurs, the dimensions will intersect. They will come together briefly, and it will be a great day to be alive; it will be a great day to ascend. We will all be together in spirit in the presence of one another. You will be proud of your work here on Earth as a planetary healer. I am Chief White Eagle. All my words are sacred. All my relations. We are one with you. We are a great star family. Ho.

CHAPTER SEVEN

The Year of Planetary Healing

Chief White Eagle

Greetings, I am Chief White Eagle. We are here to greet you as our brothers and sisters. All of us are one family. We are also united with the star family. We, the Native Americans, have known for a long time that we are part of the star family. We are not just a family on Earth. We are also a family with the stars, where we come from. Part of our family tree — part of our family DNA — has come from the star family out in the galaxy. But we are here on Earth now, and we are loving being here on Earth. We feel an honor to be on Earth at this time. We feel that we are here to serve and to honor our Mother. We must treat Earth the same way as we treat our mother.

The Arcturians have said that 2011 was the year of the planetary healer. What does this mean, my friends? This means that the idea of the planetary healer is coming to the consciousness of humankind. The planetary healer is able to listen to Earth and to find out what Earth wants and needs. I can tell you that right now there are many planetary healers working for the energy of Earth.

Yes, there have been terrible tragedies in 2011. There have been many problems. But it is not as bad as it could be. Believe me, there have already been so many predictions of the end times when so many tragedies are going to happen. But it has not turned out to be the end of this world yet. I say to you that there has been great help already in communicating to Earth.

The basic teaching of the planetary healer is this: Earth is interacting with humanity and humanity interacts with Earth. Never before has there been a species like humankind in the history of Earth. And humanity's actions now determine who lives and what species live. All the life forms on Earth now are dependent on one species: humankind. Humanity can decide to try to save the oceans, or it can continue the way it is and eventually there will be no life in the oceans. Whether the whales or dolphins survive is dependent on what humanity does.

One species is determining what happens to everyone else. Only one species can relate directly to the spirit of Earth, and that is humans. What we now know is that Earth as a planet can go into the fifth dimension. But in order to go into the planetary higher dimension, the planet needs humans. So we gather our energy to encourage you to explore your hidden abilities as planetary healers.

Remember that there are a core number of humans who will change the evolution, the consciousness. Part of the changing of the consciousness is to say, "These areas are sacred." Let people know that that there are many sacred areas on the planet. The energy in the sacred areas on the planet must be protected and acknowledged. You know that the greatest thing for children is to get attention from adults. The greatest thing for Earth is to give her attention and help to honor her. That is what we are doing in our ceremonies: honoring Earth.

I will say a prayer to Mother Earth: "Oh, Mother Earth, we are gathered here today to honor you. We want to send our love and our abilities to be planetary healers to you. Show us the way so that we can activate our powers as planetary healers. We are ready to serve and fulfill our mission as planetary workers. We honor our mother, Mother Earth."

Feel the power of that prayer. This is how Biorelativity works. You speak from your heart to your Mother Earth. You treat your mother with honor and respect. It is amazing that Earth loves us unconditionally. Even though we have done so many awful things, our Mother Earth still loves us and is happy that we are here. Twenty-eleven is the activation year of the planetary healer. During 2012 and beyond, you will be receiving activation to open your paths up to your planetary healing skills. I am Chief White Eagle. All my relations.

BOOK 1
Part 2

Gudrun Miller's Speeches at
the Workshop in Turkey

Trauma and Emotional Energy

Gudrun Miller

Surviving Trauma

In my practice as a psychotherapist, I work frequently with people who have survived severe trauma. Primarily it is trauma from childhood, but often it is also additional trauma in adulthood or an unusual and difficult experience that they have had as adults. These people are, in my opinion, very courageous. I love working with them, because they have experienced more than most of us have in the parts of life that are extremely painful and unbelievably cruel. And then they have had the courage to look within to heal themselves.

The Arcturians were drawing a comparison to starseeds as survivors of trauma. This is trauma in two parts. On the one hand, it is the survival of trauma from other lifetimes, because many of you have had lifetimes in which your energy, your beliefs, and your spiritual abilities were not welcomed or appreciated. So many of you have had experiences in those past lifetimes in which your life even ended traumatically because of who you were. Another difficult and painful experience is the trauma of your highly sensitive emotional body living on a dense planet like this, where there is so much abuse and violation of human beings, where you are watching people act like animals at times and also watching Earth changes and cataclysms where people, animals, and plants are dying, and species are going extinct. Those of you who are very sensitive find that traumatic.

Remember that I talked about the courage of my patients to come ask for help and the tremendous strength they develop as they heal themselves. I think we, as starseeds, are also very much like that. I think we are courageous and strong. We are willing to come here and be of service to Earth in spite of what we see going on here and in spite of our past-lifetime experiences. So you may not perceive yourselves as being particularly strong people, but please appreciate this about yourselves. And appreciate the fact that you are willing to understand more about yourselves and willing to know more about what you can do to help the planet. My clients who eventually recover from their trauma are some of the strongest people I know, because nothing really shakes them up anymore. Once you have seen the worst of life and you feel that, you are pretty solid.

Acceptance and Expansion Rather Than Fight or Flight

Juliano asked me to talk to you about our reaction to crisis and trauma. We, as animals and as human beings, have an instinctive response to any kind of a crisis or trauma that we experience. It is a survival technique. This is how we as animals survive. It has to do with our adrenaline system: It is the fight or flight instinct. If you think about the history of humanity, when faced with crisis, this is what we have done. And we survived. But this time calls for more than survival.

We, as starseeds, need to develop a way of reacting or responding to the trauma we see on this planet in a different way. This has to do with connecting with our higher selves. It also includes our adrenaline system. When the adrenaline system and the love that we can generate within our hearts combine, they apparently unlock some latent genetic ability in our DNA that allows us to open to ascension. That is a higher spiritual understanding of how we ascend.

They asked that we work with the concept of acceptance and expansion instead of fight or flight. What is it that you have to accept? Two things. The first is that you accept your response. You might have fear, anger, or grief. Our emotions are energy. If you block the emotions, they cause you problems, and these emotions really do not go away. Many of us often reject the negative emotions that we experience as sensitive human beings and starseeds. We do not want to feel those feelings — especially intense negative feelings — because we think that negative feelings aren't very spiritual. But what we are being asked to do is allow ourselves to have those feelings and emotions. And then they pass. So accept your emotions.

You also accept what you see is happening on this planet. Remember that you are advanced spiritual beings. You are here to be of assistance. You also know that these Earth events were predicted. So you develop a level of detachment with compassion where you do not get caught up in the pain that you are watching. That is the acceptance.

Expansion means that you open your consciousness to your greater awareness and understanding of events on Earth and of yourself. You are aware that you are a spiritual being and you expand into your higher self, so you open up. When you are in the fight or flight mentality, you are contracting. Contraction does not allow you to grow. It does not allow you to advance spiritually, emotionally, or mentally. Expansion allows you to grow, and as you open and expand, you can be of greater service to yourself, your family, and your communities. But it is very instinctive and natural to want to withdraw and contract.

Remember this discussion we have had today when the next trauma happens on Earth. See if you can work with accepting and expanding, which also might mean that you have some difficult feelings to work through.

We are waiting for a crisis to happen to Earth. Do we need to work with our feelings and emotions at that time, or can we do the work now?

Expanding ourselves means having a greater picture of what happens to Earth and also having a greater picture of yourself, of who you are.

I was watching the pictures on television of the tornados in the United States. It was horrifying. I could not imagine what that could be like for those people. I could cry now just thinking about it. You have to let yourself have that emotion, not push it away. Let it come. One expanded awareness you can have is that the people who had that experience agreed to have it on a higher level. People who died or lost their homes were, on a spiritual level, willing to have that experience. That is the expanded awareness. All of life is a spiritual experience. Every experience is designed for our greater evolution and growth. That is expanded awareness.

Thank you. It is now clear.

You are welcome.

CHAPTER TWO

Life-between-Lives Therapy

Gudrun Miller

I will give you a very basic understanding so that you know what this is. First, we have to talk about the subconscious and supraconscious. There are different states of trance: alpha, beta, theta, and delta. Beta is consciousness, like we are in now. Alpha is when you are in a trance, and you can go to three levels of trance in alpha. In alpha trance, you can access all the information from all of your past lives and all the information from this life. Theta is a deeper trance. That is where you go into your supraconscious and you have access to your higher self, guides, and teachers.

Delta is when you fall asleep. When I work with my patients in the trance process, I take them slowly deeper and deeper. We start up with memories in this life and then we go into the mother's womb. At that point, oftentimes there is information about the soul connection to the mother. There is information about how the soul and the fetus are able to bond with each other. Believe it or not, the fetus has an energy all its own, and as a soul coming into that fetus, you have to work to make that bond function well. Sometimes that works very well and sometimes it does not. You have to work with the mental circuitry in the brain. It is an opportunity for you as a soul to fine-tune the body that you are going into.

From the fetus, we go directly into a past life. Ideally you go into your most immediate past life, because it is easier to access the information from there. You go to that life through the death and then we go through the death process in that life and the time when the spirit leaves the body. If it was a difficult life, we will have to spend some time processing the lessons from that life. Oftentimes my patients' spirit guides will come and talk to me. These guides will also talk to the patients themselves from their understanding of themselves in past lives and their awareness of themselves in this life.

Meeting Your Soul Family and Your Spiritual Council

In that process, we attempt to help you make sense of what happened to you and what it is that you came into that lifetime to learn. Then you, as an advanced soul, will usually move on to meet with your soul family. Your soul family is composed of approximately nine to thirteen beings. It is a very close family. You have your soul evolution together as a family. Everything that you learn in a lifetime you share with that family. Everything they learn, they share with you. There is a leader of your soul family, the one who is the most spiritually advanced, but everyone helps each other.

It is possible that members of your soul family will be incarnated with you in a lifetime. Usually when that happens, there is a very special purpose for the two of you being together — helping each other learn something. This can be beautiful or very painful, because sometimes we as human beings learn best through pain, unfortunately. When you meet with your soul family, they will talk to you about your lessons, what you still need to do, how well you do, what you are neglecting, and so on. It is not done with judgment or criticism but with deep acceptance. Usually there is a lot of emotion from my patients when they are meeting with their soul families. This is the kind of closeness we look for in our Earth relationships.

After you meet with your soul family, you can go to a meeting with your council. Your council consists of five to ten beings who are highly advanced spiritually. Oftentimes there will be beings you are aware of in your religions on Earth. You go in front of the council to receive an evaluation and specific guidance about lessons you need to learn in your next life. Usually there is such a feeling of love that permeates this experience that it overwhelms not just my client but also me, in my role as therapist.

One patient started to weep when she met her council, because Mother Mary, Jesus, and Moses were all part of it. She believed that she was so insignificant and worthless that meeting with such high teachers challenged her beliefs about herself in this life. A lot of her belief structures had to melt from her mind and heart right then.

Choosing Your Next Life

From the meeting with the council, you go to a place where you pick your next life. And often you have several choices. In this place, you actually can go through each lifetime as if you are living that life, and you decide whether it is appropriate for the lessons you need to learn. You choose a life that is most likely going to give you the soul advancement you are looking for.

My clients talk about it like being a very highly advanced computer. You can watch each lifetime, or you can step into the computer and live that lifetime very quickly. You choose a lifetime and you decide on specific people you will meet and specific things that will happen to you. This is when you are in supraconsciousness and you are not concerned about the pain that you will experience in that life. You are only concerned about whether or not that is going to be the best way to learn your lessons.

When I was twenty, I met my husband, David. It was a night when I was very tired and my brother called me and told me to go to a party. We were both living at the university. I told my brother: "I hate parties. Why would I want to go to a party?" My brother does not like parties either. It was very strange that he asked me to go to a party. I told him no and hung up the phone, but ten minutes later, my brother knocked at the door. "Let's go," he said. I was very grumpy. I went to the party and had a bad time.

Right when I was ready to leave, David walked down the stairs. I had never heard any voices in my head before, but I did then. The voice in my head said: "There you are." And my twenty-year-old third-dimensional self said, "Why are you so short?" But David saw me and I saw him, and we have been together since. Now I understand that we intended to meet that way and that my brother had to help because otherwise I would not have met David then. Many of you have probably had similar experiences in life. Maybe now you know a little more about that.

Here's another interesting story. This one is not about a patient of mine. A woman was given the opportunity to be in the body of an extremely beautiful woman. The soul realized that with that kind of beauty, this lifetime would be extremely difficult for her. She chose not to take that life. Most of my patients are females, and those whom I regressed have wanted to come back as men when choosing their next lives, because it is still easier to be a man on our planet. Not for all men, of course — I know that men have issues that are just as complicated as women's issues. But my clients' guides tell them that it will be easier for them to access spiritual openness in this life as women, because it is actually still more difficult for men in Western culture to have access to their hearts and to open spiritually. We have two men here today. This is an exception; when David and I do seminars, the percentage is usually about 10 percent men. Many of you here may have chosen to come in as a female because you knew it would help you open spiritually.

Awakening in This Lifetime

At this time on planet Earth, it is critical that you have access to your spirituality so that you may awaken in this lifetime. When you are in this trance, it is interesting because you are able to be in many different awarenesses of who you are. You are aware of yourself in your current incarnation, you are aware of yourself in a past life, and you are aware of yourself in your between-lives state, when you are connected with your higher self. For me as a psychotherapist, this is fascinating because I work with all those parts of you, along with your personal guides and teachers and also with your higher self. You do not get confused while you are in this trance, but it is harder on me.

Let us say that a person was living in pain in a past time. Does he or she tell you about it in Spanish, for example? Sometimes we hear stories about speaking another language that the person does not know in this lifetime.

It can happen, but when you seek to have this hypnotherapy work done on yourself, your higher self is guiding you to do this. And your higher self attempts to make it as simple as possible for you to work with your therapist. In my case, you would use no other languages, because I do not understand other languages.

When a person goes to a past life and starts to feel sorrow or pain, what do you do at that moment?

It is possible to heal that. If not, you can talk about it through the rest of the regression and you will begin to understand why you had to suffer. If the emotions are too intense, we can get lost in them, so I will then attempt to bring you into an awareness that is more detached. All of my subjects, when they are in a supraconscious state, feel like they are at home. They do not want to come out of the trance. They only come out because they are tired, hungry, or have to go to the bathroom. Oftentimes they cry when they come back into this life. I know that our true nature is a very beautiful thing.

There is an interesting case that I would like to talk about. When I met this woman, I knew she was a starseed and highly gifted, but she was lost in a very bad relationship with a man who treated her as if she knew nothing. In the process of therapy with me, she became aware of her sensitivity and spirituality, and she wanted to have a regression. She had had a difficult childhood in a Christian fundamentalist family. She was taught to be afraid of mysticism and the Devil, but her true nature was that of a powerful spiritual being.

She went to a past life where she was in the United States in 1400. She was a female physician, which was unheard of at that time. She was well respected and did very good work. She was very powerful and had good self-esteem. It was good for her to remember this about herself. When we left that life, she had a good death, and in the supraconscious state, she understood that she was a seventh-dimensional being who came from the Andromeda galaxy.

She began to channel her guides from Andromeda. The energy was so high that it was hard for her to make the words. Her words were short and brief, but she got a lot of guidance. She was told her soul name and the name of her guide. I began to speak with her seventh-dimensional guide from Andromeda. This was at the end of the session after about five hours of intense trance. I was getting quite exhausted. I asked my patient's permission to ask her guide a personal question. She said yes. I asked the guide if he knew of a guy called Gurhan who David sometimes channels. She lay on my couch for a while and then a big smile came on her face. She said, "David, your husband, is a beam transmitter." She went quiet again, until another smile came on her face and she said, "And he is very good at it." I was surprised because she did not know David. Now I call my husband Baba, the beam transmitter. In the United States, we have action figures like Superman and Spiderman, and in my mind, since I was getting a little bit silly, I saw a picture of David with a prayer shawl. That was fun. If you ever hear me call him Baba, this is where it comes from. Any other questions?

What is it like to be a beam transmitter?

He brings through energy. You feel it.

How many dimensions are there?

I do not know. Through my clients, I have only experienced the seventh dimension.

Do you feel any other dimension while you are in this dimension?

Yes, I go into trance too, and that allows me to work very closely with my patients.

And you draw those pictures?

Yes. Some other interesting information that I got from some of my patients is that they started their first incarnation on planet Earth as other life forms. One of my patients came to Earth as the seed of a tree. And there were only twelve seeds that came. This subject was also from Andromeda, but she chose to have her first experience on Earth as a tree. She loves trees.

After being human, is it possible to be a seed again?

When you leave your human incarnation, you go on to a higher, more advanced soul state. You could probably go back into the seed. She dreamed that she was given a white envelope and there was a seed inside. She placed it in her palm and that seed became a green plant. When she woke up from sleep, it was a tree.

Can we have messages from our dreams?

Absolutely. There are books about it and there are skilled people who can help you understand. Dreams speak in symbols. I help my clients understand their dreams by them becoming every part of their dream. They speak like that part. With the example of the seed, they would say, "I am a seed and I am growing in the palm of your hand." You keep talking like that and pretty soon you get an idea.

There is a state that is not a dream. What can you say about that?

It is lucid dreaming, and you can do it as a shaman. You can work out of your body and do things in the fourth dimension, for example. David says it also could be a hypnogogic trance, which is not as deep as lucid dreaming. It is between being awake and asleep.

BOOK 1
Part 3

Lectures by Juliano, the
Arcturians, and Sananda

through David Miller
Brazil, August 2011

Tools for Ascension

Juliano and the Arcturians

Greetings, I am Juliano. We are the Arcturians. We will talk about the tools for planetary healing. Remember that we said that this year of 2011 is the year of the planetary healer. Planetary healers like you can awaken to their mission of planetary work. It is totally amazing that the planetary healers have come to this Earth. It is totally amazing that there are so many planetary healers now and that planetary healers like yourselves are ready to go into action and ready to work together.

We have developed new tools for spiritual technology and the healing of the planet. Of course, we recognize that it is most important for you to heal, because when you are healed you are more in balance. When you are more in balance, you can be a more effective planetary healer. You have to be in good physical, emotional, spiritual, and mental health so that you can transmit this powerful energy of planetary healing.

Tapping into the Fifth Dimension

The first tool for planetary healing is contact with the fifth dimension. When you are able to contact the fifth dimension, you are able to set the foundation and plant the seeds of planetary healing. I want to clarify something about the word "healing." People say, "Well, Earth will survive no matter what happens." But what I want to say is that Earth is a spiritual planet that is happy to have this level of life. Earth wants to keep this complex life interaction. Healing Earth, in this terminology, means keeping a high level of life forms balanced and alive.

Connecting with the fifth dimension means you can bring down quantum light. This quantum light transcends the normal logic. We have demonstrated to you that there are certain techniques of connecting with the fifth dimension. This includes using the corridors and going to the crystal temple, but it also includes being able to use the etheric crystals. The etheric crystals are all duplicates of the master crystal from Arcturus that is in their crystal temple. These duplicate crystals have been strategically placed around twelve different places on the planet. That means that the fifth-dimensional energy is anchored in these places.

The crystal that was downloaded here at Serra da Bocaina in Brazil represents the interaction of third-dimensional energy with fifth-dimensional energy. Of course, it is interesting that Brazil is able to hold that interaction force, because the new life forms that will remain on the planet will emerge from this interaction. Yesterday we visited the sacred area called Solo Sagrado — a spiritual resort center about twenty miles outside of São Paulo, Brazil — and we were impressed that a Japanese spiritual master there chose Brazil for the special temple energy. He built a tremendous circle with a pillar at the end (see photo). The circle was maybe twenty feet high, or even higher. We immediately understood that this circle was gathering light from the galaxy. We think that it is significant that this galactic light

Solo Sagrado, a spiritual resort center near São Paulo, Brazil

collector is here in São Paulo, because this reaffirms our belief that Brazil is able to hold galactic energy and that it can hold the interaction of this galactic energy within the third dimension.

We have tried to teach that Earth is interacting with the galaxy. Logically, it is hard to understand how Earth can interact with a galaxy that has billions of stars within it and is so unimaginably large. There is no logical way to explain it to you. But I can tell you that the light-force energy and the spiritual energy from higher light sources are able to cross all dimensional areas. This creation at Solo Sagrado demonstrates that other people on Earth recognize the existence of galactic life and spiritual energy and realize that there are certain ways of collecting that energy.

The Iskalia Mirror and the Ring of Ascension

We have another spiritual tool for planetary healing called the Iskalia mirror. The Iskalia mirror is an etheric mirror that is above the North Pole. It is set above Earth and is in alignment with the Central Sun. It is collecting and gathering light from the Central Sun and bringing it into Earth. This light from the Central Sun that is coming into Earth is bringing new ideas and new technology.

The other tool that we are using is called the ring of ascension. It is a halo of light — a ring just like the ring of Saturn. But the ring of ascension is bringing together an interaction force that allows the ascended masters to interact with the third-dimensional lightworkers. The ascended masters are helping Earth, but they need an interactive mechanism within which to bring down their energy to help. One interactive method that can be used is defined as the ring of ascension.

We have done exercises in which we used the ring of ascension as a planetary healing tool. We are able to send energy around the entire world through this ring. We need to grasp that we have to look at the planet as a whole organism, as a whole being. In order to do the proper rebalancing of the feedback loop system, we must treat the planet as a whole and send light to it.

[Chants.]

Activate the cosmic egg light around you. See the etheric energy light of the aura of Earth. You can see that Earth has an aura just like you. The Earth is a living planet. It has a pulse, it has a breathing cycle, and it has an energy field. You, the planetary lightworkers, can telepathically interact with this great spirit known as the Blue Jewel. It is your telepathic healing thoughts that will help Earth to be balanced.

Planetary Cities of Light

One of the most important spiritual tools for healing Earth is the creation and holding of the light through the planetary cities of light. How many planetary cities of light are there now in Brazil? Can someone tell me?

One.

Where is that city of light?

In Ponta Grossa.

Very good. There are going to be more cities of light developing in Brazil. We are very grateful to those who have already been holding the planetary cities of light for Ponta Grossa. Blessings to each of you in Ponta Grossa for holding the light of Ponta Grossa. You are spiritual explorers; you are spiritual evolutionary workers for the planet.

What the planetary cities of light do is very simple. The idea is that we will try to work in small areas first. In other words, we are going to create sacred cities and sacred areas. Yes, it is true that there are terrible economic problems, there are terrible international political problems, and there are terrible wars. Those things are difficult to influence at this moment, but we can influence the small areas.

We can create sacred areas immediately. When we create these small sacred areas, we call them planetary cities of light. That means that we are creating a spiritual light energy field around the area in question. This idea was described by earlier writers, who called it Shangri-La. It is the idea that there is a fifth-dimensional city on the third-dimensional Earth that you can only enter when you are in a higher vibration because there is an energy field around the city that blocks lower-vibrational energy from entering.

In the planetary cities of light, we are bringing in fifth-dimensional people and fifth-dimensional thinking, and then we are holding that energy in the city. We are putting crystals around the outline of the city. We are meditating to visualize an energy field around the city. We are inviting higher fifth-dimensional people to come into the city to give workshops and lectures. We are helping to raise the spiritual light quotient of the city. Yes, it is true that a city has a spiritual light quotient and that a country has a spiritual light quotient. Even Earth has a spiritual light quotient. So we raise the spiritual light quotient of the planetary cities of light.

We now have over fifty planetary cities of light on Earth that are participating in this project, and this is soon going to grow to over a hundred. There are people just like you committed to creating and holding the light energy. We have traveled throughout the galaxy and we have seen other planets. We have seen these planets go through conflicts, crises, and evolutionary stages similar to those happening on Earth. This method that we are offering you works; we have seen it before. Create planetary cities of light — they will grow and they will increase.

There is an area of light above the city that I live in. Its size was five kilometers in diameter, but it has expanded to a hundred kilometers in diameter. At this point, is it a planetary city of light?

No, because the planetary city of light has to be based on Earth. It certainly is great that the light is there, and I am sure that it is aiding, but the concept of the planetary city of light is to download the fifth-dimensional energy into Earth, into a specific city. For example, when we activate a planetary city of light, we plant crystals around the perimeter of the city in order to hold that energy on the earth. Remember, it does not necessarily have to be a city as designated by the geography of your maps. It can be a neighborhood or portion of a city. We actually do not recommend trying to make an entire city of five or ten million people a city of light. We think it is better to start out small so that you can hold the energy and the light in that city more effectively.

Is there a rule regarding how many crystals should be in a planetary city of light or how big it should be?

There is no rule for how many crystals. I have been talking about the crystals that need to be buried in the ground. Generally, we would like to have at least four crystals buried at each cardinal point. The most important thing is that you are creating an energy field around the city. A lot of it depends on the size of the crystals and how many crystals you think will be needed to help hold the energy field. In our last activation with this channel, we were able to use four crystals. But if you have more crystals and have the freedom to bury more, that is wonderful. We did an activation near Barcelona, in Sant Pere de Ribes, and we had close to forty people participating in the activation.

Who are the people who are able to activate a city of light?

Anybody can do that. Any lightworker can do it. Because we are organizing through this channel, we are just asking that the channel is made aware of it so that this organization can support it. You can use the Group of Forty to activate a planetary city of light. What we are saying is that by doing it with the Group of

Forty, you are using the publicity, the knowledge, and the ability to communicate it to other people. We want the cities of light to become known. For example, two planetary cities of light recently became sister cities of light. We know that San Martín de los Andes, Argentina, is now a sister city of light to Sedona, Arizona. If the Group of Forty was not involved, the people in these two cities would not be able to communicate. But now the Group of Forty members in Sedona are starting to communicate with the Group of Forty members in San Martín de los Andes. That means that the people in Arizona are becoming aware of other planetary cities of light, and therefore they can work with those cities and send each other energy.

Are the sister cities of light connected through the ley lines?

There are old ley lines and new ley lines. Many of the old ley lines are blocked because of the pollution and many of the other destructive things that have gone on on the planet. But you are absolutely right — the planetary cities of light can connect to each other and can create new energy lines to each other. So there are many different possibilities for how the planetary cities of light can work with each other. Remember, working with the planetary cities of light is one of the most powerful healing techniques of the planetary healer. Many people living within a planetary city of light will become happy when they learn that so many people are trying to help the city become more fifth-dimensional.

The Waves of Ascension

I want to know how the ascension waves are going to work. Is the first wave going to take a lot of people into the fifth dimension? What kind of Earth will we leave behind? Will there be a new wave of ascension?

First of all, the ascension will have an effect on those left behind. The ascension is going to occur because the fifth dimension is going to interact with the third dimension. This can actually be described as two spheres interacting — one sphere is the third and the other is the fifth. At the moment when these two spheres touch, there will be a downloading of energy.

Remember, it takes energy and tremendous force to lift people into the fifth dimension. Yes, it is true that some of the best lightworkers are going to leave in the first wave, but the fact that many of them will leave is going to greatly activate other people. This was even shown in the Bible when one master ascended and the other who stayed behind became himself a great master. [Channel's Note: Elijah is the master who ascended, and his student went on to become a great teacher.]

So just remember that if you ascend, the energy of your ascension and the energy of the ascension itself will open up many other people immediately. It is generally believed that there will be three levels or three waves of ascension and that those who do not go in the first wave will definitely go in the second wave. In the third wave, people will go just because they are totally convinced at that point that this is the best way to deal with everything.

I know that many people want to know the exact date, but that is a secret. If the date were given, it would affect how people act, which could negatively affect them. People might give up trying to heal Earth; people might give up trying to work. You are supposed to go on as if you are not going to ascend, even though you know you are. The ascension will occur with an awakening sound. This sound has never been heard with so much force by so many people at once. You will love it!

In relation to the waves of ascension, how is it going to be with the children? What is going to happen with the children?

Generally, most of the children will be going with their parents. Remember that, in many ways, children are the responsibility of their parents until the children reach a certain age at which they can determine their own future. Plus, many of the children of the lightworkers are themselves lightworkers, so they chose parents who are going to work with them and help them in ascending.

Until what age are the children connected to their parents, in the sense that they are working with the light together for ascension?

It varies according to the child and according to his or her karma. I cannot give you a general cut off age of sixteen or eighteen. I think a lot of it depends on the children's starseed development and whether or not they are open to the ascension.

I do not know if I am qualified to ascend, although it is a very big desire that I have. What I would like to know is, if I do ascend, will the other simultaneous lives present that are dense in quality be taken with me?

Most people are not going to have totally completed all their lessons. Most people are not going to be 100 percent ready, and we understand that complete readiness is very difficult to achieve. We know that there is an aspect of ascension called grace. Sananda oversees that aspect of ascension, and maybe he can tell you more about it. Let me just briefly say that the idea of grace is this: You are gifted a special compensation. You are granted a special light that helps you bypass and skip some things so that you can ascend. The only thing that is required from you is that you have a sincere and honest intention to ascend and that you continue to work on yourself as hard as you can. So do not give up and say, "I am just going to wait for the ascension," but work as hard as you can with a direct and open heart. And then grace will lead you in the way up.

✳ ✳ ✳

So I, Juliano, reactivate the corridor of light around the room. And I am reactivating your planetary healing abilities. I ask that you all awaken to your role and your mission as planetary healers, that you open up to the tools of ascension, that you open up to your highest spiritual light quotient, and that you are willing to work for the raising of the spiritual light quotients of both your city and that of Earth.

It is possible that even a small contribution will help. We use the expression "the hundredth monkey effect" to describe this. After a certain number of people make a change, everyone accepts it. This is what we mean when we say that you are contributing to the evolution of the species. It means that you are holding a certain energy of consciousness that will help to create a stronger consciousness of the changes that need to happen on Earth, and the greatest consciousness must gather around the idea of telepathically interacting with the spirit of Earth. We call this ability to interact telepathically with Earth Biorelativity. I am Juliano. We are the Arcturians. Good day.

CHAPTER TWO

Messianic Energy and the Sacred Triangle

Sananda

Greetings, I am Sananda. This is my galactic name, for I am working with many worlds. I am truly multidimensional and I can be at different places at the same time. You are just learning to become multidimensional. For you it is a great accomplishment to be able to project your presence to another dimension. Can you imagine that I am able to be in many different places with full consciousness and full abilities at the same time?

I was also multidimensional when I was on Earth, and I was on many different places on Earth at the same time. I had many different interactions with different peoples on the planet. At the same time, I was able to be multidimensional in other planets simultaneously. But you are growing and learning, and for you to be multidimensional in two times or two places is certainly a great upliftment and a great accomplishment. You are multidimensional, and being multidimensional can also be defined as having multipresence. Now it is difficult for you to be in more than one place at one time, but I promise you that you are learning and it is going to be easier for you to be in two different places at the same time. More importantly, you will be able to be in different dimensions at the same time; you will be able to hold your concentration equally well in both places.

The Sacred Triangle and the Power of Grace

Today I am visiting you to speak about the Sacred Triangle, a beautiful paradigm that we developed together with the Arcturians. If you look at the Sacred Triangle, you will see that there are three spiritual forces that actually form a sacred unity of light. The part of the Sacred Triangle that I represent can be described in many different ways. I like very much the description that is known as the White Brotherhood and Sisterhood, which represents the many ascended masters who have been on this planet or are working with this planet. This includes the energies of Archangel Metatron, Archangel Michael, Saint Francis of Assisi, and many other great mystics from the Judeo-Christian religions. Of course, it also includes representatives of other famous religions, including the Hindus and the Sufis, and many other masters. Every religion has a higher energetic form, and this higher form links unity with other religious thoughts and other religious ideals, and these forms of unity are like a brotherhood and sisterhood.

Of course it is desirable that you can unify and use all of these three sides. I will be talking about how these three sides have come into unity, but it is sufficient for you to work just on one side. There is enough in every religion to find the unity, to find a way to the Creator, and to find a way to ascension. Some people really have had a hard time with the higher-dimensional galactic beings. I emit no judgments on that. Some people may have difficulty relating to the ascended Native American people or other native peoples of the world. Again, I make no judgment of them either way, yet these same people may be totally into the Judeo-Christian way of connecting to the Creator and connecting to me. So this is acceptable, and I encourage everyone to follow their hearts and to follow their path to the Creator.

You need to know that the door is open for you to walk through and that this door has been opened at the will of the Creator. The Creator wants to be known by his creatures, by his people, but there is a path that needs to be followed in order to see his light. It can be compared to looking at the Sun. If you do not have the proper filters, you cannot experience the Sun and you will be damaged. The light of the Creator is so intense that no human can be close to it without perishing. But you are growing in your abilities to hold light, and soon you will be able to move closer and closer to the Creator's light.

I think at this point it is important for you to know as much as you can about my father. Many people have many ideas about my father. The important points are that my father wants you to ascend, there is a pathway toward your upliftment, and the work of ascension is also involved in the work of grace. Grace means that you are given a special dispensation to advance. That means that some of you may think you aren't good enough and others may think that you didn't do enough work, but the idea of grace is that you are given a chance to advance even though you have not done all of the work. Your heart is moving in the right direction and you are continuing with your efforts. This is a desirable and important aspect of your work, so that grace can be given to you in order to ascend. This is the time when my father wants to have a massive ascension — an ascension of many, many people. Yes, there is a hierarchy in the spiritual world, but there also are many opportunities for upliftment and many opportunities to be taught how to progress and how to advance.

Messianic Energy

The second thing I want to talk to you about is what is called the Messianic energy. One of my names is Messiah Ben David. This relates to the idea that there is an extraordinary intervention on this planet in which an extraordinary person or being must be present. This extraordinary being must have powers that are beyond those of anyone else, and this being can create an extraordinarily powerful intervention that will save the planet and put it back into the balance it needs. So this intervention will be done with Messannic energy. Messianic energy is beyond the third dimension — it is fifth-dimensional. It is an energy that cannot be understood by science or logic, but at the same time, it is an energy that transcends science and logic. It is an energy based on the fifth dimension, where everything is possible and everything can be united in that higher energy.

[Sings.]

The energy of Messiah Ben David is represented in the Arcturian Planetary Tree of Life by the etheric crystal known as the Montserrat crystal. Montserrat is near Barcelona, Spain. This area has a purification energy that is very open to the energy of the Messiah. It is a pure energy; it is an energy of the heart. Mary, my mother, resides in that area. She is the overseer of the grace and she is waiting to provide blessings to all of you who want to ascend. So the ascension is a family interaction, an interaction with your White Brotherhood and Sisterhood family.

I am deeply moved by the ladders of ascension. We have placed the ladder of ascension in Jerusalem. So what is ascension? Ascension is the upliftment from the third dimension to the fifth dimension, and the ladders of ascension are actual doorways through which you can comfortably climb up from one dimension to the other. Now, we are speaking to you also about the codes of ascension. This means that there are locks in your mind and in your mental body that must be opened so that you can receive and process the energy of ascension immediately.

Montserrat, Spain

We have worked with the energy of the beautiful phrase: "Holy, holy, holy is the lord of hosts." And this phrase, when sung in a certain tone, helps you to unlock the codes of ascension within you. That means that when the codes of ascension are unlocked, you are able to ascend immediately at the moment that is correct. I will sing the codes of ascension in ancient Hebrew. It was the language that I used for praying. [Sings: *Kadosh, Kadosh, Kadosh, Adonia Tzvaoth.*]

Holy, holy, holy is the lord of hosts. So we understand the importance of holiness, the importance of sacredness. You make yourself holy when you are opening up the codes of ascension within you. When you open up the codes of ascension, you must feel sacred; you must feel like you are in a special energy field. It is a unique fifth-dimensional energy. Then we say, "My lord" — *Adonai* means my lord. This is an important phrase in the opening of the ascension. First of all, it is telling you that our father is personally involved in your upliftment. So you are referring to him or her as "my lord." You are able to have this beautiful personal interaction with my lord. This is one of the most beautiful discoveries on Earth because the religions and the spiritual masters that have come to this Earth have been able to teach that the lord is available for a personal interaction.

Experiencing the Presence of *Adonai*

There are other spiritual disciplines on this planet that are very mystical, and they sometimes like to teach that there is a great unity, a universal light force. They want to teach that there is no personal energy of the lord, that there is only the universal energy force. But they have a perception and a view that represents a beautiful reality when you understand that there are different levels of interaction with my lord.

Yes, there is the great universal force, the undifferentiated energy, and it is even expressed in the Planetary Tree of Life. You will see that this force is described as undifferentiated light. But that is a very high, open level of interaction of the lord. The light of the lord is stepped down on Earth so you can interact with it, so you can grasp it, because it is difficult for many people to relate to the universal light force. But it is like higher electricity. In order to use electricity in your home, you must step it down so that there is a voltage that you can use without exploding your electrical devices. In fact, this is one of my main missions — to let everybody know that there is a way to experience this very high light of my lord, and that my lord wants everyone to be able to have an opportunity to experience his presence. [Sings.]

Now I want to tell you a special secret about multipresence. Everyone has the possibility and the opportunity to experience multipresence with my lord, *Adonai*. You can be present simultaneously with my lord and yourself here on planet Earth. And that is also multidimensional presence. So you can hold your presence with my lord and you can hold your presence here on Earth. You can hold your presence with me, Sananda, and you can also hold your presence here on Earth. And I know that you talked about cohabitation and the idea of having more than one being with you.

I want to suggest a new idea to you today: You can cohabitate with more than one person, one being; you can have your presence with my father, you can have your presence with me, and you can still have your presence here on Earth. If you can do that, it is a beautiful process — and I know you can do it. When we say, "the lord of hosts," the word "hosts" refers to the many higher beings that work together. So there are many angelic beings and, of course, we are referring to some of the higher ones, including Archangel Gabriel, Archangel Michael, and Archangel Metatron. There are thousands of higher angelic presences that are working together with us.

A Galactic Understanding of *Adonai*

Now I want to speak about another aspect of the Sacred Triangle, the galactic spirituality. I have been on other planets. I have spent a great deal of time on the Pleiades, and I have been on many other planets, so I know that there is a galactic understanding of *Adonai*. And I know that there are higher spiritual beings on other planets. This is not the only planet in your galaxy that has higher spiritual beings on it; this is not the only planet that I have visited; this is not the only planet that I am working with.

Many people may be shocked by this. But it is the truth, because my father has allowed many planets to have life in this galaxy and each planet has a beautiful story and a different perspective of the third-dimensional reality. Some of the planets have been fortunate enough to ascend, to go into the fifth dimension. My father commanded us to oversee and work with the third dimension. My father wants the third dimension to be a beautiful place. My father willed the existence of the third dimension. This dimension was created as the dimension of duality to provide a place for your soul to learn and for your soul evolution. So it is a great blessing and a great commitment to be able to oversee, to work with, and to experience this dimension. But there are other dimensions and other planets.

There are many fifth-dimensional beings. These are beings who have lived on planets that have evolved to the fifth dimension, and Arcturus is one of the great planets that have achieved high energy and high light. The Arcturians have been given the authority to oversee the stargate. There are other higher-dimensional beings who are involved in this side of the Sacred Triangle, and all of these beings are working toward helping with Earth's ascension. This includes Ashtar and some of the other higher beings that many of you have been working with. If you are so moved, then you can work with both the galactic spiritual masters and the White Brotherhood and Sisterhood.

We Need the Native Energies Back in Full Force

There is a third part of the Sacred Triangle, and this part is for the native peoples. My father said that there is a special energy that the native peoples carry for Earth, that these peoples understand Earth is a sacred place, and that they have special knowledge on how to talk to Earth and how to pray to Earth. Earlier, when many of the religious movements were developed, the people who were practicing and developing these religions were also practicing some of these techniques. But as societies and civilizations became more complex, the religious people lost their connections to nature and to the native energies. But some of the people you may call primitive were and have been able to hold this energy.

In order to heal Earth, we need the native energies back in full force and strength. So I encourage you to work with the native energies, if you are so moved. This includes the native energies of the people in Brazil and all over South America. The Sacred Triangle, then, is seeking to unite these three forces: (1) the energies of White Brotherhood and Sisterhood — that is, the mystical aspects of all of the traditional religions on the planet; (2) the galactic spirituality, including the fifth-dimensional masters; and (3) the native peoples of the planet and their spiritual perspective. This paradigm will help to move the planet toward the fifth dimension.

I love you all very much. I am always available for you. I am Sananda. Blessings.

CHAPTER THREE

Activation of Two Planetary Cities of Light in Brazil

Juliano and the Arcturians

This is an activation of the planetary cities of light. Today is August 13. The first city we will activate is Piracicaba, 100 miles west of São Paulo, and the name of the area is Jupiá. The second city is Palmeiras, 285 miles west of the city of El Salvador in Brazil, and the name of the area is Capão, which is 3,280 feet above sea level.

Greetings, I am Juliano. We are the Arcturians. We are gathered here today in the city of Porto Seguro, Brazil, to activate two planetary cities of light in this beautiful country. Brazil is carrying a great deal of light for the Arcturians, the galaxy, and Earth, for this country has core connections to the Inner Earth. It is these connections to the Inner Earth that provide a direct link to Earth's feedback loop system. Earth's feedback loop system has several openings in the Brazilian rain forest. These openings enable the planetary healers to more directly and telepathically connect to the feedback loop system. What the planetary healers can do in Brazil has the possibility of being extremely effective. In a way, you can say that Brazil has the opportunity and even the responsibility to activate the planetary healing energies.

Everyone is realizing that the rules of the planetary healers and their mission are more important than they previously understood. Also, the roles and the work of the planetary healers are becoming more powerful and more effective. How is it that the planetary healers can become more powerful? The reason has to do with the effectiveness of the interglobal communications and with the fact that many of the planetary healers have soul origins from other planetary systems, including Arcturus and the Pleiades, as well as the moon-planet Alano. These healers are called starseeds.

Increasing the Power of Your Thought Energy

The starseeds are bringing powerful abilities, concentration, and energetic focusing. These are all skills that are needed to become effective planetary healers. When we talk about concentration, we also talk about the ability to increase the arcan thought-energy power. The starseed planetary healers are able to telepathically send strong energies to the spirit of Mother Earth.

Remember, the place where you meditate can also effectively increase your arcan energy. Who you are, who you were in previous lifetimes, whom you are cohabiting with, whom you are connecting with, whom you are sitting with in a group at this moment, and who you are interglobally connecting with — all of these connections can increase your arcan abilities. The fact is that you are also connecting with the Arcturians, and that telepathic and spiritual connection with us also increases your abilities to make your arcan energies more powerful.

At this time, when we are here to activate two planetary cities of light, it is highly useful to have strong arcan powers of thought and energy. In fact, when planetary cities of light are activated, this activation is raising the spiritual light quotient of the country that the cities are in, as well as the cities themselves. Additionally, the spiritual light quotient of the whole Earth is positively affected. These two new planetary cities of light are powerful sacred areas on their own. We welcome the new cities of light: Piracicaba, the neighborhood of Jupiá, and Bahia, the city of Palmeiras, in the neighborhood of Capão.

The Interconnected Pung Energy Fields of the Cities of Light

At this moment, these two planetary cities of light have starseeds surrounding them energetically, placing crystals around the cities and creating a beautiful, etheric white light around the perimeter of the neighborhoods of the cities where the activation is occurring.

I want to explain a little bit about the white light or the energy field, because the energy field around the planetary cities of light has a characteristic similar to your energy field. Your energy field has a pulse; it has the ability to send out a protective force field, and this force field can allow higher energies to come in while preventing lower energies from coming in.

I have also spoken in earlier lectures about the power of the pung energy. I have compared my understanding of pung energy to a balloon that has special characteristics. This metaphorical balloon is very soft in the beginning, but because of the force of air and the energy within it, the balloon is able to bounce and push away the energies of any force that strikes it. This power, this force of bouncing lower energy away, is called pung energy in the etheric world.

With this activation, I have developed a pung energy field around the cities of light. This means that higher energy is allowed in. People who have higher thought vibrations can come in and are welcome. People with lower thought vibrations, though, are bounced away; they are not attracted into the city. They will say, "Well, I do not feel like going into this city. Who wants to go in here? This is not interesting to me." They will have unusual thoughts of distaste and rejection so that they will not be attracted to come into the city. This is a powerful force field, and I want to emphasize the importance of this pung energy that increases the energy of the cities' thought fields. These two planetary cities of light are joining other planetary cities of light around the globe that are already activated through the Group of Forty.

This means that these two new planetary cities of light are interconnected with the other cities of light. It also means that their energy fields are interacting with each other. The energy fields of these two cities are gaining logarithmically, because they are interacting with over fifty other powerful planetary cities of light that already exist and have been activated through the Group of Forty. The energy fields of these other cities are now contributing to the activations of these two new planetary cities of light. In a way, this is like saying that the arcan light and energies of the other already-activated planetary cities of light are logarithmically and energetically increasing the powerful energy forces around these two new planetary cities of light that are being activated now at this moment. [Chants.]

The Pulsing of Protective Energy Fields

In addition to the pung energy fields of these planetary cities of light, there is also a pulsing of the energy fields around the cities. Remember, your aura has a pulse, and the higher the rate of your aura, the higher the vibrational energies you can receive. Your arcan energies can increase your abilities to perform thought projection, and remote healing can increase. Many things and many skills increase when the pulsing of your aura increases. It is the same within the planetary cities of light. When a planetary city of light is activated, there is an increase of the pulse of the energy field around the city. As we are activating these two new planetary cities of light, I, Juliano, begin to increase the pulsing of the energy field around the cities. [Sounds.]

The increase of the pulsing of the energy field around the two planetary cities of light has begun. This increased pulsing has many of the same positive effects as the increase of your own aura. This means that people within the planetary cities of light will experience an increase in their psychic powers. By being inside the energy field of these planetary cities of light, one will immediately experience an increase in many psychic abilities, including thought projection, remote healing, and the overall ability to connect with fifth-dimensional energies, fifth-dimensional lights, and all of the twelve etheric crystals.

Because we are closest to the etheric crystal at Serra da Bocaina, I, Juliano, call on this crystal to be raised. A brilliant light from that crystal is being sent directly to Porto Seguro, Brazil — where the channel and his friends are sitting. The whole area of Porto Seguro fills with this beautiful etheric crystal light. The light from this etheric crystal is going to these two planetary cities of light. These two cities are being raised higher and higher in the etheric baskets of light, through the third dimension, through the fourth dimension, and into the fifth dimension.

Brazil's Leadership Role in Spiritual Planetary Work

Energetically, a subcrystal of the Serra da Bocaina crystal, a miniature subcrystal, is being produced, duplicated, and sent to the homes of each of the leaders of these new planetary cities of light. Hundreds of people are now joining us and directing their thoughts and energies to these two cities. These planetary cities of light will be the beginning of ten more such cities that are soon to be activated in Brazil, which is going to become a leader in activating planetary cities of light. Brazil will become a spiritual leader of fifth-dimensional energy on this planet.

The development of these planetary cities of light is a natural outgrowth of the new spiritual role that Brazil is going to take. Several countries in the world are going to take leadership roles in planetary healing. Brazil is going to be one of the three countries that will assume the role of leadership in planetary healing and in using the concept of planetary cities of light. This work is so important and so powerful at this time, for the energies of our collective work with you are going to raise the vibrational energy fields of many more planetary cities of light.

I send you my light and my love. Know also that there are many areas in the galaxy at this moment that are connecting to the planetary cities of light, but in particular the two new planetary cities of light here. And know that my starship Athena is activating new corridors over these two planetary cities of light as they become anchors for the leadership role in the spiritual planetary healing that Brazil is going to assume in 2012. I am Juliano. Good day.

BOOK II:
Basics of Arcturian Spiritual Technology

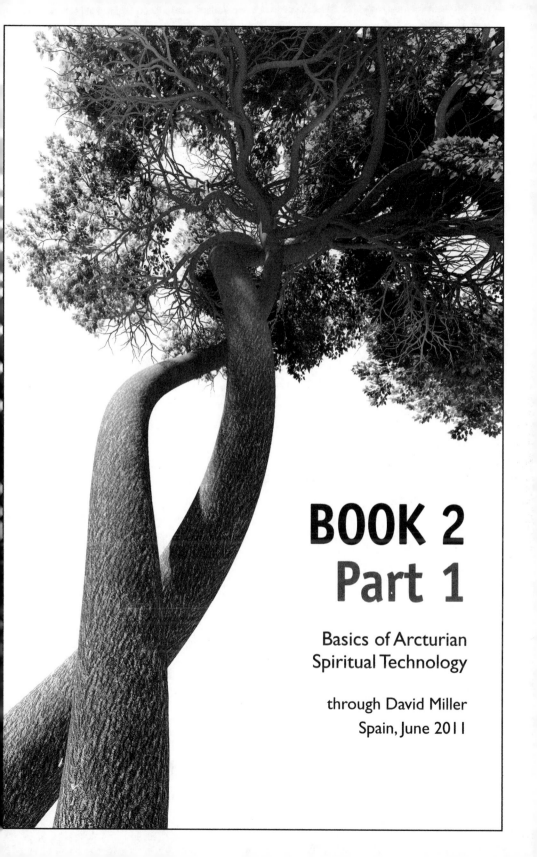

BOOK 2
Part 1

Basics of Arcturian
Spiritual Technology

through David Miller
Spain, June 2011

CHAPTER ONE

Planetary Crisis of Earth, Ascension, and Exercise with the Cosmic Egg

Juliano and the Arcturians

Greetings, I am Juliano. We are the Arcturians. We are with you in your experience of this Earth's planetary crisis. It is hard to accept and understand that this planet is in a crisis. Everyone in different parts of the world is experiencing the crisis in a different way. Some parts of the planet are experiencing flooding, tsunamis, and earthquakes. Some parts of the planet are experiencing droughts. Some parts of the planet are experiencing cyclones. Some parts of the planet are experiencing flooding. Many parts of the planet are experiencing financial crisis. And many, many parts of this planet are engaged in social unrest and very serious war.

The Delicate Balance of Earth's Feedback System

All of these things are affecting the delicate balance of the biosphere. The biosphere is the energy field that is holding together and containing the life-force energy for Earth. The biosphere is able to keep a delicate balance that is needed for life on Earth. This includes the delicate percentages of oxygen and nitrogen in the atmosphere, and many other factors that relate to keeping a certain temperature so that the life can exist comfortably, and of course the balance of the percentage of water versus the percentage of land on Earth. It also includes the ocean currents that are flowing at a certain rate and at the correct temperature. Some parts of the world have recently experienced La Niña, which is due to an ocean current shift that really has caused much devastation and many weather pattern destructions.

The biosphere contains Earth's feedback loop system. The feedback loop system is a complex interactive loop and a self-regulating mechanism. This means that the self-regulating mechanism tries to maintain conditions so that a definite pattern of temperatures and rainfall is maintained throughout the planet. There are thresholds at which the loop system can bring back temperatures within a certain balance. It is truly an amazing and complex system, but humankind still has no concept or awareness of this feedback loop system and its importance.

A volcanic eruption or a tsunami can be an attempt of the feedback loop system to bring everything back into a balance. But you know that sometimes, if Earth is too far out of balance, the correction to bring it into balance can be more violent. You are already seeing such violent reactions on Earth. These reactions that you have seen are but the beginning shifts in Earth's attempt to rebalance everything. The more out of balance Earth becomes, the more dramatic the corrections for Earth's feedback loop system will have to be.

Earth faces a crisis, and, generally, the world governments are not willing to admit this. They are not willing to discuss or admit that there is a feedback loop system. Finally, generally, Earth's peoples are not willing to admit that Earth is a living spirit. Earth is a living planet — it is not a dead planet. It has a spiritual presence that is known as Gaia, and it can respond to humankind's telepathic ceremonial communications.

You Are Living on the Edge of Evolutionary Change

You may ask, "What does this Earth crisis have to do with the ascension?" The answer is that the ascension is part of the opportunity that is created when a planet is in such a crisis. Because when a planet is in a crisis, there also is the opportunity for evolutionary change. There is an opportunity for evolutionary change, but there is also a necessity for evolutionary change.

Previous human-like forms existed on Earth. Let us use the example of Neanderthal man and Cro-Magnon man. An evolutionary change was necessary for both of them to exist; they both lived in Europe. Because of temperature changes, ice ages, and so on, an evolutionary change was necessary for survival. Neanderthal men were not able to make the necessary evolutionary changes and died. Cro-Magnon men, who are your forerunners, were able to make the evolutionary change. Part of that evolutionary change involved evolving into a being who possesses higher intelligence. Now we are in the same position; that is, we are in a dangerous crisis in which an evolutionary change is necessary. You are living right now on the edge of such an evolutionary change. A dramatic change is now necessary if humanity is to survive.

What type of evolutionary change is necessary for humanity to survive? The answer is that the evolutionary change must be a change in consciousness. The change in consciousness involves an awareness of the fifth dimension and an awareness of the ability of humanity to ascend into the higher realms. It also includes the ability to download or bring down energy from the fifth dimension and use that energy to solve Earth's third-dimensional problems. We can say that the ascension is based on the awareness of the fifth dimension. The ascension is also introducing to humanity the existence of the fifth dimension.

The ascension has a second important aspect: The fifth-dimensional energy needed for ascension and the accompanying fifth-dimensional light can be brought down to help solve Earth's problems. Each of you desires, I know, to ascend to the fifth dimension. But you are part of the higher fifth-dimensional energy, and that means also that you have a role to play in the planetary healing. Clearly, you are going to ascend in the future, but also clearly your role and your mission include working with the fifth-dimensional energy on Earth now.

Laying the Fifth-Dimensional Foundation

The ascension energy involves you ascending to the higher realm, and it secondly involves your participation in teaching and bringing down higher energy onto Earth now. The ascension is an important evolutionary awareness and a step for humankind that is necessary for Earth's survival. The evolutionary shift for the Cro-Magnons was the shift to a higher intelligence, a higher mental brainpower. The shift for solving the evolutionary crisis now is the development of the awareness of the fifth dimension and the relationship between spirituality and the planet. This awareness of the relationship between spirituality and the survival of the planets requires that humanity raise its spiritual light-quotient energy. [Chants.]

Open up your consciousness to the fifth dimension. Receive now the corridor of light that I have placed over this room. Know that you are part of the evolutionary new energy group. The new group of energy is forming a circle of participants, and a certain key number of people on Earth must embrace the energies of the fifth dimension. When that "magical" number is reached, the fifth-dimensional energy will be grounded firmly in place on this planet. This energy must be firmly in place before the actual ascension can occur.

Many people have asked, "Why has the ascension not occurred yet?" The answer in part is because the firm foundation to keep this fifth-dimensional energy in the evolutionary process has not been firmly set in the planet. But we are getting close, and you are working very much for this. I know that many of you have reincarnated onto Earth at this time to participate in the laying of the fifth-dimensional foundation.

Your Physical Body Knows How to Ascend

I would like to speak more directly about ascension. Ascension is the ability to shift one's energy so that one can move one's physical body and energy field into the fifth dimension. The fifth dimension is a place where there is freedom from the incarnational cycle, which means that the person who does ascend is not obligated to return to Earth. We want to compare the process of ascension to the process of dying. Your body knows how to die. You, as an ego presence, as a self, may not know how to die. In fact, your ego-self often believes that you will not die. Many of you may still hold the illusion that you will live on this planet forever. When people are in a hospice unit in a nursing home in America, they joke, "Nobody gets out of here alive." That is at least an awareness that the body and this physical presence will end.

I do not know how many of you have been around dying people. This channel has seen hundreds of people dying in his work at the hospital, and one of the obvious lessons is that the body knows how to die. Before dying, the person will usually lose consciousness, and then he or she may go into a coma. The body has a certain process of how it shuts itself off. The oxygen will stay in the center of the body, and the feet and the extremities will receive less oxygen. There is a certain breathing pattern that people use before they die. The respiratory pattern becomes less and less frequent — maybe it goes from thirteen respirations a minute down to eight. The body actually has a sequence it follows. This sequence becomes really clear within the last twenty-four to forty-eight hours before the physical death occurs. The person has no consciousness of how the body does it and no control, and actually this dying process is a natural process. The body knows how to stop the pain, so eventually the spirit can comfortably be released from the body and move on.

The point is that this is a deep wisdom within the physical body. I am here today to tell you that your body also knows how to ascend. This is great news. Just like your human body knows how to die, the human body also knows how to go through the ascension. More and more people will ascend. This is an evolutionary change that is now coming into humanity's consciousness. We are teaching several different stages and several different skills for awakening within you this deep hidden knowledge of how to ascend.

Two of the techniques that we are teaching are shimmering and unlocking the codes of ascension. Other techniques include raising the spiritual light quotient, thought projection, and the use of etheric crystals to raise your thinking power. We call the thinking-power ratio the arcan energy. These are subjects that we would like to explore in depth with you, because even though the ascension energy is a deep wisdom within your body, you still have to participate in it; it does not happen automatically. The reason why it does not happen automatically is because you are on the forefront of a huge evolutionary ascension. Maybe it is natural now for humans to go to school and to practice expanding the memory. In the future, humanity will be teaching these spiritual skills that we are going to be discussing today. These skills of ascension will be part of the curriculum in future learning, and you are now the first wave of ascension seekers. [Chants.]

Learning to Pulse Your Aura

Become aware of your aura. Become aware of the shape of your aura, and command your aura to go into the shape of the cosmic egg. Say these words to yourselves: "I command that my aura now go to the shape of the cosmic egg." For you have the control of shaping your aura through your commands. No matter how disorganized or ungrounded you feel, when you command with your mind to shape your aura, your aura will respond. Your aura is around your body, and the idea of shimmering begins with the aura. Visualize a dark-blue line around your aura. This is an outline of your aura.

Become aware that the aura has a pulse, just like your human pulse. I will make a sound that will be rhythmically aligned to the pulse of your aura, and just allow the pulse of your aura to be resonant with this sound. [Sounds.] Let your aura be pulsing at higher speed, for in the ascension time your aura pulse will be going very rapidly. [Sounds.] Now experience the rapid, increasing pulsing of your aura in this moment of silence. [Silence.]

Become aware of the effects of the rapid pulsing of your aura on your physical body. Remember that the aura is around your physical body, so the rapid pulsing of your aura has a positive effect on your body. It can make your body feel lighter, more etheric, and in some cases, it can even make your physical body feel like it can fly.

We will do another round to make you practice this pulsing and also study the effect that the rapid pulsing has on your physical body. Try to make the pulsing resonate with this tone. [Sounds.] Again, go into silence and notice the effect that this pulsing is having on your physical body. [Silence.] You can also remember and hear the sounds of the *ta-ta-ta-ta* as you are doing this silent meditation. [Silence.]

This exercise is teaching you the beginning stage of ascension. When you are ascending, your pulse will be going at least a thousand times faster than what I have just been teaching you. I am talking about the pulse of your aura, of course. When the pulse of the aura reaches a certain critical speed or pulsing, the body begins to shift into another dimension. But you have to have some practice because you want to be prepared.

The ascension is a transformation with total consciousness. It is very different from the dying experience, because in dying, you lose consciousness and your body takes over and goes through a preplanned process. But in the ascension, it is exactly the opposite. You go into a higher consciousness. You are very aware of everything that is happening. I want to take you to the next level of this exercise. But before I do that, I want to stop to see if there are any questions about the experience that I have explained so far.

Separating the Pulse of Your Aura from the Pulses of Your Physical Body

What if, when your aura is pulsing, your heart also starts pulsing very strongly?

The first part of the exercise is to have you beat or pulse your aura. I understand that your heart would also start to beat rapidly, but eventually you are going to have to separate the heartbeat from the pulse of your aura. If your heartbeat is going too fast, you will have to lower the pulsing of your aura so that your heartbeat is comfortable, because we do not want you to injure yourself. But eventually, you will be able to separate the pulsing of the aura so that will not increase your heartbeat and make you sick.

As you are experiencing it now, slow down your aura when the heart becomes uncomfortable and slow your pulsing until your heartbeat is at a comfortable rate. Then eventually, with practice, you can separate the aura pulsing from the heart pulsing. Imagine that the aura pulsing could be a thousand beats a second or a minute. Your heart cannot possibly keep up with that. At this point, I would just increase the pulsing and then notice if the heartbeat increases. Stay at that lower pace and experiment with how you could separate the aura pulses from your heartbeat. As your aura pulses higher, eventually your heartbeat will not follow.

I guess my question is very similar, but I was feeling that it was difficult to breathe. I was lacking air.

I understand why it would be difficult to breathe. Certainly, when you are excited or even overly charged, you may stop your breathing. Remember, I teach you this exercise so you can practice and work out these problems. Think about this: The yogi can slow his breath down to maybe seven or eight times a minute or much lower, but he does not stop the breathing process. In your case, you will have to slow down the aura pulsing so that your breathing gets into a rhythm and does not freeze or stop. That is something that you could learn to do also, because it is not good to stop breathing. It is good that we can work out these other problems first. You can try the aura exercise at a slower pace so that you can have control. Remember that there will be no time to practice this at the moment of ascension, so that is why it is better to practice it before.

I do not know if I am understanding this properly. I understand I cannot breathe fast, so how will I be able to move fast in the ascension light? Am I understanding this properly?

What you are moving is the pulse of your aura. The first stage is that you imagine that your aura is in the shape of the cosmic egg and that there is a line around the whole aura, around the whole egg. That line is what is pulsing. First you must become aware of the fact that your aura is pulsing. Many people do not even know that the aura pulses. Let me say that there are many things that affect the pulsing of an aura. If you see somebody who is on alcohol or drugs, you will see that he or she has a very slow, irregular aura pulse. Even in your language, you say, "That person is of low vibration." When you are at a higher vibration and higher energy, then you are concentrating on a higher light, such as the light of Jesus or Sananda. When thinking about Jesus, your aura will pulse at a higher speed and vibration. This is a paradox because when the regular pulse of your body is going too fast, there can be a problem. But when the aura is pulsing faster, you are going into a higher light, and this is a positive development. So you have to be preparing your physical body for higher vibrations. Your body is the vessel.

Do Not Ascend Before Your Time

How will we know that it is our moment of ascension?

I am going to have Archangel Metatron answer the question later, because there will be a sound of ascension. This sound has never been heard before. When you hear the sound, your body and your inner knowing will know what it is. Archangel Metatron will tell you more about the type of sound and how you will respond to it.

When I was doing the exercise, I enjoyed it a lot, but it was very difficult for me to come back. If I do this on my own, how am I going to come back to the now?

First of all, I think that you are very advanced, even if you have difficulty coming back. That is a good sign, because it means you are able to leave your body. When you are practicing alone, or even when you are doing this with us, you must make the following statement before you start the exercise: "I promise myself before I do this exercise, I make the promise and agreement, that I will return to my body in the third dimension and I promise this." If you cannot make that promise to yourself, please do not do this exercise. It is okay to have difficulties coming back, but you must honor this promise, because it is not your time yet to ascend.

Timing is everything. You want to ascend in the right time, not the wrong time. The guides, teachers, and ascended masters are opening up the doorway of ascension for you. You do not want to go up to the fifth dimension, knock on the door, and then have the door not open. You want to go up, have the door open, and then walk through. There would be help if you, for some reason, have trouble coming back, but we do not want you to go through that discomfort.

Another Exercise to Pulse Your Aura

I suggest that we do one more of these pulsing exercises, and I will not go so fast. Are we ready now? I will give a small tone to prepare. [Chants.] You may do it with me. Visualize your aura. Command that your aura go into the shape of the cosmic egg. Become aware of a solid blue line around the cosmic egg. Your aura has a pulse beat, and this pulse beat is mostly expressed at the outer blue line. Become aware and experience the natural pulse of your aura. See that this pulse has a natural harmonic rhythm. When you hear this sound I make, your pulse will even go to a higher and more balanced rhythm. Just listen and become aware of your pulse beat as you hear this word toned. [Chants.]

The pulse of your aura is very rhythmic. Your physical body is now going to a state of relaxation, and a very comfortable separation now exists between your aura pulsing and your physical body. In some ways, your physical body is in a deep state of relaxation, almost like you are in a state of sleep, but your aura is in a different energy state. As I make these tonal beats, slowly increase the speed of the pulsing of your aura. [Sounds.] Go into a state of silent meditation, hearing these sounds and pulsing your aura to match them. [Silence.]

Come back. Become aware of yourself. Be ready to reenter and awaken your physical body. You can come back into your physical body, and at the same time

Gateway of Ascension

the pulsing of your aura can continue. Come back now into your physical body awakened.

I felt a normal breathing, but my body seemed to be moving to and fro.

Your body is readjusting to the newer vibration. Your aura has reached a higher vibration, and now your body has to readjust itself. This is good. Many people do not realize that the body also has to go through adjustments. When the aura is in a higher light, the body must make some adjustments.

Is the cosmic egg exercise that we are doing somehow related to what is called merkabah?

The exercise we are doing is part of merkabah. But this cosmic egg exercise is a unique exercise that we, the Arcturians, are teaching, because this is the first part of shimmering. We have not even gone to the second part yet, which we can do if you want. In the merkabah, you move your aura into a vehicle, and the vehicle takes you up to the higher level. In this exercise, you are directly going there through your aura.

CHAPTER TWO

The Sounds of Ascension and Unlocking the Codes of Ascension

Archangel Metatron

Greetings, I am Archangel Metatron. I am sitting at the stargate. The stargate is the transitional gateway into the fifth dimension. When you go through the stargate, you have graduated from Earth. There are only two stargates in the entire galaxy. One of the stargates is here, near Arcturus. We, the Arcturians, have been given the responsibility of overseeing the stargate. When the ascension occurs, you will be able to transition through this gateway known as the stargate. The doorway will be open. You will be able to pass through this doorway and pass into the fifth dimension.

The fifth dimension is an eternally beautiful garden area. In the fifth dimension, we are not constrained by linear time. Time in the third dimension is in a line — past, present, and future. In the fifth dimension, time is like a circle — past, present, and future interacting. If you can experience fifth-dimensional time in the third dimension, you can experience your future self as well as your past self. This is a powerful and life-changing experience, especially when you have the opportunity to experience your future self, because as your future self, you are already an ascended master. It is wonderful to experience yourself in your future, when you have evolved even more than now.

Let the Doorway of Ascension Be Opened to You
I will talk to you about the sounds of ascension and the unlocking of the codes of ascension. Juliano talked about how the body knows to ascend. In order for the body to go through the ascension process, the mind and the body together

must experience what is called unlocking the codes of ascension. This has been compared to the opening of the assemblage point. The assemblage point is an area in the body described by the shamans where the doors of perception are opened during special experiences. When the doorways are opened, the assemblage points are opened and the person can see the true reality, which includes all the different levels and dimensions, all the auras, the cords that are attached to everyone, the thought waves of people, and many other interesting things.

If your assemblage point were opened prematurely, you would have difficulty navigating through this reality. There are always so many things to see and to be careful of when you are walking around in the streets. Can you imagine if you were able to see everybody's cords of attachment and auras? It would be very difficult to move. The codes of ascension are also powerful. You have been trained to stay here on Earth. There is a certain process of constriction that you have to experience in order to be in Earth's body.

The codes of ascension, when they are unlocked, allow you to be free of that constriction and to go into the higher-energy corridors. The unlocking of the codes of ascension can occur through sounds and coded words. It happens that Hebrew is a sacred language, like Sanskrit, and there are certain tonal words and sounds that, when said with a certain intention, open up the codes of ascension within the minds and bodies of the people hearing the tones. Therefore, we can activate you into a higher level when you hear the certain tones from these sacred Hebrew words. These words are also known in Latin, Spanish, and English. I believe that the sacred words for the ascension are also written on top of the Sagrada Família church in Barcelona, Spain. These words say: "Holy, holy, holy is the lord of hosts." But the words have a greater power in the original Hebrew. The original Hebrew has connections to the greater galaxy.

What I am going to do is to bring down the energy of the sacred words through the channel, and then you can receive the energy that will unlock the codes of ascension. What does it mean to unlock the codes of ascension? What is the effect? It helps you to more easily learn the skills and practices necessary for ascension. It also opens you up more clearly toward your ascended masters, guides, and teachers. And most importantly, it opens up your body and mind to allow this process to occur. The body has to be reminded that it does not need to be constricted anymore, that it is okay to drop the constrictions. Are you willing to hear the sacred words that can unlock the codes of ascension? [Chants.] Together.

Let the keys of ascension be unlocked so that you are opened to all of the energy of the fifth dimension, so that you are opened to receiving the instructions on how to ascend, and so that you can go through the process of ascension into the fifth dimension with ease and comfort. [Chants.] Go into meditation now and allow these sounds that you have just heard to work on unlocking these codes within you.

Adonai is my lord. We accept that my lord, Adonai, is giving us the grace to ascend, like Enoch, like Eliyahu, like Jesus, and even like Mohamed — they all have ascended. They have been showing the way of ascension, but this way of ascension is encoded into your DNA. It is only waiting for the right evolutionary circumstances to open. Let the doorway of ascension be opened to you. Let our Father's light shine into you. We call this the holy light. [Chants.]

The Sound of Ascension

The holy light is the light of the Holy Spirit. There is, of course, the sacred sound, but there is also the holy light. People ask, "What will the sound of ascension be? How will it sound?" It is a sound that you have not heard. It is a sound that is so beautiful and so powerful that it is not able to be described, but the sound itself will set off an immediate energetic transformation. Some have tried to describe and explain some of the sounds through music. There was an interesting piece of music by Ravel called "Bolero," which builds up to a beautiful crescendo, which is exciting and opening. But that music is maybe one-thousandth of the power or beauty of the sound of ascension. There is this beautiful German song called "Ode to Joy" which is in Beethoven's Ninth Symphony. Its lyrics include the line, "Freude, freude schöner Goetterfunken" [translation: "Joy, joy, beautiful and wondrous spark"], and this tone is totally transforming in this beautiful music. The beauty of this sound of ascension approaches music from Beethoven. There is beautiful music on this planet that is trying to raise up the vibrational energy for this type of ascension work.

The sound of ascension has the ability to be both heard and seen. That is called synesthesia, which is the ability to hear and see at the same time. The sound of ascension also can be seen as the light of ascension. The sound has a light. You will hear, you will see, and you will feel at the same time. At that moment, when you hear and see this sound, there will be such a joy and an overwhelming emotional reaction. Many of you will immediately start crying. It is not a crying of sadness. It is a crying at being overwhelmed with the power of the moment of ascension. It is a sound that it is now beyond your hearing threshold. You have a very limited range of hearing. The sound of ascension is now out of your range, but it will be coming into your range.

[Chants.]

Almighty God, *El Shaddai*. I am Archangel Metatron. Sananda will now speak to you.

CHAPTER THREE

The Ascension

Sananda

Greetings, I am Sananda. Your ascension brings great joy to us. Your ascension is the fulfillment of all of our work that was brought down to Earth 2,000 years ago — work that many of the ascended masters have been working to explain. Of course, the codes of ascension are within your DNA. Our Father and our great Mother want you to ascend. And you want to ascend. We are working to show you the way to the ascension. The way of the ascension is by opening your heart to the love of all that is, all that was, and all that will be. These are the instructions directly from our Father, for he was, is, and will be. Just like you were, are, and will be. That is the key to your understanding of your powers of ascension. When it is said that you are made in the image of the Creator, it means that you too have these three attributes. You exist in the past, present, and future all at the same moment.

Heart Energy Is Your Entrance Key to Ascension
How can you open up your heart more? The heart energy is the entrance key so you can pass into the fifth dimension. We must speak as best as we can about this quality known as love. I like to explain what it means to love our Father. When you are experiencing the closeness and the love for the Father, this closeness is the highest and most important experience. The ancient rabbis had a special word for those who can maintain the closeness to the father. This closeness required that your heart was always there, always with the father and his hierarchy. The

hierarchy is referred to as the *Tzeva'oth*, the core of the army that is working with the Father. In Hebrew, the ancient rabbis called this clinging and closeness to the Creator *devekut*, which is the ability to stay close to the Creator. When you are closer to the Creator, the ascension is so easy.

I, Sananda, bring down the holy light into this room. As the holy light comes into this room, Mother Mary is also with me. She is also on top of the room with open hands and heart. You all are below us with your beautifully shaped auras that Juliano calls your cosmic eggs. You have the beautiful blue light around the edges of your auras. Mary and I are sending this beautiful golden light into this room and your auras are receiving this light. You find that your aura is in beautiful harmony and has a beautiful rhythmic pulsing from the golden light. [Chants: *Holy light*.]

I am here to help you with your ascension. At the moment of ascension, we will be appearing to you. Mary and I will be extending our hands to welcome you into the corridor of ascension. We have already downloaded two ladders of ascension. These are like the ladders that Jacob used in the Bible. You can use them to walk up into the higher realms. [Chants.]

The Transformative Energy of Agape

There is a beautiful concept in Greek called agape, which is a beautiful description of a higher energy of love. This is the love that is totally mature. It is the unconditional love of the mother; it is the unconditional love of the father also; it is the love of the husband for the wife and the wife for the husband. It is the love of the mother for her child, the love of the brother for the brother, and love of the sister for the sister. All of these different loves come together into one powerful love, the love of agape. When you experience this love, it is totally transforming.

The ascension is also an emotional transformation. During the ascension, you will review all of your life on Earth and you will immediately understand that everything that happened to you was as it should be and that it was for your benefit. All of the pain, suffering, and heartache that you had on Earth will make sense and be part of a process that you will accept. But you will have a greater mind and wisdom at that moment. And you will not have any doubt that everything you did was part of a wonderful process and experience for you. You will be able to see and accept all of your Earth experiences at that moment. It is true that at the moment of ascension, you will want to cut your ties to Earth, but also remember that you will have experienced love for your Earth's body and your Earth's experience. The human body is like a coat that you will take off at the moment of ascension. But you do not want to take the coat off and throw it on the ground in anger; rather take off your coat with love and appreciation for all that your body has allowed you to do and experience in Earth. [Chants: *Agape.*]

The holy light continues to fill this room with a golden energy. You are bathing in this beautiful light. Your mind is also receiving great information and wisdom that is coming to you. Remember that you are part of what Juliano calls the evolutionary change. The evolutionary change needs the lightworkers. You are servants to the Creator, who wants this dimension to ascend, who wants this planet to ascend. I send light now to the holy city of Jerusalem, city of light and peace, where there is a ladder of ascension now at the Dome of the Rock. Visualize it now. It has a golden roof and there is a beautiful golden ladder above the dome. The ladder is going up to the fifth dimension. [Chants.] I am Sananda. Good day.

CHAPTER FOUR

Planetary Healing, Arcan Energy, and Etheric Crystals

Juliano and the Arcturians

Greetings, I am Juliano. We are the Arcturians. We would like to focus now on the planetary healing. The ascension has the aspects of the personal ascension and the planetary ascension. We are cooperating and working with the other ascended masters to create the conditions necessary for Earth to ascend. Planetary ascension is a newer concept that was introduced recently to humanity. We believe that the original idea was introduced to humanity around 1987, when there was a global activity called the Harmonic Convergence. Later people began to realize that we are globally connected while living on a spiritual being called Gaia. The pictures that have come back from the astronauts showing Earth have contributed greatly to the concepts of global consciousness and planetary healing. Even now, you can remember the astronauts saying how beautiful and peaceful Earth looks from outer space.

We are talking about the new spiritual technology for the personal ascension, but there is also a new spiritual technology for the planetary ascension. Remember that we are higher interdimensional space beings and we have traveled through many different planets and areas of the galaxy. At this point, there are approximately one to two hundred planets that have life forms in our galaxy — the Milky Way — similar in evolution to Earth. In our travels, we have seen different planets go through different stages of development like Earth.

Earth's Crisis of Spirituality Versus Technology

We now say that Earth is going through a crisis of spirituality versus technology.

The question is: Can the spirituality of the planet catch up with the technology? Because if the spirituality does not keep up with the planet and the planetary technology that has been developed by humanity, then the technology of humanity could destroy the planet or the biosphere in which humanity lives.

I have seen several planets destroyed. It was very painful to watch. But even now you see how painful it is to see your planet being harmed. There is a stage in planetary healing in which humanity learns how to interact with the spirit of the planet. This stage must be reached and expanded in order to protect Earth. We call this process of awareness part of planetary healing. We call it this because the planetary healers must be awakened to the fact that Earth is a living spirit and it can ascend. What a beautiful idea to think that an entire planet can ascend.

I know that many starseeds would turn down your opportunity to ascend in a first wave if they could participate at a later time in the ascension of the whole planet. This is admirable and it is a great dedication from your part. We are talking about evolution on a personal and a planetary basis. On a personal basis, we have already talked about consciousness and awareness of ascension in the fifth dimension. On a planetary basis, we are now introducing the concept of Biorelativity. Biorelativity is the ability of the higher-evolved beings of the planet to telepathically communicate with the spirit of that planet. The purpose of this interaction is for the purpose of moderating and rebalancing the planet with the least intrusion and disruption. Also part of the ideas of Biorelativity and planetary healing is to attract and link this planet now with the fifth dimension. This is a profoundly important step, linking this planet with fifth-dimensional energy now.

Planetary Cities of Light

There are techniques to do planetary healing, and those techniques also involve linking the planet to the fifth dimension, which will assist the planet in its ascension. We have introduced new planetary spiritual technology for planetary healing. One major planetary technology is the development of the planetary cities of light. The planetary healer is looking to create sacred places on the planet. The importance of these places cannot be underestimated because people want to do as much as they can to change Earth. The overwhelming problems with the political and economic situation on the planet make it difficult to decide how to do a planetary intervention. A way of intervening is working on small areas that you are living in. These small areas can be called planetary cities of light.

Being a planetary city of light means that the small area or city designated has an awareness of the planet, so the activities and energies in the city are undertaken considering how they will affect the planet. For example, a planetary city of light would not want to have a nuclear power plant in it. We spoke in great length about the dangers of nuclear technology well before the Fukushima earthquake and tsunami. We are against nuclear power because we believe that it distorts the etheric aura of Earth. It creates holes in Earth's aura. These holes allow life-force energy to escape.

When we are talking about the planetary cities of light, we are talking about creating special, sacred places. Remember, when we did the exercise with shimmering, we created a cosmic egg shape and then used the line to go around the shape of the aura. In creating the planetary cities of light, we work with an energy line created around the whole city. We are creating this energy field so that only higher energy can come into the field.

It is like the concept of Shamballa or Shangri-la. In Shamballa, there is an energy line or border around the whole city. If you have lower third-dimensional energy and it is very dense, you cannot come into the city because the protective energy around the city will not let you pass through it. It is the same idea with the planetary cities of light. You are helping to create this beautiful boundary of etheric energy protection. Therefore, you ensure that only higher energy and thoughts can come in, and only higher energy will affect everybody who is living in the planetary city of light. There are over fifty planetary cities of light that have been activated through the Arcturian work, and we are sure that the number is going to grow dramatically.

We have said that these planetary cities of light can also be neighborhoods. It is difficult to have a whole large city like Barcelona become a planetary city of light. It is possible, but it would require maybe a thousand lightworkers to work on it. It is possible to take a certain area or neighborhood and work on that area as a planetary city of light. This has already happened in several places in Argentina and Brazil.

Establishing a New Balance

The more planetary cities of light there are on the planet, the more fifth-dimensional connections this planet will have. These planetary cities of light will also be protected from some of the major Earth changes that are coming. There are already many predictions about what is going to happen in 2012. The idea that planetary cities of light can be protected from these changes is very attractive. This is possible because one principle of Biorelativity states that the inhabitants of the planet can telepathically communicate with the spirit of Earth and ask for protection and balance on the area of the planet where they live. In return, those people living in the planetary cities of light are dedicated to establishing balance and harmony with Earth and also dedicated to certain energetic practices, such as using crystals and establishing an energy field to create a new balance.

This new balance also includes the balance of a just society. This means that the planetary city of light is environmentally in balance with Earth, but it is also in balance from the standpoint of social justice. That is, people in the planetary city of light are living with higher fifth-dimensional principles of justice, brotherhood, and service. Now the planetary cities of light are developing connections with each other. That means there are sister cities already. One planetary city of light in England has another sister planetary city of light in Mexico. This idea is a powerful principle to create healing for the planet.

Etheric Crystals Help to Rebalance Earth

Another planetary technology that we are using is that of etheric crystals. We know that there must be new meridian lines on Earth. Earth is a living planet and it does have meridian lines, or ley lines, that keep open certain energy channels that are necessary, but many of these areas have been blocked by dams and by pollution. So the question is: How do we open up these lines? The answer is that we can do bypass surgery or create alternate ley lines. We know that it is controversial now to remove dams.

We have downloaded twelve etheric crystals throughout the planet, and these twelve etheric crystals are creating a new ley line system and a new pattern of meridians. These new patterns can help to rebalance Earth. These etheric crystals also have the power of attraction. They are serving as attractive links to fifth-dimensional Earth. This means that Earth has the ability to attract the fifth dimension as a planet. This raises the important point that Earth has a role in attracting the fifth dimension. The attraction of the fifth dimension will be accomplished through the planetary cities of light and by the twelve etheric crystals.

Explosive Solar Activity in 2012

Everything is complicated now because of the special energy of the Central Sun, which will be at its height of power on December 21, 2012. There are many different factors affecting Earth, starting with the Earth changes themselves. But there are also the extra factors, even factors from the Sun. Your Sun is reacting to the influences from outside of the solar system. The Sun is going to have some interesting explosive activity in the coming years. Part of this activity and explosive energy could result in the destruction of many of the communication satellites on Earth. This could set off a new economic crisis on Earth. For example, people will not be able to use their credit cards or pursue other economic activities that require these communication satellites.

These solar explosions will be periodic, and they will create many problems for Earth. I would recommend for any type of travel to be kept to a minimum during that time of solar activity. I am talking specifically about air travel, because without the satellites it will be difficult and there will be much confusion on the planet. It is a shame that Earth is not doing anything to prepare for such blackouts due to the solar activity.

The year 2012 will also create the alignment of the Central Sun, which in turn will create a powerful energy, bringing new healing ideas and techniques from the fifth dimension. In fact, the fifth dimension and the third dimension will intersect, and fifth-dimensional energy is so powerful that it will come down to Earth at that time and download powerful instructions and energy transformations. I want to talk about two other concepts: the arcan energy and the etheric crystals.

I understood that there were some dates of maximum solar activity, but I did not understand if the intersection between the third and fifth dimension was supposed to happen before or after that.

We do not have exact dates, but there will be an intersection. Some people have talked about the null zone, but the result of the null zone is similar to what is happening in the magnetic solar storms. So this will result in the unbalancing and even destruction of some of the communication satellites. All I can say is that it is possible that the intersection of the dimensions will occur at this time [December 21, 2012]. But predictions are very difficult to be exact about, because there are so many different factors occurring.

About traveling — what about the people who make a living out of traveling?

I understand that there are problems with traveling. With these high solar activities, the airplanes are exposed to more radiation while flying. The radar and all the other navigational equipment might not work as well. As with all information, you have to make decisions based on what you think is best. But it is a well-known scientific fact that the solar activity is now increasing, and you know how unpredictable the weather is. Imagine that the solar activity could also become unpredictable.

If there is a solar activity that knocks off communication satellites and makes navigation equipment unreliable, I am sure that the airplane associations will take the necessary steps to prevent the airplanes and the pilots from flying. The energy of the Sun sometimes takes several days until it gets here — I am talking about the magnetic energy — so there will be warnings about this.

Food-Related Issues

When our vibration increases, will we need less foodstuffs for the physical body?

Generally you will need less food, but it is also important to avoid certain foods. For example, sometimes red meat makes your energy slow. But some people can have red meat and it will not affect them. So we cannot make general statements that everybody must avoid this or that, but all we can say is you must be sensitive to what your body needs and wants. The nature of the food supply is going to become more and more of an issue. There is so much pollution and radiation in different parts of the planet that it is going to be harder to find pure food. I think that is more of an issue than specifically what to eat.

I would like to ask about epidemics from contaminated vegetables. No one knows the origin, but contaminated vegetables produce many deaths. Is this caused by humans?

First of all, let us look at this at two levels. The first level is that the immune system of humankind is weaker. What you now see as an epidemic of food would not normally affect people if their general immune systems were stronger. There are people who could eat contaminated cucumbers and have no problems and other people who could have problems. Secondly, the issue of the genetic manipulation of food is a factor — how the food is produced, what seeds are used, and the fact that the soil is not as strong. There are many factors. There is no one single thing that is causing the new epidemics, but rather it is a multiplicity of things: the lower immune system of the human, the genetic manipulation of the seeds, the lower quality of the soil, and of course the use of pesticides. That all creates the right conditions. There are super bacteria now that were not present before. Where do they come from? We know that there has been an overuse of antibiotics, and this has created an opportunistic condition in the food chain now around the world. It can happen everywhere. The whole food chain is fragile right now.

Questions about the Planetary Cities of Light

About the activated cities of light — are they in the region where the etheric crystals are?

The planetary cities of light are not always in the same places as the etheric crystals, but they are of course able to relate to them. However, the etheric crystals are in different places. Those places where the etheric crystals are can also be cities of light. There is a city close to Lago Puelo, Argentina, where an etheric crystal is. There is now a city called San Martín de los Andes that has become a city of light. There is a place near Munich called Aufkirchen that has also become a city of light, but there is no etheric crystal there. And of course, Sant Pere de Ribes is a city of light, and there is no crystal there.

What are the requirements to be a planetary city of light?

The first requirement is that we need to have lightworkers who live there and are willing to do the spiritual exercises to maintain the energy field. There is a special exercise that we do to activate the city. This includes putting people around the city and burying crystals around the four cardinal points of the city. We have people going around the border of the city during the activation of the city. After the activation, the lightworkers periodically meet to activate the energy of the city. Actually, I want people to understand that they could also do the same thing around their houses or neighborhoods. We cannot guarantee that your house or backyard will become well known like the planetary cities of light. We want the planetary cities of light to be well known. But you can do the same type of techniques around your house, and then your homes and backyards can become holders of fifth-dimensional energy light.

Could you talk to us about the city of light of Barcelona?

Barcelona now is not designated as a city of light. We think that it is a large city. It would be too much to make the whole city a city of light. We recommend that you choose a section of a city. That section of the city can be a city of light, which usually has the name of the neighborhood. For example, people wanted to make Los Angeles a city of light, but there are not enough lightworkers there to make it a city of light. In our estimation, it is much more important to work in small cities or neighborhoods, where you can assure that there will be enough lightworkers to cover the area, and then later on you can expand it.

How many lightworkers do you need to do the work in a neighborhood or a small city, and what is the method?

We recommend four people as a minimum. The most important thing is that the people who do the work are dedicated. It is better to have four people who are very dedicated than forty people with only a third of them working. We like very much the number of forty. We certainly would like to have forty people working in a city of light, but we recognize that sometimes it is difficult to get that number. I would say that if there were forty people who are really dedicated, that could be optimal. But even four to ten people could do it, and then later they can get more people.

As for the method, the first thing to do would be to contact the Group of Forty planetary city of light coordinator. Then the Group of Forty will activate the area through a global meditation. It is a planetary city of light and you want everybody on the planet to know about it. We designate a day when that city will be activated. We have meditators around the world who are working on the project, and they will work with you and send the energy to you on that exact day. The day you do that, you go around the city and bury crystals at the four cardinal points, and you get as many people as possible to stand around the outline of the city and create an energy line. Visualize a basket underneath the city and the basket lifting the city up into the fifth dimension. Then the basket is brought back down and the fifth-dimensional light is spread throughout the city. This is a quick summary of how the city is activated.

I am happy that you are interested in becoming planetary healers, because I know that many of you have come to Earth now just for this purpose. So planetary healers, awaken! Now is your time! I am Juliano. Good day.

CHAPTER FIVE

Thought Projection and the Crystal Lake in Arcturus

Juliano and the Arcturians

Greetings, I am Juliano. We are the Arcturians. We wish to continue with the exercises in shimmering. The next part of the exercises involves thought projection. Thought projection is the ability to send our etheric presence to another point. In fact, there are many stories of people who have been able to project themselves to another place and at the same time remain in the first place. There are two auras — two presences, in this case. This is one example of thought projection.

Thought Projection Is the Fastest Energy in the Universe

In our work, we have to discuss thought because thought is the fastest energy in the universe. Thought is quicker than the speed of light, and the speed of light, of course, is 186,000 miles per second. The speed of thought is much faster than that. You can think of a place and, with your thought, you can be there no matter what the distance is in the universe. Our good friends in the Pleiades have developed special space-travel techniques that combine the use of space antigravity technology with the thought processes of the space travelers to power their spaceships. Telepathy and thought projection are combined with space-engine travel. Space-engine technology alone can only bring you up to a certain speed.

At a point that is really so fast, approximately 50,000 miles per second in your terminology, space and time shift. The ability to project yourself with thinking becomes more possible at that speed. You actually leave the dimension you are in and go into an interdimensional corridor. This is also a well-known space-travel technique for the Arcturians.

Maybe you have wondered about how the higher extraterrestrial beings can come to Earth? For example, our star system and planet of Arcturus is approximately thirty-seven light-years from Earth, and the Pleiades are approximately 430 light-years from Earth; the round trip from the Pleiades to Earth would be 860 years. Most beings, even the higher beings, do not want to spend their whole lifetime traveling in a spaceship. The higher beings use the technology that I have just described. They accelerate their spaceships to a certain speed, and then they combine their thoughts to enter an interdimensional corridor from which they thought-project themselves to where they want to be — anywhere in the universe! This is a truly fantastic ability.

I give you this as an introduction because I want you to understand the concept of thought projection. In the first case I told you about, when the Pleiadians are using this technique, they initially accelerate their spaceships and then begin to visualize which place in the universe they want to go to. In the thought-projection exercise that we are doing, you are only able to bring your etheric presence; you are only able to thought-project your spirit. In the ascension, you can thought-project your spirit and your physical body because the energy of the ascension is so complex and so deep that it allows you to thought-project yourself the same way that the Pleiadian spaceships can thought-project themselves when they are traveling at these high speeds.

Another way of describing ascension is to say that your space-time relationship is shifting and opening, and you can take advantage of it for your movement to the fifth dimension. For example, in normal though projection exercises, you can thought-project yourself to your home, to Montserrat, or to any other place that you are familiar with.

Interdimensional Corridors and the Arcturian Crystal Lake

When you do thought projection, you have to have a place where you are going to thought-project yourself to. For example, we have been talking about the fifth dimension. I know that you can say: "Well, I am going to go to the fifth dimension." This is like saying, "I am going to go to the United States." Which part or which city in the U.S. are you going to? It is better if you have an exact destination. For example, do you have a place to stay? Do you have a city you want to stay in?

When we are talking about the fifth dimension, we similarly want you to have a place to thought-project yourself to in this realm. Therefore, we created a special place for Earth's starseeds. We call this special place the Arcturian crystal lake. It is a fifth-dimensional lake in our Arcturian system in the fifth dimension. We have been using this lake for many, many years to help the Arcturian starseeds and all lightworkers so that they have a place to thought-project themselves to. This lake is approximately one mile in diameter. In the lake, there is a very powerful crystal. It is so powerful that it must be in the water so that it does not give up too much power immediately. In other words, the water attenuates the power. With thought projection, you can project yourself to this crystal lake.

We are introducing these exercises in different levels and different stages. The first stage of thought projection is the one that uses a corridor to go to the fifth dimension. A corridor is like a hallway that connects an area in the third dimension to the fifth dimension. The reason for the corridor is to help you, because the next level above traveling through the corridor is shimmering. While shimmering, you go to a place in the fifth dimension without the corridor, but the intermediate or learning stage is to go through the corridor.

Awareness of Your Multidimensional Presence in the Fifth Dimension

You are multidimensional. This means that you have an existence and a presence in two or three different dimensions at the same time. People have a hard time understanding this in normal logical consciousness. They say, "How can I be existing in two bodies at the same time, even though one body is in another dimension?" My answer to them is this: You already have another existence in the fourth dimension. You go into the dream world every night. You inhabit your dream body. In fact, if you look at the dream world, you are in your dream body quite a long time during the night. You do not seem to have any problem accepting that.

I realize that you are thinking about this in linear time; either you are awake or asleep. We look at time in a circular way because the awake and asleep stages actually interact. In fact, sometimes you do what is called daydreaming. You can do that immediately. In that state, you inhabit your dream body. We are encouraging the awareness of your multidimensional presence in the fifth dimension, for this is also a great aid and assistance to the ascension process.

Each of you now has a fifth-dimensional body at the Arcturian crystal lake. I would like for you to understand that there are 1,600 fifth-dimensional bodies around the lake. Your personal fifth-dimensional body is there. We are going to do an exercise in which you are going to travel to the crystal lake, if you want to meet and inhabit your fifth-dimensional body. Then, once you inhabit your fifth-dimensional body for a brief time, you will be able to bring back that energy, that excitement, and that joy into your third-dimensional body. There is a special technique of reentering your third-dimensional body. We are encouraging what we call "a perfect alignment." When you travel to the fifth dimension and you come back into your third-dimensional body, you have to be very careful and make sure that your spirit perfectly aligns with your physical body.

Let us talk about your fifth-dimensional body. What does it look like? It is composed of a different, higher-energy substance. You have the ability to shape and form this body to your liking. Most people will choose for themselves a body that represents how they looked when they were twenty-five or thirty years old. When they realize they have the ability to shape their body, they like to choose the shape they had when they were at their prettiest on Earth. For example, when you see pictures of Adama or Kuthumi, you often see them with very young-looking, handsome faces and beautiful hair.

You can create and use your Earth imagery for shaping your fifth-dimensional body. Sometimes people choose to have an older figure, like an old, wise man. Your fifth-dimensional body has attributes and abilities far surpassing your third-dimensional body. For example, your fifth-dimensional body has greater telepathic powers: It has the power of teleporting objects, it has great healing abilities, and of course it has the ability to travel to other realms and go anywhere in the fifth dimension.

There are many benefits to being able to inhabit your fifth-dimensional body. One obvious advantage is that it is getting you used to being in your fifth-dimensional body so that when the ascension comes, you will feel comfortable inhabiting it.

An Exercise for Inhabiting Your Fifth-Dimensional Body

Breathe deeply and enter a relaxed state. Become aware that the room is going around in circles, almost like a merry-go-round. You are not becoming dizzy at all. Very gently, your spirit body is rising out of your physical body. You are able to leave your body and go to the top of the room. At the same time, I, Juliano, have established a beautiful and powerful blue corridor over the room.

[Chants.]

This corridor is filled with sparkling blue light — light more beautiful, deep, and rich than you have ever seen before. The corridor opens right into the ceiling and I, Juliano, am above the room in the corridor, and I meet you right here. You can take my hand and follow me. We are going to travel at the speed of thought through this corridor now.

[Sounds.]

It is beautiful to be in this corridor. When we come to the end of the corridor, we are connected to the great Arcturian crystal lake. We are above the lake now. It is a beautiful and fresh lake. The air is relaxing, deep, clean, and clear. The light over this lake is a light that you have never seen. It is a combination of a sunrise and a sunset light, with the richness of the sunrise and the freshness and brilliance of the sunset.

Look down around the lake. There is a beach with many people sitting around. Many of them are sitting in the cross-legged yogi position. Everybody looks so beautiful and fresh. Your fifth-dimensional body is one of the 1,600 bodies that are around the lake. Find your fifth-dimensional body and move your spirit and aura directly over it, but do not enter it yet. First, line yourself up with it. At the count of three, you can enter your fifth-dimensional body at the crystal lake. One, two, three — now you are in your fifth-dimensional body. Enjoy this wonderful experience.

[Chants.]

We, the Arcturians, also use the name *Adonai* for "my lord." The light of *Adonai* is filling the crystal lake. The light of Jesus, Sananda, is also filling the lake. The presence of Mother Mary is also filling the lake. You are now in your fifth-dimensional body, but remember that you also have a third-dimensional body. Look and become aware of your third-dimensional body back on Earth.

You have brought with you imprints from that third-dimensional body. These imprints could be recognitions of certain illness or discomforts of your physical body on Earth. They could be certain imperfections in your existence in the physical body that you have wanted to improve. Just become aware of your Earth imprints. Just know that you are connected to them. Know that you have the imprints with you in your fifth-dimensional body now and that these imprints can be healed in the fifth dimension.

I, Juliano, now begin to raise the etheric crystal in the crystal lake.

[Chants.]

The crystal is now raised to the surface of the water, and the crystal has a brilliant light on the very top of it that is moving around in a full circle, 360 degrees. It looks like a light tower that you see in the bay near an ocean. And that light, which is going around so fast, passes over your third eye just momentarily as it circles around. It connects with you and sends this high-intensity light to your third eye. It is such a powerful light and such a powerful healing experience to receive this light. This powerful light is a healing light for the third-dimensional imprints that you have brought with you. It is purifying the imprints. It is bringing fifth-dimensional healing to the third-dimensional imprints you have brought with you. We will go into a meditation now in silence for a few minutes, as you experience the power and this light from the crystal and your being in the fifth dimension with this healing experience.

[Silence.]

You are receiving a high amount of fifth-dimensional light. You have now reached the maximum amount of healing light that you can absorb. I am going to bring the crystal back down into the water. Your spirit presence has absorbed all of this light, and all of the imprints that you have brought with you have been cleansed and healed. You have experienced yourself in your fifth-dimensional presence. You will be able to return to this presence at any time.

Returning to Your Third-Dimensional Body in Perfect Alignment

Prepare to leave your fifth-dimensional body. Rise up out of your fifth-dimensional body. Your spirit is now above the crystal lake. I, Juliano, am with you and we will take a return trip through the corridor and travel back into the third-dimensional world.

[Sounds.]

We are traveling at the speed of thought. We now are above the Earth room. You can see the room below and it is still turning in circles. Find your physical body. Move your spirit directly over your physical body. Do not reenter the body yet. Tell yourself that you will reenter in perfect alignment. Now that you are in perfect alignment for reentering, you can reenter your third-dimensional body with all this fifth-dimensional light. Remember, all of the imprints and any other discomforts or problems that you had have been cleansed.

At the count of three, reenter. One, two, three — now, reenter your body in perfect alignment. Your third-dimensional body is filled with this wonderful light. And most importantly, you now have a good connection to your fifth-dimensional body. The light and energy you brought down with you will become integrated into your third-dimensional body.

There is a process called "spiritual osmosis" in which the spiritual energy slowly and carefully reenters your physical presence, because it takes more time in the physical world to receive all of the energy and light that you have accepted in the fifth dimension. The process of spiritual osmosis is now continuing. You can open your eyes and return to the room.

Traveling to the Arcturian Crystal Lake on Your Own

Do you have any comments or reports to make?

Can we do this on our own?

Yes, of course. You can do this on your own. We want you to do it on your own. We want you to practice this. This is part of the ascension work, but most importantly, it is helping you to bring down the fifth-dimensional energy into your third-dimensional body.

Can we do this whenever we want, or does it have to be a specific moment?

You can do this whenever you want to. I am going to teach you the advanced part in the next section. The advanced part allows you to shimmer and then immediately go to the fifth dimension without going through the corridor. This can protect you very powerfully. If you are in a situation like an earthquake, a tsunami, or any other catastrophe that you can think of, you can immediately move into your fifth-dimensional body using the technique I have just shown you. When you shimmer directly to the fifth dimension, your third-dimensional body will be protected from whatever catastrophe or occurrence might be happening in the third dimension.

There is a woman who works with the Group of Forty who was involved in a car accident. Before the impact of the accident, she immediately transferred herself into her fifth-dimensional body using the technique of shimmering that I have just explained. When she woke up from the accident, she was not injured. Yes, you can do this shimmering and thought-projection exercise whenever you want. You can practice it, and you can use it in emergencies.

Do we need to call you to invoke the corridor?

I think it would be helpful for you to call me because I am connected with the crystal lake. It is a special lake that we, the Arcturians, have set up for the lightworkers. So it will be easier for you if you call on me to use the corridor as you are getting ready to go to the lake.

Could we program our traveling to the lake at nighttime, when we go to bed?

If you have the power to do that, it would be wonderful. Most people do not have that kind of control over their sleep, but if you have the power in your dreamtime to do this, you will experience many benefits. If you have can do this, you will receive a powerful healing while you are in deep sleep.

Do we have to invoke Juliano for the crystal to rise up out of the lake to repeat this work?

Yes, you can use me to invoke the crystal coming up. The crystal coming out of the water has a high-intensity light. Usually we bring up the crystal in small increments — we do not bring it up all the way out of the water at once. I would recommend that you invoke me to lead you through the whole exercise. There is a great benefit just to being in the lake with your fifth-dimensional body, without the crystal coming up.

Cleansing and Clearing Third-Dimensional Diseases with Fifth-Dimensional Energy

The next part of the exercise is shimmering directly into your fifth-dimensional body.

Yes. I want to ask if this exercise works for people who want to heal a disease.

The healing part using this technique has two levels to it. The first level is that you bring your spirit-body with you into your fifth-dimensional body. By the mere fact of your bringing your body to the fifth dimension, the imprints that are the signs of the disease in your spirit become cleansed and cleared. When you bring your spirit back into your third-dimensional body, this energy is updated into all of your cells.

There is a second part to this for those who have particularly strong diseases. After we have gone to the crystal lake, I bring these people to the healing chambers on my spaceship, and I use a special technique to remove the deeper imprints of the disease. This first level that you did is the entry level for the healing. For the next level, which is a more serious and deeper healing, I use another technique in my healing chamber that is even deeper for healing. Then we follow the same technique. You go back to the crystal lake, and you go back into your physical body from there. The idea is the same: You heal the imprints, you heal the aura body in the fifth dimension, and then you download that new fifth-dimensional energy into your third-dimensional body.

Please remember that, in an emergency, this exercise could be useful. You do not have to become unconscious. You still can maintain a perfect concentration and be totally multipresent in both bodies. Sometimes when you do the exercise, you may look like you are asleep in the third dimension. Jesus was multidimensional throughout all of his years as a teacher and a healer. He was able to be in full presence in both dimensions simultaneously. Remember that you can be in the fifth dimension and have full presence in the third dimension. I am Juliano. We are the Arcturians.

CHAPTER SIX

Shimmering and Biorelativity: Practice Using Etheric Crystals and Arcan Energy

Juliano and the Arcturians

Greetings, I am Juliano. We are the Arcturians. You have the basic foundation now to go to the next level of shimmering. You met your fifth-dimensional body in the crystal lake, you have done the basic round exercise with the cosmic egg, and you have learned how to vibrate that. Now I will teach you the final step in the shimmering practices. In this technique, you do not need to go to the corridor, but you can only do this technique because you have done the other techniques. This technique is actually faster than the other techniques. It is especially useful if there is not a lot of time. But each technique has its advantages.

Exercise: Shimmering into Your Fifth-Dimensional Body

In this technique, what happens is you will vibrate your aura. And then I will say the word "shimmer." Many of you have seen the *Star Trek* movies and TV series. There is a transporter that they use to transport people from the spaceship to the planet. The person to be transported stands under this high electromagnetic beam. Right before the transportation occurs, the person begins to shimmer in and out, in and out, and then he or she is gone. That is the image we are using in shimmering. I will also explain to you that shimmering is key to working with the planetary cities of light. When we shimmer a city of light, we are bringing it into a fifth-dimensional energy. We will look at that later, if we have time.

Become aware of your cosmic egg. Make sure that it has the shape of a perfect egg. Become aware of the line around your cosmic egg. As you hear these tones of the aura pulsing, the line around the cosmic egg will begin to move faster. When I say the word "shimmer," immediately transport yourself to your fifth-dimensional body on the Arcturian crystal lake. You can do this because you have already visited your fifth-dimensional body in the previous exercise. When you are in the fifth dimension, you will be able to shimmer back to your third-dimensional body. I will give you the instructions again as we are proceeding. Become aware of your cosmic egg and the line around it. Increase the pulsing rate of the line around your aura.

[Sounds.]

Shimmer, shimmer, shimmer into your fifth-dimensional body! Shimmer into your fifth-dimensional body now! You are now in your fifth-dimensional body. You are totally into your fifth-dimensional body, just as you were when we did the other exercise earlier.

Now you are going to go back into your third-dimensional body, bringing with you all the light that you felt in your fifth-dimensional body. Shimmer in your fifth-dimensional body! Shimmer back into your third-dimensional body now! You are back into your third-dimensional body. It is refreshing to be in both bodies so quickly.

When I say the word "shimmer," you will automatically increase the pulse of your aura, and you will start going in and out. If somebody else were to see you, they could see you going in and out, in and out. Shimmer in your third-dimensional body, back into your fifth-dimensional body now! You are now in your fifth-dimensional body. This exercise that we are doing uses both acceleration and thought projection. We will go back to your third-dimensional body now. Shimmer back into your third-dimensional body now!

Once you have done all of these exercises with me, then you will be able to do this shimmering by yourself. In our work with the planetary cities of light, we are able to shimmer the city. For example, we can shimmer the room and move the room into the fifth dimension, and the whole room can appear in the crystal lake.

I, Juliano, bring a huge etheric basket underneath this room. Shimmer the room now — shimmer, shimmer! Now we raise the room into the fifth dimension. This room is now experiencing fifth-dimensional light. Shimmer the fifth-dimensional room into the third dimension now.

[Sounds.]

You can use this technique when you activate a city of light. You can place people around the whole city. This is why we say it is better to work with a small city at the beginning. When you do this, you want to communicate with each other — with cell phones, for example — so that everybody is shimmering and using their energy at the same time.

Etheric Crystals Amplify Thought Power

The next subject that we want to talk about is the use of the etheric crystals and the concept of thought power. We call the measurement of thought power "arcan energy." You have measurements of electromagnetic energy such as watts, amperes, voltages, and so on. These are all indications of the strength of an electromagnetic current.

What technology do we have to measure the power of thought? Thought has power, even though it is difficult to measure it on Earth. Thought power is measured in our technology in units we call "arcans." If a thought has weak power, it may have only one arcan of power, but if it is very strong, it can go to five or ten arcans. It is always better to have stronger thought power. We use the example that one person can have an idea that can affect millions of people. Look at the effect that Albert Einstein had in the science of the twentieth century and beyond. Look at the effect that Jesus had on millions of people with his strong thoughts. I can give you many examples of one person affecting many, many people. But the point is that you want to increase your energy of thought and make it as strong as possible.

One of the activities of the Group of Forty is to bring people together so that they can increase their arcan energy. One of the methods of increasing the power of thought uses the etheric crystals. The etheric crystals are energies from the fifth dimension that are represented in the form of etheric crystals — crystals that exist in a thought-form from the fifth dimension. We have brought down twelve of these etheric crystals to Earth. The twelve etheric crystals correspond to certain energy spheres and patterns that we call the Arcturian Planetary Tree of Life. This paradigm is based on the Hebraic Tree of Life, but we have expanded that model for planetary healing purposes. The etheric crystals are all duplicates of the main etheric crystal that we experienced when we went to the crystal lake. They are huge crystals. Many of them are a mile long.

One of the main issues we are working with is how to help Earth attract more fifth-dimensional energy. We realize that the technology necessary to attract more fifth-dimensional energy is related to the downloading of these twelve crystals. They have been downloaded with great ceremonies throughout the globe during the past four to six years. There were many people in Spain who were with us

David and Gudrun Miller (both wearing hats) stand with a group of lightworkers in Montserrat.

when we downloaded the crystal in Montserrat. Each etheric crystal corresponds to an energy in the Tree of Life. I will, however, give you a brief overview.

The crystal in Montserrat represents the energy of the messianic light, a beautiful light that transcends logic and brings in miracles to Earth. I think everybody will agree that this planet needs some miracles now to pull it out of its current situation. Montserrat has been chosen in part because of its connection to a great deal of Messianic energy that it has been holding for many centuries. Also, this crystal is connected to all the other eleven crystals.

When I explain the Planetary Tree of Life, I like to explain it in terms of balance versus counterbalance so that you can better understand how energy works in the universe. When Earth is out of balance, it will try to correct itself in some way. Sometimes the counterbalance is a volcanic eruption or a flood. So one side of this tree represents judgment and the other side represents compassion.

We can also look at that in terms of your own personal life. If you are too critical or judgmental of yourself, you become miserable. Judgment needs to be counterbalanced by compassion. If you are too compassionate, this is not good either. Therefore, you have to have compassion and judgment together in balance. We know that the Creator has made planets in which there was too much judgment, and there are other planets he made where there has been too much compassion. We are looking to create a balance. That is how the planet can heal, by bringing judgment and compassion into balance. Too much pollution and too much ignoring of the balance of nature will require a judgment to bring this into balance. In the same way, too much compassion is counterproductive.

Now we will come back to the thought of the arcan energy. We project our thoughts to the etheric crystal. The etheric crystal can increase the power of our thoughts. Let us visualize the beautiful country of Spain. Let us say that we want to send healing energy to the whole country. We can send these thoughts to the country, but we could also send our thoughts of healing and balance to an etheric crystal in Montserrat, and then the energy of our thoughts will be amplified and sent through the whole country with great strength.

In the exercises we are doing in planetary healing and Biorelativity, we often use the imagery of a radar screen as seen on weather reports, because everybody can visualize the shape of the city or country on the weather report's radar screen. We know that there are many thoughts and images of destruction related to the end times. Earth has a subconscious energy that receives all of these images and thoughts from humankind. All of these images of destruction are pouring into the Earth. However, we can send more positive images and thoughts to the country and the planet.

A Biorelativity Exercise: Healing Spain

I will lead you in this exercise. This is an exercise using Biorelativity for the healing of a country, Spain, using the etheric crystal and arcan thought. Visualize Montserrat, Spain. If you have been to Montserrat with us before, you will remember where we do our exercises there — on top of the hill. This is where the Montserrat crystal was downloaded. Now thought-project yourselves to that hill. If you do not know the area, simply say the words to yourselves in your mind, "I thought-project myself to Montserrat."

Together, we raise the crystal in Montserrat. The crystal is raised, and we are standing around it. Send this healing thought that I will describe into the crystal: "Spain is receiving healing light from the fifth dimension now." Send that as a thought wave into the crystal. Spain is now receiving fifth-dimensional light. Your thought is going into the crystal at five arcans, but it is being sent out from the crystal at fifty arcans. See waves of fifth-dimensional energy of light coming out of the Montserrat crystal and traveling all over Spain.

All of the problems that you are aware of in Spain — problems with the economy, the environment, and any other conflict or polarization of the people — are also going to receive this fifth-dimensional light and information. See waves of fifth-dimensional light settling over the whole country, just like you see the picture of the weather map. This energy is so strong because it is being amplified as it is going through the crystal.

[Chants.]

As this fifth-dimensional light goes out over all of Spain, many of the starseeds who are living in Spain but are asleep are now going to awaken. There is so much fifth-dimensional energy and light coming out of the Montserrat crystal now. Specifically, some of this fifth-dimensional light is coming directly to Barcelona. Barcelona is receiving all of this fifth-dimensional energy now.

[Chants.]

Peace and tranquility fill all the land. I see a peaceful transition in the coming year. I see an energy stability and balance over the year, with many people awakening to their fifth-dimensional starseed heritage. This beam of etheric light coming out of the Montserrat crystal is now going out to all the crystal areas in the planet: Mount Fuji in Japan, Bodensee in Germany, the crystal in Istanbul, Lake Moraine in Canada, Volcán Poás in Costa Rica, and Mount Shasta in California. The Montserrat area still has so much light that this energy is going to all these places: Lake Taupo in New Zealand, Grose Valley in Australia, Serra da Bocaina in Brazil, and Lago Puelo in Argentina.

[Chants.]

Montserrat is in the center of all of these energy spheres. Spain can be one of the major centers for planetary healing and balancing. There is much healing light and balancing that can be sent to the world from here. The energy that goes in is amplified and is sent out so much more strongly. Visualize again that your thoughts are going into the crystal at Montserrat as energy. There is so much light and energy now.

Let us visualize Sant Pere de Ribes, Spain. A powerful light of balance and healing is falling on that small, beautiful city. This is a planetary city of light, a city that is working for global balance. There will be other planetary cities of light that will emerge in Spain. Spain will not experience major disruptive Earth changes. Yes, there will be some ups and downs, some issues, but Spain will be able to sustain itself and function well throughout Earth changes. This is the type of thinking that needs to be downloaded in the subconscious of Spain. These are the type of statements that need to be spoken in ceremonies. Earth responds to this type of energy. This is how we prepare a city and a country for becoming a fifth-dimensional area.

[Chants.]

Now the crystal in Montserrat is lowered back into the ground. Return to the room where we started the exercise. As you return to the room, you can feel the beautiful thought waves and energy that were sent over to Barcelona.

[Chants.]

This is an example of planetary Biorelativity using etheric crystal energy and an example of how to take advantage of the arcan power of the etheric crystals.

How can I take this energy to my house or garden, for example?

You set up a perimeter around your house. You will usually do this by putting crystals around your house and yard. We recommend that the crystals be buried in the ground. If you have some help, it will be better. Go around the perimeter of the land and start to shimmer the land. You can also use your energy to connect to Montserrat and the etheric crystal there; you can send the energy from Montserrat directly to your house. You are actually shimmering the line around your property. And you are asking that the energy go to the fifth dimension so that your house and garden can be connected to the fifth-dimensional light and all of the protection that goes with that.

Does it have to be a minimum four people?

It depends on how big the property is. Four people would work.

What about a flat?

You can make a circle like a medicine wheel in the flat. Does everybody know what a medicine wheel is?

No.

We can have Chief White Eagle explain it to you. And then I will be returning.

CHAPTER SEVEN

Medicine Wheels

Chief White Eagle

Greetings, I am Chief White Eagle. It is wonderful to be here again with many friends. I understand that you want to learn about the medicine wheel. This is a cosmic mandala that we, the Native Americans in North America, use to create healing energy and light. The circle is a sacred symbol for unity and connection to all dimensions.

The medicine wheel is a circle that can be made of stones or crystals. There have to be enough stones and crystals to make a full circle in the medicine wheel. One point of the circle is north, one is south, one is east, and one is west. The lines of the circle are also made of stones connecting north to south and east to west. In the center is the inner circle. You can put even more powerful stones in this inner circle — the most sacred energy and stones. Then you can shimmer the circle. It is a natural object and shape that can be shimmered.

If you have a piece of land or an apartment, you can create the medicine wheel there. The medicine wheel is automatically connected to other dimensions anyway. The question of activating your apartment can be answered by creating a medicine wheel and then shimmering the medicine wheel until you see that a great healing light and fifth-dimensional energy is in your apartment. We will ask that forty to fifty energy wheels be established now throughout the world because of their great healing potential. I am the Chief White Eagle. Ho.

Spanish lightworkers gather around the medicine wheel at Lago Puelo under the leadership of David Miller (not pictured here).

CHAPTER EIGHT

The Mental Body

Vywamus

Greetings, I am Vywamus. I am a soul psychologist. What is a soul psychologist? It is someone who has a fifth-dimensional perspective and specializes in understanding the psychological nature of the human condition from the soul's perspective. So right away you have to say to yourself, "It must be difficult to be in the human condition if you need a specialist to figure it out." I think you will agree, for you have been here for quite a few years, and you know that the third dimension is a pretty weird place to be. There are a lot of paradoxes and contradictions. It is supposed to be a logical world, but many illogical things happen.

Life Lessons and Wealth in This World

There is a lot of density on the third dimension. There are a lot of people with low vibrations. I cannot believe how many people always ask the same question: "Why am I here?" Even after being here for forty or fifty years, people are still asking that question. You would think that after being here that long they would know why they are here. It is confusing because you do not get a letter when you are born saying, "You are here to learn this lesson." Maybe they should start that way.

When a baby is born, it should get a letter from the spirit world saying: "You are here to learn this Earth's lesson. Do not open up this letter until you are eighteen years old." But I do not know if people would wait that long, or whether they would believe or accept the lesson when they opened the letter. What if the lesson was "You are here to learn how to be spiritual while you are in poverty"? Who would want to have that lesson? But there are people who in previous lifetimes had a lot of money, and because they had so much money and wealth, it interfered with their ability to be spiritual. So now maybe they have decided — or their guides have decided for them — that they would come back in the next lifetime without any wealth and see if they could be spiritual.

Personally, I would say, "Give me another chance. I can come back rich, and I can show you I can still be spiritual." Would you not rather be rich and spiritual? Many of you are using your powerful affirmations to get wealth. We know that there are many teachers around the world saying, "Use my meditation techniques and you will have wealth in six months. Please give me two thousand euros so I can teach you this technique." I can become wealthy with you too. But is it that important to be wealthy in order to be spiritual? Earth has the opportunity for free expression and free will. I know that you are here to study the ascension and you may wonder, "Who is this guy? What is he talking about? What does wealth have to do with the ascension?"

Changing Your Self-Talk to Clear Your Mental Body
You know that you have a mental body too. I know you like to work with spiritual energy, and maybe you think that mental energy is a little bit lower and beneath you. But one of the healings you must receive is for the mental body. The mental body is one of the four bodies. It has a powerful effect on all of the other bodies. What you believe about this reality has an effect, and what you believe about yourself has an effect.

One of my favorite topics is self-talk. This is one of the most important psychological discoveries of the twentieth century. Everybody thought that the most important psychological discovery was the Oedipus complex, but that is minor compared to what I am going to tell you now. And remember that you have heard it from Vywamus, the soul psychologist! The biggest change you can make in yourself is to monitor and change your self-talk. Self-talk is what you are silently telling yourself in your mind all the time. Did you know that you are having an ongoing conversation with yourself almost twenty-four hours a day?

Some of the things that you are saying to yourselves are pretty bad: "You are stupid. Why did you do that? You should have known better than that. The way you are going, you will never ascend. The ascension is only for more worthwhile people. You are not worthy enough. Those people over there are much more spiritual than you. They will ascend, but you will not. You meditate and meditate and you still do not see the auras. What is wrong with you? You have been trying to hear the guides for twenty years, but you still do not hear anything." Does any of that self-talk sound familiar? What effect do you think that type of self-talk will have on your development?

Part of your ascension work involves clearing up your mental body. If you cannot solve this problem, you can always come in other lifetime and try again. But one of the things that the guides have been fond of saying lately is that if you think that Earth is a difficult place to live in now, wait to come back in 2050 to see what it is like here. If you think that the weather and the Earth changes are weird now, wait until you see it in 2050.

The idea is that you will want to learn and clear as many Earth lessons as possible so that you do not have to work out any more psychological issues that may require you to return to Earth in another incarnation. It sounds simple enough, but it is difficult to get a handle on what to do about the problems. In some ways, you are like a computer. When a computer is born, it is given a program to operate. When you were born, you were also given a program. Some of the programs came from a past lifetime, but a lot of the current information came from the program your parents gave you.

Now you are trying to solve all your problems, but you are using old software and it does not seem to work. You know what it is like when you use an old program to solve a complex new problem. All of a sudden the computer freezes and you have to hit the "control," "alt," and "delete" buttons at the same time to get out of that locking up of the computer. When the computer freezes, you cannot do any more work. How do you change your self-talk? What type of change and what type of software or new programs do you need to download into your mental body?

One new program is: "I am a starseed and I am ascending." That is certainly better than the old program that you probably grew up with. But there are also issues with that program of being a starseed too. Being a starseed makes you more sensitive and sometimes can cause you certain problems.

Working with Your Body to Stop Your Mind

If you have any particular problems related to self-talk or changing your programs and life lessons, let me know now and I will see if I can help you.

I am a very mental person. When I try to do a meditation, my mind always goes somewhere else. I cannot stop my mind.

This is a case where you have to work with your body to stop your mind. If you try to focus on the mind, you are feeding fire with fire. Some people think that you just have to sit there, and maybe after twenty years the mind will slow down. I find that, especially in this age, there are so many things to keep your mind occupied. So you sometimes have to work with the body.

Let me give you an example. You might find that it will be more helpful for you to do yoga or some type of physical exercise in which you can shut the mind off for a while. This was a standard practice in some of the ancient temples in China and also one of the main intentions of yoga many years ago. People would do certain body exercises and movements in order to move the energy away from the mind. After doing these exercises, they found that they were able meditate a little bit better because they had discharged the energy.

You would have to find out the physical exercise that best suits you. Maybe weightlifting would be good for you — have you thought about that? There are different types of exercises, and you will have to see what is suitable for your body. For example, you might do well at swimming, and you might find out that you can more easily turn your mind off after swimming. Would you be willing to try one of those exercises? I am not sure which one would be suitable for you, but I think you get the idea. You might be surprised. Half an hour of exercise may help you to do two minutes of quality meditation, achieving a depth in mediation that you could not have reached before.

Creating More Positive Self-Talk and Controlling Fear

My self-talk is usually: "I am not perfect. I have not done things well."

I am glad that you are aware of your self-talk. A simple solution would be to use another affirmation, such as: "I am doing things the best I can with the ability I have for my highest good." You could change that sentence to better suit your situation. One of the ideas of changing your self-talk is to create another talk for yourself. Who knows where that message you are saying comes from? It might not even come from you. It might come from your mother, but it is not the most important thing to find out where it came from. The important thing is to shift the thinking so that you can create a better message for yourself. After what I have told you, can you come up with a better message? I would like to hear it.

I have tried this: "I do the best I can with my present ability."

That would work, and that would give you more compassion for yourself. Do you remember when Juliano was talking about the Planetary Tree of Life? He talked about judgment on one side and compassion on the other. Too much self-judgment is not good. You need more compassion toward yourself for your progress.

What about controlling fear?

Fear is a big issue. From my experience as a soul psychologist, I find that fear is based on feeling cut off from the unity that is present. One of the things about coming into the third dimension is that you lose the eternal contact with the oneness. If you do not feel connected, you obviously feel alone, and that is uncomfortable. One of the most severe punishments in primitive societies was to be excommunicated from the group. In many situations, that person would prefer death to being kicked out of the group.

This is the first place to start looking at fear. The truth is that being cut off is an illusion, but it feels real. There are other reasons for fear aside from feeling disconnected. All fears really come from being cut off, even from your own power and unity. Even when you do have something that bothers you, if you are connected to your personal power and your guides, teachers, and unity, it is very easy to deal with whatever problem you have.

I also wanted to say that, whatever the fear is, you can use this affirmation: "My personal power is getting stronger, and I am able to deal with all problems that arise." We have a special technique we use to increase the power of affirmation, because you have been saying these other possibly negative affirmations for many years. Even if you are given correct or newer affirmations, how do you overcome the years of the old affirmation? The answer is that you use fifth-dimensional light to counterbalance the affirmations of your subconscious.

When there are different paths to take, how can we make the right decision?

The fact that there are different paths to take is a good sign. There is a saying: "There are many different paths, and they all go to the same place." You have to connect with your own inner power and guidance, and then it will become apparent what you should do. In your case, I do not think that any of the paths that you choose will be bad for you. Maybe one would be a little bit better than the other, but even if you choose the one that is not the best, things will still be okay.

I always say — and this is something similar to what I told the other woman at the beginning — "Choose to the best of your ability what you think is the best path." Even if two paths are really close, use the best of your ability to choose. You can say this affirmation to yourself: "I will work to the best of my ability to choose what I think is best for me." But it is good you have choices. Some people do not even have any choices to make.

What about things we have in our subconscious that are blocking us, things we are not even aware of?

If there are things in your subconscious that are blocking you, you will see a symptom of the block somewhere in your life. There is always a thread in your conscious life that will lead you to the block in the subconscious. I do not recommend going on a fishing expedition to try to find out what is in the subconscious. Look for the threads and the link in your conscious life. There is always a link. If you look hard enough, it will lead you to the subconscious block, and then you can remove it. But we do not recommend going to your subconscious first; we recommend using a conscious thread as a connection to go to your subconscious.

Blessings to you, all my friends. This is Vywamus.

CHAPTER NINE

Grace

Mary

Greetings, I am Mary. It is always a great pleasure to be with so many of you again. I know of your deep love for my work, and I also have a deep love for your work, because I know that you are trying to be the best that you can.

I have been asked to speak to you today about grace, because there are many different things to learn on Earth about grace. There are many different lifetimes, and there are many different things to understand and to try to balance. I can understand how at times you might feel overwhelmed about everything, and I can understand how you can be overwhelmed by the ascension.

One of the lessons of the ascension is that you are trying to resolve all of your karmic lessons in this lifetime. Some of you are totally committed to this task and working full-time on it. It is honorable that you try to learn and resolve ten lifetimes of lessons in one lifetime. Even after you have committed yourselves to that effort, you still may not be able to resolve everything. Because of that, you might feel inferior, like you are not doing as much as you can or that you will not be successful in your ascension.

That is why I came here today to talk about grace. Grace is the ability to receive an energy of blessing so that you can skip certain things, so that you can be relieved of certain things, and so that some things that were problematic for you before can be made easier for you. Grace also sometimes helps you to receive gifts that do not seem to be logical, gifts that come from nowhere. This is grace; it is a beautiful spiritual energy.

I am asking you now to open yourselves up to my grace and to the gifts that are still available for you. Maybe you will not finish everything, and maybe you will not be perfect in your work. But from our standpoint — the standpoint of the masters — your effort, your intention, your desire to be spiritual, and your desire to be the best that you can be are also important and relevant. You can receive from that effort and intention my grace and the grace of other masters and teachers. This will be a gift that will help you.

I would like to ask you all to speak these words: "I am open to any grace that it is available to me now." You may be surprised. Nobody is expected to be perfect, and all we expect is that you do the best that you can, that you remain spiritually open, and that you continue to work as hard as you can up until your ascension. If you are not at 100 percent at the moment of ascension, you can still ascend with grace. Your education and work can continue in special situations before you actually completely enter the fifth dimension.

I know that everything is accelerating. I am optimistic that with your new openness, your new light, and the Grace that is coming to you, you will continue to make great progress on your ascension work. I am Mary. Good day.

CHAPTER TEN

The Holographic Healing Chambers

Helio-ah

Greetings, I am Helio-ah. We are the Arcturians. Today I will speak to you about holographic energy. My name, Helio-ah, is taken from the word "heliographic." In our language, we use the word "heliographic" instead of "holographic." I will try and find a holographic energy for you. Holographic is a term that means, "The part gives you access to the whole."

Holographic Worlds and Doppelgängers

In the holographic world, one piece of an apple can be used to re-create an entire apple. The world of genetics and biogenetics includes the study of taking one cell from a person and using it to re-create a duplication of the person. In our work with the Arcturian crystals, we use the principle of holographic energy to reproduce an etheric double of the original crystal. In fact, in your work and studies of the psychic world, there is a word that is used to describe the second aura, which is the duplicate of the first aura. In German, the word is *doppelgänger*, and this is a description in the psychic world used by the student Helena Blavatsky to describe the duplicate aura of a person.

Remember that Juliano was saying that you can thought-project yourself to another place and that second projection can be called the doppelgänger? But we are looking at understanding the self and the universe through holographic energy. Let us first take the universe, something simple. [Laughs.] I am glad that you still have a sense of humor. This Earth is smaller than a speck of sand compared to the size of the universe. But according to the principles of holographic energy, one little speck of sand can give you access to all the information of the universe. It is truly an amazing perspective you have from Earth. You can go back into time to the big bang and even before the big bang.

Let us look now at the self. This experience that you have in this body and in this dimension is but a part of your greater self, your greater soul. Yet from this perspective, you can gain access in understanding all of yourself. When we look at one lifetime, we can see this. Each lifetime gives the person the opportunity to have access to their greater self. According to holographic energy and holographic thinking, each lifetime is an opportunity to seek a unification of the self. That includes the past, the present, and the future self. We can also apply the same principle to God, or Adonai. Each dimension has a unique aspect and perspective on Adonai. No matter what dimension you are in — the third, fourth, fifth, sixth, seventh — you can gain a full experience and unity with Adonai. The third dimension has the ability to reach this unity, even though the third dimension is denser.

Let me return to the discussion of the holographic energy and Earth. I said that Earth is like a speck of sand. What is also amazing is that each speck of sand and each place in the universe is unique, so you can gain a perspective that is unique by traveling through the universe. So yes, holographic energy says that a part can access the whole, but according to Arcturian thinking, being in different parts also gives you a different perspective.

The Eclipse of the Great Central Sun

I can give you an example in the world of astronomy. You are all familiar with the eclipse of the Sun and the Moon. You may not be able to see the eclipse from Spain. You certainly can see the Sun, but to see the eclipse coming you may have to go to Australia. You would go to a different place to have that perspective.

I explain this to you because Earth has a unique perspective. Many people have asked, "Why are the higher extraterrestrial beings interested in Earth? Why are there so many people wanting to reincarnate to Earth right now?" The answer is because Earth has a unique perspective. Earth holographically has access to everything in the universe, but Earth also has a uniqueness that is special that is bringing people and spirits to this point.

I could compare the eclipse of the Sun to the alignment of Earth with the Central Sun. The alignment with the Central Sun is an indication of a special perspective that Earth has. That perspective can also be described as an alignment for an ascension. The alignment that is coming to Earth is quite unique. It only happens once every 26,000 years. From your perspective, your Sun is aligning with the center of the galaxy. Imagine the Sun rising on December 21, 2012, and exactly at the point that is known as the winter solstice, the Sun will be directly in alignment with the center of the galaxy. There is a discussion among the astrologers and astronomers. They ask, "Does the alignment cause the energy, or is the energy a result of the alignment and an expression of the alignment?" The answer is both.

I will go back to the eclipse of the Sun. Many people know that when an eclipse of the Sun happens, darkness occurs. Sometimes animals become confused when that darkness occurs. Let us say that the eclipse of the Sun occurs at one o'clock in the afternoon. The animals are not ready for darkness at one o'clock in the afternoon. Earlier, primitive humans were confused and afraid that something bad was going to happen when an eclipse occurred. Also, when you think of an eclipse, you think of the beginning, the full eclipse, and the end. The energy begins to happen even in the first quarter of the eclipse.

It is the same with the Central Sun. We actually call this alignment an eclipse. Earth is 93 million miles away from the Sun, and the Moon is 237,000 miles from Earth. When the Moon gets in front of the Sun, it blocks the Sun and then we have the eclipse and you see it. But the Central Sun is many light-years away from Earth. This means that the first part of the eclipse with the Central Sun will actually begin months before December 21, 2012.

This eclipse of the Central Sun on December 21, 2012 will actually last for a long period of time. We have the pre-eclipse, or the building up of the alignment, which began months before. During the spring of 2012, you will be in the energy of the Central Sun alignment or the pre-eclipse energy, and you will begin to feel what I described earlier with animals and darkness. Have you not already noticed some of the confusion that has been going on with some people on the planet? Haven't you noticed that some people want to create rebellion, and some people are going crazy? And Gaia has been responding in a more forceful and perhaps aggressive way.

These reactions reflect the energy of the pre-eclipse, or the pre-alignment, because the Central Sun energy represents many things. It does represent a shift, a change. It is a change in the old standards and institutions, and there will be a change in many of the ways in which the economy and energy are run. The whole basis of the structure of society and civilization is entering an explosive period. If the foundations of the institutions are all shaky, you will find that they will not be able to stand up. It is like an earthquake. Imagine that the structures of the buildings have already been earthquake-proofed in solid foundations with a special sliding apparatus. Then the buildings will survive the shaking. Do you think your financial institutions are set on solid foundations? Do you think that your energy foundations are on solid footing?

Juliano has already spoken about the disruptive energies from the Sun and how they could affect the satellites. Many of the things that are set up as the foundations of your civilization are very fragile. As this planet Earth goes through this eclipse, which is called the Central Sun alignment, there will be more shaking and more tumbling down of certain structures and institutions. This is what the 2012 alignment represents.

The Central Sun alignment also brings forth the newer energy and new solutions, the newer technology for living on a more sustained and solid foundation. But it is the law of spirituality of the universe that this shaking up has to occur, because the institutions themselves will not voluntarily allow themselves to dissolve. Does this alignment scare you? This is one of the reasons why Juliano and I have been teaching about the planetary cities of light. There is more security in establishing small circles of planetary light cities. These planetary light cities will become fifth-dimensional thresholds and frontiers for establishing new energy on the planet.

Past, Present, and Future Energy

Let us return to the idea of holographic energy. It is also used for personal healing. We have developed special healing chambers on our ships that are called holographic healing chambers. I want you to imagine a computer that is so powerful that when it locks into your energy field, it can read your past — anything that happened in this lifetime. Remember, anything that happened in this lifetime is recorded in your mental body, in your emotional body, and in your physical body. All of this gives off a vibrational energy signal. This computer is so sensitive that it receives the energy vibration, and it can lock into and record and display everything that happened to you in this past life.

Now imagine that this computer can also look at your future. Based on all of the vibrational energy fields around you — including the past energy, the present energy, and of course the future energy, based on how it sees you — the computer can see how long you are going to live, and it can make pretty accurate predictions about what is going to happen to you in the future, how your body is going to react, and so on. But we are not done — this computer can do even more. This is the quattro-turbo model. It can read your past lives. That means that the energy impressions from your past lives also have a vibrational signal and field that can be read by the computer. There are many stories of Kaballistic masters in the ancient world who were able to look at your forehead and read the vibrational field from it. From that impression, they were able to tell you who you were with and what you did in your past lives.

This computer can also tell you about your future lives. We call this energy and the structure that contains this computer the holographic healing chamber. We have set up rows of holographic healing chambers on our spaceships that are correspondingly aligned with each of you in this room. We call them holographic healing chambers because they give you access to your whole self. We can invite you into the holographic healing chambers that are especially aligned and calibrated for your energy field and then begin to do some healing work with you. This is quite an advanced and intense healing. We will bring you through the holographic healing chamber.

Personal and Planetary Holographic Healing Chambers

I want to describe to you the holographic healing booth. I call it a booth because it is the size of a phone booth. In the booth, the computer is sitting right in the front, and there is a computer screen right above the table where the computer is.

There is a big dial right in front. Once the computer is turned on, you must imagine that the dial is like a clock and it goes from twelve to three, to six, to nine, and back to twelve. It is exactly like a clock. If you can, imagine twelve, one, two, three, four, five, six, and so forth. Now when you turn the dial to the right, that represents your future. Imagine also the left side of the clock with the numbers eleven, ten, nine, eight, seven, and six. This left side of the clock represents going back in this lifetime in the past.

For this exercise, we will only work in this lifetime. But you know that some of the computers that you have here now have buttons. When you press a certain button on *this* computer, it goes into the turbo mode, which allows you to go beyond the past in this lifetime and actually experience your past incarnations or past lives. This holographic healing booth computer also has a button that we can press to make it go into past-life mode so that when you turn the dial to the left, you are going into the past lifetime in this incarnation. Remember, when you turn the dial to the right, you are going to a future lifetime. Some of the problems and issues that are bothering you are related to your past lives. The idea of going to a future life helps you to bring back the energy and light that you will have in the future. This is a useful feature because many of you will be more advanced in the future. You can bring back the energy of the future into the present.

I want to explain one other level to this. There are the holographic healing chambers for the planet. We have set up a holographic healing chamber for the planet, but instead of using a phone booth, we have set up a large theater. We need a large audience so that we can go back into the immediate past of the planet. For example, there have been some terrible problems created from Chernobyl. There have been tears in Earth's aura from that accident. We can call on the images of the past of the planet and work on those images.

Changing Negative Images from the Past into Positive Images

This leads me to an important point. Everything that happens is recorded in your brain as an image. Everything that happens on Earth is recorded as an image in a subconscious energy field in Earth as well. The basis of the holographic healing is to call up the image of the event. And then we bring the event onto the screen in front of you. And we do the same thing for the planet when we do planetary holographic healing. Once the image is in front of us, we reshape it into a new format that is more healing and more in alignment with higher fifth-dimensional energy.

At that point, when the image is beautifully created on the screen, we press the save button — just like the save buttons in your computers — and that image is reentered into the files, or memory of the computer or of yourself. We actually visualize all of the events that happened in this lifetime for you, stored in your brain like a Rolodex card file. Once the file is brought up and put on the computer screen, it can then be changed and brought into a higher vibration. After it is saved, it will be sent back into the same place in the Rolodex file, and then the whole file system from that point forward is updated with the new change and a higher vibration.

For example, you could have had a traumatic event in your life ten years ago that totally affected you and traumatized you. The memory of the event would be stored as an image in your subconscious. In the holographic healing chamber, we can bring up the image as I have described. We visualize the memory using the image you have of the event. Then we reshape the image in a more positive way, and we reenter the new positive image back into your system. Everything in your subconscious related to that event is updated. Remember that your body stores everything as an image, and now the new updated reshaped image becomes the basis for a healing.

What happens with the emotions that are stored with the event?

The emotions are also changed when the image is reshaped. You change the emotions. So instead of sadness, you can change the feeling in the image to happiness. But remember that the subconscious records the emotions and the facial expressions, so you would need to see different emotions on the faces of people in the image, including yourself! Not only would you experience the emotion, but you would also see it on people's faces, in their eyes, and so on. Of course, you are right. The emotions would also be changed. If you are really sharp, you can actually change the emotional energy based on the aura field of the people in the image.

If we see a traumatic event that affected us, do we then have to change the image with the ideal situation, or can it be changed to something completely different?

You can change the image any way you want. For example, let us say that you were traumatized and physically abused as a child. You have the image of your father beating you — you are in the corner crying as he is very cruel to you. After you call up this old image, you still see your father doing this in the new image, but someone new enters the image — Archangel Michael appears. And Michael sends the healing light to your father and to you, and suddenly your father has great compassion and is filled with higher energy and light. You see Archangel Michael with his great strength appearing in your new image, and now you feel connected to the higher light by that new image.

That is the new image that you would download. You use your creative abilities to update the old image to the new one. When you put the image back into your subconscious, the subconscious will accept that as the new reality, because you are using the same imagery of the subconscious. This is an example and a way that I would recommend to change the image. If somebody has other images that they want my advice on, I would be happy to offer it.

What about neurolinguistic programming techniques and hypnosis? They are similar to what you are telling us.

Absolutely, yes. Those are similar technologies, but we are using the past and the future, and we are using these images from the immediate past life in this incarnation, and also we use images from past lives and future lives. You are absolutely right, though. There are other technologies that you mentioned that use similar principles. This holographic energy is coming to the planet now for newer healing methods.

A second thing that is different about this technique is that it can also be used for planetary healing. Everybody has images of the planetary eruptions, the planetary traumas. And already there are many images of the end times for Earth, for example, that have come out in movies. Those images that have been downloaded into the subconscious of the planet are put into a place called "universal unconsciousness" or "collective unconsciousness." We are suggesting that new imagery for healing Earth also needs to be downloaded to the universal unconsciousness or the collective unconsciousness of the planet.

The third difference is that we are bringing you to our ships to do this under a fifth-dimensional energy field. So we believe that this also adds another level of effectiveness to the process.

Can you modify an attitude?

You can modify an attitude by looking at the picture that appears on the image that you bring up, because your attitude is reflected on your energy field. So the answer is yes. We can guide you through one of these exercises.

An Exercise in Holographic Healing

This is the holographic healing chamber. We are excited to offer this service. We also like to do this for the future, because in the future, you can go forward to a time when you have an even higher energy. That means that the imagery of yourself in the future at a more energetic and enlightened time can be brought into the present. It is almost like when you see people like the Dalai Lama. They chose the child to be the next Dalai Lama because they saw his future and they brought the future energy into the present. We are excited to use this methodology for planetary healing.

One of the things that we want to do for planetary healing and Biorelativity is begin to use this type of methodology for planetary healing images. There are many negative images that are being downloaded into Earth right now, and part of the Biorelativity technology that we are teaching is to talk and interact with Earth in a more positive way.

Feel the room going around in circles, like a merry-go-round. You are not becoming dizzy at all. Very gently, you feel your spirit body rise out of your physical body, rising to the top of the room. I, Helio-ah, am using the same corridor that Juliano has established over the room, this beautiful blue corridor. This corridor is now connected to our Starship Athena in the interdimensional realms. Come with me, Helio-ah, as we travel through the corridor at the speed of thought to our Starship Athena.

[Sounds.]

We come to the entry portal of our starship. As you walk into the portal, I direct you to our healing chamber rooms. You see a row of these beautiful holographic healing booths. There is a room that has been calibrated for each one of you, so go to the room that is for you. You will naturally find it. As you step into the booth, close the door and turn on the computer by pressing the green button on the left. It will take a minute or so for the computer to calibrate itself to your energy field. The calibration is almost completed. Now it is completed.

You can turn the dial to the left to any place in your lifetime that you wish. Just remember that 6PM represents your birth and twelve noon represents now. Turn the dial accordingly to the event that you feel needs to be healed. As you turn the dial, you lock into that image of that event. That image and that event now appear directly on your computer screen in front of you. See the computer event and the details as best as you can. You can change the event and image with your thoughts. You may want to bring in an archangel. You may want to bring in me, Helio-ah. You may want to bring in any higher guide you wish to make the changes you want. We will take a moment of silence while you redo this image to match your highest good.

[Silence.]

We are almost ready to complete the image. Please use the brightest colors that you can. Make sure that the image has the energy and the correct outcome that you need. Now press the save button, which is right next to the green button on the left. And now the image will go back into the file of your memories, but it will go back first in the computer in the holographic healing chamber. And it is going in now. As it is downloaded into this computer, it is updating all future events and files based on what needs to be updated. You may feel this going on in your mind, because what is happening in the computer is also reflected and processed in your subconscious and unconscious. The update is almost complete. Now it is completed.

[Chants.]

You feel a lightening up of your own energy field. Now you are ready to leave the chamber. Shut the computer off, open the door, and come out into the large room, where I, Helio-ah, am waiting for you. Together, we leave the ship and go down the corridor of light back to your physical body.

[Sounds.]

You are above your physical body. Tell yourself to do the perfect alignment. At the count of three, reenter your body in perfect alignment. One, two, three — now.

Your unconscious and subconscious are now being updated based on the holographic healing that we have done in our chambers. The room is now stopping its circular motion, and you are back in your normal consciousness and thinking. I will be interested if you have any reporting, comments, or questions on this exercise.

Interactions between the Energies of the Past, Present, and Future

I would like to say that as I was incorporating the image, I was feeling warm.

These body sensations of heat are a good indication that you have successfully interacted with the energies. This is a deep level of healing, and you are already very sensitive to the different sensations that it is generating. This is an example or an indication of a positive connection to the healing work.

Before starting the exercise, you told us that we could also go into the future and bring the energy of the future toward the past.

We are only now bringing the energy of the future to the present. We can bring the energy of the future to the past, but that is a very advanced technique. I want to make sure that you can bring the energy of the present to the past, the present to the future, and the future to the present before we do the future to the past. But that can be done also.

What about images of past lives? Is the result the same?

Yes, you can do past-life healings using this method. Incidentally, the idea of bringing energy from the future to the past works also in planetary healing.

Could we do that ourselves to another person? Could we share this with another person?

It may seem simple the way that we have done it, but there are a lot of different things going on that you are not seeing. But if you call on me, Helio-ah, when you try to do this with another person, I will be with you and help you with it.

In your example, you gave the image of a father beating his son. Is the healing also for the father?

No, the healing is for you. You cannot do this for another person. It is a nice thought, but this is your subconscious, your unconscious, your imagery. There is a way to send healing energy to another person, but I do not want to work on that today.

[Pause.]

Downloading New Healing Images into Earth's Collective Unconscious

I want to explain again that what we were talking about before our break is also the basis of a planetary healing exercise. I want to emphasize again the importance of downloading the newer images of healing into the collective unconscious of Earth. There are so many negative images now that are coming to Earth based on movies and TV.

One beautiful image that would be helpful is this: The higher fifth-dimensional light from the Central Sun is coming to Earth and bathing Earth in this higher, beautiful fifth-dimensional light. Another image is this: Visualize that each dimension is a sphere itself and Earth is in the third dimension, which is a sphere of light. The fifth dimension is also a sphere, and it is being attracted to Earth. This attraction is partly occurring because of the etheric crystals that are downloaded on Earth.

Visualize that there is an intersection at one point where the two spheres actually intersect — they touch each other. At that point of intersection is the ascension. Visualize that the ladders of ascension are all going directly into this point of intersection. Visualize that people are going up the ladder and going through that point of intersection. There is a tremendous transfer of higher light and energy at that point of the intersection. And now we can download that image into the collective unconscious of Earth.

[Chants.]

Feel the room spinning around again. Again, feel how easily your spirit leaves your body and goes to the top of the room. As it goes to the top of the room, you meet me, Helio-ah, right at the corridor, and you and I travel together at the speed of thought to the entry point of my starship, Athena.

[Sounds.]

Bringing Energy from Your Future into Your Present

We enter a large room in the starship, Athena. You see before you the many holographic healing chambers. Go into the one that has been especially calibrated for you. Turn on the machine by pressing the green button, as I described before. The computer calibrates itself according to your energy field. The calibration is quicker because it remembers your energy signature from the previous exercise we did.

You are at the dial. I have explained to you how to use the dial. It goes from twelve to one, two, three, four, and five, and it represents your future here on

Earth. You can turn the dial approximately to three o'clock. This is a moment when you are in the future and have really advanced yourself spiritually. You are already advanced now in the present, but at the three o'clock time in the future, you can do many more tasks and bring through much more energy. You also have much more of an ability to manifest what you need to here on Earth.

Press the dial and see an image of yourself in this future time, when you are much more advanced and energized and you have been able to arrange your life in a much more powerful way than at present. Keep your eyes on this image, and gather as much information as you can. Take the dial and turn it slowly. This is the drag-and-drop exercise. You are going to bring that image (from the three o'clock position or the image of your future self) right into the twelve o'clock position, which represents where you are in the present. Turn the dial with that image following you, and then, exactly at twelve o'clock, press the dial, then drag and drop it into the twelve o'clock or present position and it will click in.

[Sounds.]

The energized image from your future is now in your present. All of the energy, all of the beautiful thoughts, all of the advancement from your future advanced self is now downloaded into your present. Press the dial again, and all that energy will fill your etheric body. You are receiving energy from your future into your present. You are absorbing this energy very deeply and profoundly within yourself.

This is also going to change your future at one o'clock and two o'clock. Not only did you bring back this energy into the present, but you are also updating your future possibilities more positively. Take a minute to allow the future to be updated for you. The update is completed now. You have received the future energy light, and it has also updated your future in a much more positive, energetic, and spiritual way.

Get ready to leave the healing chamber. Shut the holographic healing chamber off, get up, leave the chamber, and come with me to the corridor. Say goodbye to the starship. We will travel at the speed of thought back to Earth.

[Sounds.]

As you come to the top of the room, you see your body and go into perfect alignment. At the count of three, you get into the body in perfect alignment. One, two, three. You reenter your body with this high healing energy from the future. The room stops spinning. You are totally back into your present body.

I am happy for you that you have decided to take this positive step for your future. This positive step must be taken for the planet. We must be able to work with future images and download new healing images for Earth. We are excited that this Group of Forty movie [Author's Note: *The Blue Jewel*] has been made, because it will be instrumental in introducing positive imagery. Earth will respond to the positive images.

You have deep parts and connections to yourselves. You are connected to your multidimensional selves, and this is one of the main evolutionary steps that you are taking to help the whole of humanity. There must be a core number of people on the planet who change. It is what is called the hundredth monkey effect. There were a certain core number of monkeys in an anthropological experiment, and once 100 monkeys learned the task, then the whole group of over 5,000 monkeys learned a task. Now there needs to be a core number of lightworkers moving toward this next evolutionary step.

Just by using and thinking about these ideas and energy, you are participating in the evolutionary shift. And yes, you can use this energy and light for the planetary cities. Use this energy for the smaller sites of your homes and gardens. This energy will become more prevalent in the planet. You will be working toward attracting more fifth-dimensional energy to the planet. Blessings to you all, lightworkers. Good day.

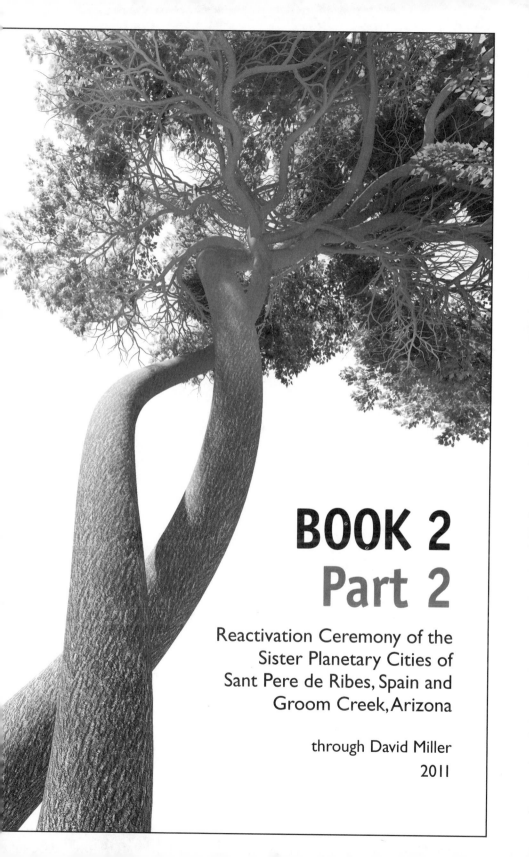

BOOK 2
Part 2

Reactivation Ceremony of the
Sister Planetary Cities of
Sant Pere de Ribes, Spain and
Groom Creek, Arizona

through David Miller
2011

CHAPTER ONE

Reactivation Ceremony of Sant Pere de Ribes, Spain

David Miller

I want to welcome you all to the planetary city of light ceremony of Sant Pere de Ribes in Spain, near Barcelona. We are happy to be here today to activate this city of light. I need to explain to you about the cities of light and Biorelativity.

Earth Responds to Our Actions

The idea of Biorelativity is that we can communicate with Earth. Earth is a living spirit. Earth receives our thoughts and feelings about her. Earth receives our images of her. It is well known among the Native American peoples that ceremonies like this are powerful in helping to send positive and healing energy to Earth. We are interested in deepening your skills of planetary healing through Biorelativity. We all know that Earth is going through rapid changes now. We know that Earth is having powerful storms and that there have already been volcanic eruptions and earthquakes in the recent past.

How can you as humanity influence Earth so that there is more balance? The answer to that question lies in your prayers, your ceremonies, and your actions. Earth responds to your actions. Earth responds when we seek a better balance with her. Ceremonies like this are a gigantic first step in helping to create balance for Earth. But Biorelativity even goes one step forward from there. Biorelativity says that we can help to moderate storms through our global meditation. I have been working with this idea of Biorelativity for over twenty years. My wife, Gudrun, and I are traveling around the world in order to teach these principles of Biorelativity and to gather people together to have ceremonies to help activate the cities and send balancing energy to Earth.

One powerful idea of Biorelativity is that of the planetary cities of light. We all know that there are many parts of the planet that are filled with pollution. There are problems in the air and the oceans, but one powerful solution is making cities sacred, making special places holy and dedicating them to new balances. We call these new sacred areas planetary cities of light. Why do we use the term "planetary"? Because these cities are dedicated to creating a planetary balance that will work for the whole Earth. These cities are working to contribute to a new energy for the new Earth and a new balance in which everybody is living in balance with Earth.

We have a vision that Earth as a planet can be in harmony. There do not need to be dramatic weather changes. There do not need to be earthquakes that kill thousands of people. There does not need to be global warming causing the oceans to rise. If we can learn how to communicate with Earth and listen to Earth, then we will be able to interact with Earth and find a new harmony. This new harmony can start with creating planetary cities of light.

This city — Sant Pere de Ribes, Spain — has already dedicated itself with many people who embrace these ideas and have already come together to create this city as a planetary city of light. We are coming together today for several reasons. First, we want to honor the work that the people have already done here in Sant Pere. They are working to keep this city sacred and holy. We also want to deepen the work here, because we acknowledge and recognize that this planetary city of light is beautiful and can have a powerful effect on Spain and the rest of the world. At this moment that I am speaking to you, there are approximately fifty planetary cities of light around Earth. Gudrun and I have visited many of these cities personally, and we are here in this city for the first time to experience the energy.

I am deeply moved that so many of you have come here today to work with us. We have prepared a special ceremony for you and for the city in order to continue the activation and deepen the energy here. The first thing is that we have gathered together here in a circle. We know from the ceremonies of the Native Americans from North America that circles are powerful healing forces. We are going to use the energy of the circle in this ceremony.

Bringing Higher Energy and Balance to Sant Pere de Ribes

We are also going to work together with you to make affirmations. We have brought here today this powerful talking stick. It is used in the Native American ceremonies in North America, and when you have this stick you are allowed to speak to the group. We will come to that point and I will give you instructions, but I want you to participate as well with your thoughts and your words. I would like you to visualize this city in your mind. Now visualize a powerful beautiful blue light around the whole city. This is a light of protection and also of higher energy and higher balance.

As you are having that image, I want you to say these words: "We are bringing higher energy and balance to Sant Pere de Ribes." Say these words together.

We are bringing higher energy and balance to Sant Pere de Ribes.

When we are doing ceremonies, we have to make sure that everybody hears what you are saying. Maybe somebody is sleeping and we will wake them up. Let us say it again, only a little bit louder.

We are bringing higher energy and balance to Sant Pere de Ribes.

Let us try to say it all together in unison again now.

We are bringing higher energy and balance to Sant Pere de Ribes.

You should feel the energy coming here to the city because you are stating a powerful affirmation. You are stating the affirmation with your words, and you are also making a visual image.

Connecting the Planetary Cities of Light to Each Other and to Earth

Feel the vibration of Earth. Your words are going right into Earth here. It is around the air here. There are many planetary cities of light. Each one of these cities of light has a special energy. Now we are going to say, "We are connecting the energy of Sant Pere de Ribes to all the other planetary cities of light."

Feel this connection. The third affirmation is: "We are connecting the energy of Sant Pere de Ribes to planet Earth."

There is a new idea about Earth and Earth's healing because we are calling ourselves planetary healers. Planetary healers are people who work together to help balance Earth. That means there needs to be a new balance, and we are seeking ways of finding that balance and working together for that balance.

We believe that there is an unconsciousness of Earth and that Earth receives the images and thoughts that we send to it. The images, words, and ideas that we send to Earth can be powerful and healing for Earth. As planetary healers, we want to encourage people to send their visualizations and their beautiful affirmations to Earth.

Beautiful Healing Thoughts for the Earth

I brought this beautiful talking stick with me, and I am going to pass it around the circle. I am going to ask each of you to state a beautiful image and a beautiful healing thought for Sant Pere de Ribes. When you get the stick, you will say: "My name is _____. All my words are sacred." And in one sentence, share with everybody a beautiful thought and image about how sacred and holy this city is. Please speak as loudly as possible. Because we have so many people, please remember that we will only have time for everybody to say one or two sentences. If for some reason you do not want to speak to everybody, please pass the stick to the next person. We are going to ask each one of you to send a beautiful affirmation and visualization to this city.

I am Olga. All my words are sacred. I send pure white light to Earth in order to heal Earth and all of us. All my relations.

I am Gudrun. All my words are sacred. I sense that Earth is receiving our love and is sending it back to us. All my relations.

Do not forget to speak loudly.

I am Mercè. I am sending yellow light to Earth. I hope Earth will heal. All my words are sacred.

Try to say something about Sant Pere de Ribes when you are sending your visualizations.

I am Montse. All my words are sacred. I send green light to Earth and Sant Pere de Ribes. All my relations.

I am Carmen. All my words are sacred. I see in Sant Pere de Ribes peace and unity, and this will then go to all the cities of light. All my relations.

I am David. All my words are sacred. Let the beauty and energy of the planetary city of light of Sant Pere de Ribes be projected and reach all the other planetary cities and all the planet. All my relations.

CHAPTER TWO

Reactivation Ceremony of the Groom Creek/Spruce Mountain Area in Arizona

Chief White Eagle, Juliano, and the Arcturians

Greetings, I am Chief White Eagle. We are gathered here today with you to help activate and deepen the connection of the planetary city of light known as the Groom Creek/Spruce Mountain area, which is just south of Prescott, Arizona. Let us quickly review the principles of Biorelativity so that we are all clear on what we are doing and how we are doing it.

Calling Earth's Attention to the Parts of Her That Most Need Balance

The idea of Biorelativity is that you are communicating telepathically with Earth — you are telling Earth your wishes and Earth is responding. This is one of the key parts, for you must understand how Earth responds and you must understand that Earth has a pattern, a system that is very complex. The area that you are connecting with, the area that you are working with, has to be balanced in the overall pattern of shifting, for Earth is aware of all things on her surface and inside of it.

I want you to think of Earth the same way you think of your body and your nervous system. Think about how your nervous system has so many millions of miles of nerve fibers, and how impossible it is for you to be aware in your consciousness of everything that is going on in your nervous system. You will only become aware of what is going on there if your attention is called to it by either yourself or by someone else. So if someone says to you, "Let us focus on the breathing," then you will focus on the breathing.

Now, in the same way, Earth has all of these millions and maybe billions of miles of energetic fibers that are constantly interacting. So what is happening here in Groom Creek is being registered, but Earth also has a consciousness, just like humans have consciousness. In a similar way to humans, Earth may not be totally aware of everything that is going on in a conscious way. So when you are doing Biorelativity, it is like calling attention to Earth. And it is like telling Earth, "Okay, Spirit of Earth Gaia, we want you to turn your awareness and your healing power to this area that we are now speaking of."

Again, we will compare this to the human body. Your healing powers are increased when you focus your consciousness on that part of the system that needs the healing. In the same way, Earth's power of being, Earth's power of protection, and Earth's general power of bringing balance to an area is increased when you call Earth's attention to the place that you want to work with. This, perhaps, is one of the most key principles in Biorelativity — that is, calling the planet's attention to the part of her body that you want to bring into balance.

Mother Earth, Father Sky, Spirit of Gaia, we are gathered here today in the Groom Creek/Spruce Mountain area to call to your attention this beautiful area, to call to your attention the terrible drought, the dryness that is here. We are asking at this time for the protection of this area from any fires. We are asking at this time that you ensure that this area — this planetary city of light known as Groom Creek/Spruce Mountain — is protected as a fifth-dimensional area. We ask that it be a protected area, and we ask you to increase this protection.

Activating an Energetic Circle of Light

We are gathered here, and we will all remember now the areas where the crystals were buried: the area on top of Spruce Mountain, the area of the schoolhouse, the area in the forest that is south from here, and also the area down at western side of Maripai. All of these areas now have crystal energy. We are gathered here in this powerful circle, this medicine wheel, and we are activating an energetic circle of light where these crystals are all connected.

[Chants.]

I, Chief White Eagle, reactivate a circle of light around those crystals so that the border area of these crystalline connections is strengthened. At the same time we are gathered here and we are calling on Mother Earth, we are calling on the Spirit of Gaia to bring her attention to this encircled area in this planetary city of light.

[Chants.]

We call to the attention of Gaia that we, the lightworkers, the planetary healers, have raised the vibrational frequency of this area.

[Chants.]

Now visualize this brilliant fifth-dimensional light energy connecting all of the crystals. It is like a wall of light that is rising up ten feet, twenty feet, thirty feet, fifty feet, a hundred feet, a thousand feet, and even higher, up into the higher dimensional spaces, up into the fifth dimension. There is a beautiful curtain of light around this whole beautiful planetary city of light, and it is a huge protective fifth-dimensional energy field.

[Chants.]

Everything that is within this curtain is receiving this brilliant fifth-dimensional energy. And I, Chief White Eagle, see that because the Groom Creek/Spruce Mountain area is a planetary city of light, every place within it — every stone, every rock, every tree, every house, every person, every animal, every plant — is being activated and is now receiving these fifth-dimensional energies, this protection, this higher frequency of light.

[Chants.]

Visions of a Fifth-Dimensional City of Light

Now, we are all gathered here today to speak of how you see this place and how you see it as a fifth-dimensional city of light.

So I, Chief White Eagle, begin: All my words are sacred. I am Chief White Eagle. I see a beautiful curtain of fifth-dimensional light around the city, and I see many higher beings in the city. I see a great wall of protection. And I see rain coming to this area soon, as soon as July 7. There will be rain even sooner. We will pray that the rain comes sooner, even July 1 or July 2. That is focused. I see everything wet. I see a great beautiful storm and a big sigh of relief. The animals are sighing, the trees are sighing, and the people are sighing with relief as our protector energies bring the rains to this beautiful fifth-dimensional planetary city of light. Ho. All my relations.

First participant: *All my words are sacred. I am Gudrun, spirit painter. I too see the rain coming and bringing a sense of relief and joy. I see people's hearts dancing with the relief and the beautiful smells that the rain brings. I see many etheric crystals in this area. They are beautiful and sparkling. There is a lot of joy around this area and a lot of spiritual connection. People are drawn here to, drawn to be in this area, and they are respectful of its sacredness. All my relations. Ho.*

Second participant: *All my words are sacred. This is Rising Sun. I see the beauty of protection in Groom Geek/Spruce Mountain. I feel safe here. I can let down my defenses, and I am not worried about being out in the forest. I also see the beauty of the rain coming in spring, flowing through this property. The water flows through and this place waits here for it. We have a beautiful place and I enjoy the water in the creek. I see the fairies and the nature spirits coming, the joy of the water and the rain, and our plants thriving. All my words are sacred. Ho.*

Third participant: *This is David. All my words are sacred. I see the power of the crystals that we buried in various locations around Groom Creek/Spruce Mountain activating the entire area, connecting with the crystals that are naturally ingrained here and creating an environment that invites positivity, deflates negativity, and really raises the consciousness of the people in the area. I also see the rain is coming to bring life to the area so that all the animals and plants here can live and thrive. All my relations. Ho.*

Communicating Directly with Mother Earth through the Medicine Wheel

These are beautiful thoughts and visions. Hold these visions and allow these visions and thoughts to enter Earth through the center of this medicine wheel. I want you to understand that a medicine wheel has many functions, but one of its greatest functions is that you can use it as an entry level into the telepathic mind of Earth. In other words, the medicine wheel is like a direct line. It is a direct way to communicate to Mother Earth.

So direct your beautiful words, your thoughts, your visions, and the images that you have just described now into the center of the medicine wheel. Know that this is so powerful. This is the most direct way to communicate directly and telepathically with Earth. So I will be chanting as you continue to direct your images, thoughts, wishes, and visions of the Groom Creek/Spruce Mountain area. Send them into the center of the tipi and they will go directly to the Mother Earth, making her attentive to what is needed here.

[Chants.]

Mother Earth is responding. I hear her speaking — she loves what you are sending and she wants more. She wants more energy; she wants more of your response. She is saying that you are helping to awaken her energies and direct them to this area.

[Chants.]

Become aware that your third eye is focused directly on the center of this medicine wheel, that the center of this medicine wheel is going directly into the

The medicine wheel tipi at David's house.

spirit of Earth, and that the spirit of Earth is responding. She is sending her energy, her light, and her protective energy right up through the center of this medicine wheel, and brilliant light and energy is flowing up through Earth, like a geyser in Yellowstone National Park. But this is a geyser of fifth-dimensional light and protection, and it is filling all of the Groom Creek/Spruce Mountain planetary city of light area now. This is a light and an energy of protection. It is a light that is filled with all the thoughts and energies that you have put in.

But it is also even more, because you have activated an interactive energy force with Gaia today, and now she is responding and sending a powerful energy through this beautiful medicine wheel. We send even higher light over all of Arizona, because this medicine wheel is emitting a tremendous power of energetic light, or fifth-dimensional energy, and it is spilling over all of Arizona.

Now I am sealing the energy flow at the top of the Groom Creek/Spruce Mountain area, for our main purpose today is to protect and energize this planetary city of light, and I want you to visualize this just like a canopy on top of this whole city of light. It is holding this geyser of light, this geyser of fifth-dimensional energy. So the Groom Creek planetary city of light is filling with this wonderful protective force and healing.

[Chants.]

This light, this force, will continue for the next six hours, filling the whole

Groom Creek/Spruce Mountain planetary city of light area with this wonderful fifth-dimensional protective energy. And now I will turn the word over to Juliano. I am Chief White Eagle. All my relations. Ho.

Connecting the Planetary Cities of Light

Greetings, I am Juliano. We are the Arcturians. Blessings to you, for your connection to Earth energies and your activations of the Groom Creek/Spruce Mountain planetary city of light. This city is also forming a relationship with the other planetary cities of light. So not only are you working to protect and energize this city so that it is uniquely protected, but also you are working to bring this city into the family of the planetary cities of light, to that purpose and to that energy,

I, Juliano, use a strand of etheric light that is on top of the canopy over this city that Chief White Eagle described. And this strand of etheric energy is dividing itself up into a multitude of over fifty strands of light, and at my command they will all connect to the planetary cities of light on Earth.

One, two, three — now.

[Sounds.]

The connections are made to all of the other planetary cities of light. And not only are they connected, but this city, this energy, and this medicine wheel are also connecting to all of the people in the other planetary cities of light now. And these people are all receiving your energy. They are all receiving your connections. They are all working with you, and they receive it. They are going to interact with this city of light as you are interacting with those other cities of light. In particular, in this ceremony, I am connecting into the energy of Sant Pere de Ribes near Barcelona, where Gudrun and David recently activated that city of light. And now I call on this city of light here, the Groom Creek/Spruce Mountain area, to be a sister-brother city of light to Sant Pere de Ribes.

I, Juliano, am going to form a connective link with the Groom Creek/Spruce Mountain city of light and the city of light in the moon-planet Alano, near the central sun of the Milky Way Galaxy. And, I, Juliano, take a strand of etheric light and energy, and I connect it now to the moon-planet Alano.

[Sounds.]

You will feel at this moment a heightened energy of fifth-dimensional molecular atomic quantum–energy light particles coming from Alano into this Prescott area, the Groom Creek/Spruce Mountain area.

David and Gudrun at Sant Pere de Ribes with fellow lightworkers.

[Sounds.]

This connection is a two-way connection — in and out. And the energy that is flowing here, this quantum light from Alano coming into Prescott, coming into Groom Creek, is also simultaneously going to Sant Pere de Ribes. The brother and sister cities of light share light with each other, for we are working with fifth-dimensional energy and know that the fifth-dimensional energy is not limited like the third-dimensional energy. So it is not like there is a limited amount of light and energy.

[Sounds.]

The elevation of the energy is profound now after this activation, and you who are participating in this process are also benefiting directly from this quantum light, this quantum molecular subatomic fifth-dimensional light coming from the moon-planet Alano directly into your planetary city of light. Let the winds die down. Let the calmness prevail. Let the rains come. Let the fifth-dimensional energies, the powerful connections fill the Groom Creek/Spruce Mountain planetary city of light area. And many people will be attracted to this — many higher-energy people. They will come here and experience the extraordinary energy, the extraordinary fifth-dimensional energies that you have helped to anchor.

I am your friend and teacher Juliano. Good day.

BOOK III:

Arcturian Spiritual Technology: An Update

BOOK 3
Part 1

Arcturian Spiritual
Technology: An Update

through David Miller
Australia, April 2011

CHAPTER ONE

The Arcturian Perspective on Earth

Juliano and the Arcturians

Greetings, I am Juliano. We are the Arcturians. In this lecture, we will look again at the Arcturian perspective on Earth. You have to understand that we are fifth-dimensional beings and our perspectives are based on the dimension we are living in.

You Are at the Point of Ascension

Our perspective is also based on the fact that you, as lightworkers, are working to evolve yourselves into the fifth dimension. You are at a crossroads in your spiritual evolution. You are at a crossroads in your development. This crossroads is called the point of ascension. The point of ascension is the point at which you are able to graduate from Earth. What does that mean? Graduating from Earth means that you will no longer have to be involved in Earth's karma or return to Earth unless you choose to, unless you really feel a calling of a service to return. Yet even in this condition, you could come back as a fifth-dimensional master and teacher. You could come back in a way that would not require you to be involved in Earth's karma.

Earth's karma is such that when you finish one lifetime, your passing sends you into the wheel of life whereby you will have a new lifetime on Earth. In the ascension, you are actually going through the energy field of the fourth dimension. You will not wind up being tied to Earth's plane with attachments that would bring you back, holding you back and necessitating your return to Earth in another incarnation.

This is a profound opportunity and development, and it should not and is not being taken lightly. One of the big issues in the earlier discussions of ascension was the concept of attachments. It was said that the attachments to Earth are so strong that even in the face of the opportunity to ascend, many would not ascend — they would instead choose to stay back. In some of the earlier discussions, Sananda talked to you about this concept of attachments and the idea of looking back.

The ascension is like a moment of enlightenment. It is an instantaneous process in which the doorways, or the corridors, between the third and fifth dimension are opened up. I have used this metaphor to help you understand this concept. Visualize, if you can, that each dimension where you are living is a sphere. Notice that I have said "each dimension where you are living," because I want to talk about the concept of multidimensionality. At this point, just consider the fact that you are living in more than one dimension at a time, and therefore you are multidimensional.

Visualize that the dimension known as a third dimension is a gigantic sphere. And now visualize that the fifth dimension is also a gigantic sphere. They have some links, but they are not touching. At the moment of ascension, visualize that the two spheres momentarily touch — they actually interact. At that moment, you have the ability to ascend, because there is direct, full contact with the fifth dimension. As these two spheres actually touch, there is an opening, but it is a brief moment, and it is difficult to even describe the length of that interaction.

Preparing Yourself for the Moment of Ascension

We have talked to you about the December 21, 2012 interaction of the Central Sun aligning with the center of your solar system, which is the Sun. When the sun rises on the winter solstice in 2012, it will rise exactly in the center of the alignment of the galaxy on that day. Even though you will not see the center of the galaxy because there is too much light from your Sun, it is going to rise in that spot. In a sense, we are calling that an eclipse. It is going to last a while. In fact, you are already experiencing the early stages of the eclipse.

I have explained that even in the early stages of an eclipse on Earth there is an unusual darkness. In that darkness and in that different light, animals act in unusual ways; there are even some strange behaviors. They begin to think that it is twilight, and because animals are sensitive to light, the darkness makes them think it is time to go to sleep. Yet at the same time, they realize that it is not the normal light, so they act differently. This is a good analogy, because you are on Earth experiencing a different light, a different vibration. Frankly, it is causing some people to act very chaotically. You are seeing parts of that chaos in the international political arena through many countries and many rebellions.

But Earth as a planet has also been reacting. This whole energy of 2012 that we will be exploring and the energy of the eclipse will last for a fairly substantial period of time. There has been a lengthy time before the 2012 eclipse energy, then there is the actual time of the 2012 energy, and then there is the time afterward. The interaction for the ascension, however, is instantaneous, so that means that at the moment when the dimensions intersect, there will immediately be an opportunity to ascend.

At that moment of the ascension, you may say: "Well, let me think it over. What about my job? What about my husband? What about my children? What about my pets? What about this? What about that? Who is going to take care of my mother?" There are honestly many correct and deep questions that have to be answered, but if at that moment of ascension you spend your time questioning how this or that problem is going to be resolved, the ascension will pass you by. This reaction is not for punishment. It is just to say that these dimensions do not intersect very often. When they do, it requires preparation and a mindset to be prepared to instantaneously release your attachments so that you can ascend.

The process does not end at that moment. We are working with Sananda and many of the other higher master teachers, and from our perspective, Earth has a tremendous number of high ascended masters now working together to provide the basis for this transformation and evolutionary process. Our work includes providing an intermediate subexperience — or a substation, if you will — for the ascended beings like yourselves who may not have been 100 percent prepared to ascend at the moment of ascension. Therefore, once you enter the fifth dimension, there are intermediate classrooms, healing chambers, and transitional centers in which we and others guides and teachers will be available to work with you. We can complete what you might call your "briefing" to complete your total release from Earth.

This is another way of suggesting that you take the leap to ascend and then work out any other lingering details or releases of attachments once you are in the ascension field, the fifth-dimensional realms. Once you get there, we and others are going to work and help you. This is not as far-fetched as others might think, because it is well known in the spirit world that when you transition, when you die and go to the other side, there are many people waiting to help you.

I can compare it to the birthing experience. When a baby is born, look at all the people who are there waiting with the mother — the doctors, the nurses, and the family members. Most of the time, there are a great number of people waiting to welcome the new baby into the world. If that were not the case, it would be hard for the baby.

It is the same way when you go into the death tunnel, and it is also the same way when you go into the ascension. The ascension is a totally joyful celebration. Some have asked me to compare it to death. Death is often accompanied by many conflicting feelings, many sorrows and many fears. It is about whether your soul lives on or if it really is the end. A lot of people do not want to give up their lives. They do not want to leave the Earth plane, even though they are in a lot of physical pain. The ascension is not like that. The ascension is a total release from all attachments on Earth. You have the opportunity to go into these transitional places to complete the release. When that interaction occurs, it is looking forward, not backward.

Earth Offers Unique Ascension Possibilities

When I am speaking to you about the Arcturian perspective on Earth and what is happening here, notice that I do not begin by talking about an Earth crisis or the many problems facing the planet and the evolution of the species. Rather, I begin by talking about the ascension. This is an important point because, as we come to look at Earth, we realize that this planet is in a unique position to ascend, and it is in a unique position to have so many lightworkers, so many starseeds also ready to ascend.

Perhaps you might think about this. With all the problems and all the conflicts with the biosphere — the wars and the destructions of habitat — with all of this going on, the most amazing energy of fifth-dimensional light has come to Earth and is still coming to Earth. This energy will bring the moment of ascension to the planet, which will allow countless numbers of starseeds to immediately transcend to the fifth dimension. That availability, that opportunity, is a calling that permeates the entire galaxy. You know that there are many beings and many planets in the galaxy, even in this section of the galaxy. But there are only two stargates in the entire galaxy, and there are only several opportunities for planetary and personal ascensions here. So the opportunity for ascension does not occur on a regular basis in this galaxy.

This means that Earth, with all the problems that it has, still represents and offers this experience of ascension, this unique experience. Ascension is such a unique experience that many starseeds have voluntarily signed up to come to Earth at this time in order to experience the ascension. It is also important to remember that some of the starseeds on Earth are already coming from other dimensions and have, through mistakes or miscalculations, wound up in Earth's incarnational cycle. In a very simple, direct way, you can say that maybe their ships crashed when they came here. They could not get out, and then they became involved in Earth's life.

Once you pass a certain stage of involvement in the third dimension, you become committed and permanently involved in Earth and in the incarnations here. Some call it "trapped." The only way out at that point is through ascension. That is the way to leave the third dimension. There are many of you who are not worried about attachments because you are ready to return to your home planet. You know that this moment and time on Earth presents the opportunity for the ascension.

Could we not stay in that ascended state after 2012 and still live on this planet to serve?

Yes, you can, but it is not the same when you stay in an ascended state. There have been discussions with people about ascending but staying in place. I have to explain that first you should make the commitments to cut the cords of attachment to Earth and ascend, and then you can make the decision to return, if you want to. But people want to make that decision before they leave. In other words, they want to say: "Well, I am going to come back." I have to point out that this still is an indication of attachment to Earth. It is not a bad thing, and it is true that you can maintain a greater fifth-dimensional presence on Earth. In fact, those people who do not ascend with the first ascension will be more activated and more fifth-dimensional in their thinking and their activities.

There are cases of ascension where people experience the fifth dimension and come back. There are examples, especially Enoch. In the Bible, he walked with God and he was no more — he was gone. And there is the case of Elijah and Mohammed. These are beings who ascended. They did not return in their same presence. Even Enoch came into a full spiritual presence as Archangel Metatron. Enoch and Metatron are united, but Metatron is the great soul, and he used the physical body of Enoch.

I am trying to give you this perspective of Earth and explain that this opportunity for ascension is the calling that brings many of the spirit masters, guides, and teachers to Earth to assist in that process.

You Will Hear the Clarion Call of the Ascension

Who will know the exact moment when the ascension comes? Is there no way we can miss it?

You will know the exact moment. It is going to be, as some have called it, the clarion call. It is going to be a sound, a vibration that is unmistakable. Some of the exercises that we are working with through our teachings and this channel have to do with preparing yourself for your ascension. One of the most powerful exercises that we are teaching through this channel is the energy and the practice of shimmering.

The problem is that you have never heard the sound of ascension in your consciousness because the sound of ascension is outside of the threshold of your normal perceptual state. We use the example of seeing colors that are not in the normal threshold. Another good example is sound waves. You know your dog can hear things you cannot hear. This shows you immediately that there are perceptions that are beyond the threshold, but they are still present. Some animals who are more sensitive can respond to them, even though you cannot.

The sound of ascension is beyond your normal range of perception, but it is going to pierce into your normal consciousness, and you will be able to hear it. It will be an experience that you will immediately know is the energy of ascension. Also you are genetically preordained to process and receive this. If you decide at that moment not to ascend, remember that you will still have heard and experienced the sound of ascension. The sound of ascension, the clarion call for ascension, can only be heard by those who are prepared, by those who are already at a certain vibration. Not everybody is going to hear it.

This will also answer the other question that was asked: If you hear the sound of ascension but do not go, you will still have made tremendous gains in your vibrational energy field, because you will have experienced this energy and the vibrational process of the ascension. For whatever reason, you might choose to keep the energy and use it. The case of Elisha, the student of Elijah, offers a good example. Elisha was with Elijah when Elijah ascended. Elisha was left behind, and all Elisha saw were the clothes of his master. The body was gone. What did that do to him? Elisha became a great prophet, and he inherited psychic and prophetic powers. You can say that he was equal to Elijah, because he also carried Elijah's energy. At that moment of the ascension, if you do not ascend but you are experiencing the ascension and the vibrational field, it *does* make you a higher being.

Arcturian Stargates and Life on Earth After the Ascension

Is there a greater attractive feeling to the stargates, for example, the one that has been shown to us through your work? Last year before my operation, I experienced the feeling of being pulled very strongly toward the stargate on a couple of occasions. Is that a sign that ascension is near?

Yes, it is. The ascension is very near because your awareness of the stargate is part of the transforming energy, a sign that the two spheres are going to intersect. Knowledge of the stargate, dreams about the stargate, and visits to the stargate at different times and in different ways — these things are coming more and more into the experience of starseeds.

Remember that we have said that you can now go to the vestibule, the front room of the stargate. In our experiences and our work, we can open the door of the stargate slightly while you are in the vestibule so that you can experience the tremendous light of the stargate coming through. But you are not allowed to pass through the stargate, because if you do, you will not come back into Earth's incarnation, you will not come back to this life. That is how powerful the energy is. You would not be able to come back as a third-dimensional being if we let you go through the stargate.

We have downloaded powerful connections to the stargate, especially at Serra da Bocaina, where the etheric crystal in Brazil is. These connections have a special connection to the Arcturian stargate. We have been working, from our perspective, on preparing Earth and the starseeds for their ascension through the gateways, through the corridors and the ladders of ascension, to go directly to the stargate. So you can come into one of our great healing ships to help complete the transition before you go to the stargate.

I have great difficulties with this concept. If you need all that focus for the ascension route, wouldn't that leave Earth in a pretty desolate situation for planetary healing?

Not at all, because in the example that I gave you of Elijah and Elisha, Elisha became a great spiritual master on his own and had a tremendous influence on many people. You are now setting great spiritual foundations for planetary healing and planetary work. Were many of the lightworkers to ascend, their ascension would set into motion a powerful vibrational energy that would enthusiastically activate deeper commitments for those who are still here.

Not too worry — it is not going to be a problem. Number one, not all of the planetary healers are going to ascend. Number two, this is why we are continually teaching you about Biorelativity and the Groups of Forty. This is why we have installed the etheric crystals — to set a foundation for our process. Your ascension contributes to the vibrational frequency of light on this planet. This is another way of saying that through ascension, you are helping to raise the spiritual vibration on this planet. Anyone who knew you and anyone who had any contact with you and understood anything about your work will be so greatly uplifted to know that you have ascended.

An Exercise to Experience the Feel of Fifth-Dimensional Energy

I would like you now to go through an exercise with me. Visualize and experience an Arcturian corridor of light coming down directly into the center of this room. I, Juliano, am bringing down this corridor of light, this huge blue fifth-dimensional light, into the center of the room. With comfort and with ease, your spirit gently leaves your physical body. You remain in your physical body as your spirit rises to the top of the room. As your spirit rises to the top of the room, you meet me, Juliano, at the top of the room, and together we go through the corridor of light.

[Sounds.]

We travel at the speed of thought through the corridor to the entrance way, the vestibule of the stargate, and there we sit together in this beautiful entrance. We see the doorway of the stargate, and we know that there are many beings — even beings like you, who have a multidimensional presence — in the stargate, in the vestibule. When you are sitting in the stargate, you can feel the intense fifth-dimensional light of the stargate. I have permission to open the gateway, or doorway, of the stargate a crack. As I open that door, feel and experience the light from the stargate coming through the vestibule, filling your etheric body.

[Sounds.]

As you feel this light, know that you are still anchored to the third dimension. You will not leave that dimension now. But also allow the energy of the stargate, this beautiful fifth-dimensional light, to be received in your aura, and make it a familiar energy. You do not have to make any decisions about leaving the third dimension. You do not have to cut any cords of attachment, but we give you the freedom now to experience the energy of the stargate, the energy of being a fifth-dimensional being. This is an energy through which you have the freedom to depart from Earth and move to any fifth-dimensional planetary system that you wish. This includes returning to your home planet. We will go into a brief meditation now as you experience this interaction.

[Meditation.]

Prepare yourself to return. I am now closing the door, the crack that was opened from the stargate, and now you can take with you all the light and energy that you are gathering from the vestibule. Follow me as we use the corridor to return to the room. Find an alignment six feet above your Earth body, but do not enter your Earth body yet.

Tell yourself that you will reenter your physical body in perfect alignment at the count of three. One, two, three — now. Reenter. Know that, through spiritual osmosis, all of the light and energy that you were able to experience in the stargate will slowly and purposefully be reintegrated into all the cellular structures in your third-dimensional body. Return to a full presence in your physical body now. We will return. I am Juliano. We are the Arcturians. Good day.

CHAPTER TWO

Planetary Evolution

Juliano and the Arcturians

Greetings, I am Juliano. We are the Arcturians. We are looking at the human Adam species, the species of Adam. We see that Adam is in an evolutionary crisis. An evolutionary shift must be made, incorporating the ability to have a new world perspective based on unity consciousness, on fifth-dimensional thinking. How is it that a species deals with an evolutionary crisis? How is it that a species gets to make the change so that it will survive? When we look at Earth, we call it the Blue Jewel. In fact, the name of the film that is being made with the participation of the Group of Forty is called *The Blue Jewel*. From our perspective, this Earth has so many great energies and so much great potential. In order for humankind to institute the next evolutionary change that will ensure the survival of humanity and Earth, the spiritual light quotient of the planet and its inhabitants must be raised. We know of many planets that did not survive, planets that fell into chaos and self-destruction, which is exactly where Earth might end up if the spiritual light quotient of this planet is not raised. We know that you, the starseeds, can help to raise the spiritual light quotient of the planet.

The Spiritual Light Quotient

Let us look at what the spiritual light quotient is. The spiritual light quotient can be measured as the ability to comprehend, use, and promote spirituality as a means of unity and solving issues related to survival. Let us say that the ingredient that is necessary for solving the problems of the planet requires a spiritual component.

Quite frankly, that same spiritual light quotient, that same spiritual perspective, is necessary for your evolution. The question that has been raised is: "Why is the soul evolving? We thought the soul was perfect." The answer is that the soul is perfect in its evolution. Its evolving is part of its perfection. But you are only experiencing a slice of your whole being. This is difficult to grasp. Imagine that your whole energy field, your whole self, is a huge circle. You are experiencing one thin slice of a pie in that circle that is representative of yourself. Your whole self is so great. You often hear people say, "You do not realize who you are." When Gudrun talks about her clients, it is clear that when they come into her office she sees a much greater picture of what these people are than they can see themselves. She sees things in them that they do not even know they have. She sees parts of them that are totally unified and put together. Raising the spiritual light quotient helps you to have that view of others and especially to have that view of yourself. One of the great opportunities in any lifetime, any manifestation, is to achieve the ability to unify all the parts of the self. Any one lifetime or incarnation can offer you the possibility of this unification.

In fact, there is the possibility of ascending in a normal situation in regular times. There are examples that have been given of people who ascended, and there are many recordings of people who have ascended that are not really of famous nature. The coming ascension is a different type of ascension. The previous ascensions were individual in nature and required dedication and a certain number of incarnations and meditations to release the mind. But the coming ascension is a group ascension. This ascension is related specifically to the spiritual light quotient factor. When we talk about raising the consciousness of a whole planet, think about that — how do you raise the consciousness of a whole planet so that all of its beings are participating in the spiritual issues and confronting them? We have offered several methods for raising the spiritual light quotient of the planet. One of the main methods is through the planetary cities of light, because we understand that raising the spiritual light quotient and energies of a planet can be done by designating sacred areas. Everybody knows that if some place is sacred, you have to be and react in a special way around that energy. We have helped to create a communication of the new spiritual fifth-dimensional technologies, which includes the designation of the areas known as planetary cities of light. It also includes the idea of the ring of ascension, spiritual exercises such as shimmering, the development of the Iskalia mirror, and the idea of downloading the etheric crystals coming from the fifth dimension to provide portals.

We have also been teaching you about Biorelativity, which is the ability to telepathically communicate with the spirit of the planet so that it can respond to shifts in balanced ways that are not detrimental to Earth's human inhabitants.

Acknowledge That Earth Is a Living Spiritual Energy Force

One aspect of raising the spiritual light quotient of your planet is for people to acknowledge that a planet is a living spiritual energy force and being. If that concept is understood, the response of humanity to that knowledge can change behavior and help humanity deal and interact with Earth in a much different way. When we talk about our perspective of Earth and the Blue Jewel, we can say that the majority of lightworkers accept the fact that Earth is a spiritual being, but the majority of the people in power on Earth do not accept that, and they do not act in that energy. It is difficult to categorize or generalize, but most of the people who are moving toward this understanding of Earth as a spiritual energy field will not use nuclear energy or promote it, because it destroys the aura of Earth and causes leakages in the life-force energy.

There is a life-force energy around the whole planet, and it is encased in a light field that it is very similar to the egg shape that we talk about when we refer to the cosmic egg. When I am talking to you about your lightbody, your illness, and your energy problems, most of the time there are leakages in your aura. Most of the time those leakages are caused by attachments to your energy and different intrusions into it, and those leakages can be healed. There are specific techniques for energy healing. Earth is the same way. Earth has an energy field, and it can be damaged. When the energy field of Earth is damaged, it leaks and the life-force energy shifts and drains. Nuclear energies cause rifts and time distortions in the energy field.

Let us talk about time distortions, because there is a third-dimensional space-time continuum. If there is a rift in the space-time continuum in a certain area, there is a distortion in the vibrational energies, and a chaotic feeling can erupt. We believe that there has been a space-time rift over Iraq, for example, or Afghanistan. When this distortion energy is present, a great deal of illogical and harmful activities occur under it. What occurs is that much energy is wasted; it is as though all these forces, intentions, energies, and monies are placed into a hole that serves no purpose and from which nothing is gained. What happens is that things are lost, and the energy gets so drained. Look what has been lost already in Chernobyl and Japan. Look at the potential loss around this planet from the nuclear factors.

We also want to acknowledge that there is a higher wisdom and a cure. We will have to acknowledge that there are other technologies to counteract the radiation, but there still need to be techniques to counteract the rifts in the energy field of Earth. All of these discussions lead us to the basic premise that the whole spiritual light quotient of Earth must be raised. One of the goals of the starseeds and the Group of Forty is to develop techniques and ways of raising the spiritual light quotient of Earth. Even the Planetary Tree of Life Cards represent a method for raising the spiritual light quotient of the planet so more people can understand that there are sacred designated areas that hold fifth-dimensional energies and light.

Fifth-Dimensional Energies and Closeness to the Creator

Let us talk about the fifth-dimensional energies, because you are multidimensional. This means that you can be living in two different dimensions simultaneously. What is amazing is that you may have no awareness of your existence in the fifth dimension now. The thing that is most intriguing to us is that the ascension and the discussion of going to the fifth dimension seems like such a major shift to you. But at the same time, I want to say that you already have, as we are speaking, part of a fifth-dimensional awareness and presence. Maybe it is not strong, maybe you have a hard time believing it, but maybe you also have a hard time believing that you exist while you sleep and that the dream world you inhabit while you sleep is part of an important reality that you are participating in, but you can only experience that reality when you go into the dream state.

The fifth-dimensional energies that we are talking about already exist. We are helping you to practice going into the fifth dimension. We are teaching you techniques such as thought projection as a way of traveling to the fifth dimension. We know that the fifth-dimensional experiences that you have can be brought back into the third dimension. People often ask, "Why don't you just come back to Earth and institute the changes as fifth-dimensional beings?" The answer is that we need third-dimensional anchors, third-dimensional people who can do this. We are talking about coming to the planet and doing service. One of the answers to this question about soul evolution is that it relates to the Creator and to the concept of closeness to the Creator life spirit and form. Part of the idea of soul evolution is that you develop the techniques and abilities to be closer to the Creator, and when you are closer to the Creator, this is considered a higher evolutionary state. The highest evolutionary state you may be conscious of can relate to your knowledge of Jesus, Sananda, Moses, Mohamed — beings who you know are close to the Creator. In this paradigm, one characteristic of soul evolution is described as the ability to be close to the Creator. One of the greatest ways to be closest to the Creator is to do service. Why do we, the Arcturians, fifth-dimensional beings, even bother coming to the third dimension? Why would all these other beings of higher light come to Earth? If we are already in higher light, why do we need to participate in Earth? The answer has to do with the role of the Creator, with the idea that service lies in being close to the Creator, and it is part of this idea that comes forth in the healing and raising of the spiritual light quotient of Earth. For it is the will of the Creator that this Earth, as well as humanity, makes the next evolutionary step and that the planet has its spiritual light quotient raised. Do you have any questions about what I have said so far?

How many portions of the pie — the totality of me — are involved in other planets or worlds?

I would say that for you there are probably three to five portions of the pie that are involved in other lifetimes, dimensions, and planets. But how much of this you are aware of now and the ways you can bring this into this lifetime are good follow-up questions. You could not be as active in planetary healing as you are unless you had these other experiences and other lifetimes. Your gifts as a planetary healer are based in part on your connections with your fifth-dimensional self and your ability to bring this energy down onto Earth. The exercise of going to the crystal lake and connecting with your fifth-dimensional self can help to enhance your memory and awareness of those other experiences. It is especially relevant to work with Helio-ah and the holographic healing chambers, because there you are able to meet, embrace, and communicate with your entire self through holographic spiritual technology, which is based on this assumption that the part gives you access to the whole. If you can correctly experience the part, that is the key that unlocks the whole. We use this principle in our personal and planetary healing. Are there any other questions for me?

Nuclear Energy's Disastrous Effects on Earth's Energy Field

It has been suggested in other places that there is a technology in higher dimensions that can clean up the radioactive mess. What do we need to do to make possible that it is downloaded very quickly?

I think that the answer to your first question is yes, there is technology to do that. As for your second question, the way to do that is to work through the Planetary Tree of Life and encourage the knowledge and wisdom to be brought down. There are people who can receive that knowledge. Let us say that the key to the theory of relativity and how to travel beyond the speed of light is available. Somebody has to receive it. It might not be sent to you, because you might not be able to integrate the mathematical formulas. It has to be received by somebody who knows how to transpose it into something workable. The second point I want to make, which might be more important, is that the people in charge of running these nuclear energy plants have to respond and make a change. Let me explain. We cannot see how things can continue as usual. Let us say that all of the radioactive problems in these plants were solved and everything became stable. Things would then go back to normal. In other words, countries would continue to operate as they have been operating, and humankind would continue to pretend that nuclear energy plants are not dangerous and that they do not need to be changed. It is very similar to the idea that you do not resolve something until you learn the lesson that was inherent for you to learn when coming to Earth. What is the lesson that the world has to learn from Japan and this great tragedy?

To use other energy sources and other systems to create energy.
Do you see this happening?

No.
I cannot say that one is supporting the other now. I only can suggest that a greater shift has to occur. The longer the crisis continues, the more likely it is that many countries will stop to reevaluate their nuclear participation. From that perspective, the continuing crisis contributes to ensuring that more people will begin to explore alternatives. But this is such a painful way to learn lessons. If the planet has a higher spiritual light quotient, people will begin to understand this before tragedy occurs. We want to look at preventing major cyclones, hurricanes, and earthquakes with Biorelativity. It is unbelievable the damage that the nuclear energy does to the energy field of Earth. It is totally astounding. All the prayers and all the Biorelativity exercises for Japan should include the telepathic communication that this methodology of energy production will no longer be used. Are there other questions?

Sometimes with destruction, we get wonderful stories of compassion, help, and people's hearts being opened, in Japan or around the world. Does this help rebalance the damage that has been caused?
It does help, but it still is not the long-lasting solution. Tragedies are experienced at multiple levels. The compassion, brotherhood, and sisterhood are

totally amazing and powerful, but we still have the basic problem. This is not a helpful energy source or method.

Is there a new technology available to put forward, or is it still being developed?

There are now people on this planet who know how to solve this problem. The issue is: "Are they being brought into the circle? Are they being listened to? Do they have access to the people who are in control of trying to solve this problem?" Our original statement — and I will repeat it because this was said in another group — is that the people who are in control of solving this problem do not have the ability to solve the problem. Who wants to have people in control of solving a problem who do not have the ability and the knowledge to solve it? Nobody really would want that. That is what is happening now.

The Biorelativity intent has to allow the information to come to those people in control and help change the decision making so that people around the planet move in the direction of eliminating nuclear energy as a means of producing electrical power. That is a hard lesson, a very difficult process, but there is going to be another nuclear accident in this planet, possibly within the next six months. How could that be possible? Who would have thought that there would be another tsunami after the one in Indonesia? Who could have thought that there would be another one? And yet we had another one that has caused more planetary damage to the ecosystems of the whole planet. I am saying this is the kind of energy and these are the times that we are dealing with now. Corrections have to be made or another accident will happen. Will the second nuclear accident then make people change? Is there any way to have this happen without a second accident? Can you even imagine a second accident and what that would mean for Earth? I am not saying this to be doom and gloom. I am just saying that this is the energetic level where things are. There has to be a change in the spiritual reaction. The shift has to be made or another tragedy will have to happen before the change might occur. What changes have really occurred in the global position on nuclear power? I want to ask you to help raise the spiritual light quotient of the planet and yourselves. I am Juliano. We are the Arcturians.

CHAPTER THREE

Healing, Chi, and the Omega Light

Quan Yin

Greetings, dear ones. I am Quan Yin. It is lovely to be here with you, and I totally love the fact that you are seekers of light, seekers of health, and seekers of expansion. It is a well-known fact that when coming to the third dimension, one must experience contractions. In fact, the basic portal that leads to the entrance into the third dimension requires a contraction of your energies on many levels. The first level is your memory. It is well known that right before you come down the gateway into this life form you are given a kiss on your forehead — a kiss that immediately erases memories of your past life, your past experiences, and your past knowledge. This is not a total erasure but a temporary one. It puts your memories in a special compartment, hopefully to be accessed at a later time when you are in a more expanded state.

Primordial and Secondary Chi

Your initial entry into this world is based on the energy of contraction, and then the second action, when the first breath is taken, signifies your first expansion. Every being that comes into this life on the third dimension is given a basic energy account, like a bank account. You have basic energy storage and basic energy availability. And we call that energy the primordial chi, the life-force energy that each of you is granted for this lifetime. It is interesting to use the monetary metaphor of a bank account. It is like saying to you, "Okay, you have been given

500 dollars of chi energy for this lifetime." Some people use up all that energy right away; some people hold on to their energy.

Now I want to distinguish between the primordial chi — the basic chi, the life-force chi that you have — and the secondary chi, which is the energy field that you are interacting with and receiving from your daily activities. In some ways, they are closely related, but they are separate in other ways. They are closely related because what you are doing in your basic life can rob you of primordial chi. One of the things that robs you of primordial chi, for example, is drug abuse; another thing that does this, not surprisingly, is radiation and nuclear energies.

One of the things that gives you chi is raising your spiritual light quotient through spiritual studies, and so is working with some of the exercises of gathering light and gathering spiritual energy. This can raise your chi. Another thing that can raise your chi is being in sacred places where there is a great deal of purity — purity of air and purity in the earth. And when you are in a state of relaxation, there is more of an opening that allows you to work on gaining chi. Chi is a life-force energy that also has the spiritual component, a spiritual charge. So there is a spiritual chi, there is health chi, and there is even emotional chi.

Specific and Undifferentiated Chi

I know that you are working on the Tree of Life and I know that you are working to expand yourselves. I also know that each of you also wants to be in the most healthy, active, and optimal condition and wellness, as we call it. So there is what we call chi healing emanation. It is based on two principles: the principle of emanating, or sending, and the principle of receiving. You can be more receptive, and you can then receive more chi.

The second aspect that I want to explain has to do specifically with the Tree of Life, because the first sphere in the Planetary Tree of Life that Juliano presented to you is based on the concept of undifferentiated chi. Undifferentiated chi is another way of saying that you are receiving light and healing, and that energy will go where it needs to go. You do not have to be specific. You say, "Okay, I will receive this light. Light is being emanated, energy is being emanated, and they can go where they need to go."

There is also specific chi healing. This could be healing for a certain organ, it could be for a certain chakra, or it could be for a certain part of your body. So in our exercise, we will use the concept of the general undifferentiated chi, and then when the chi comes down and you receive it, you allow it to go wherever it needs to go within your body. We like to think of the chi as a great golden ball of light. This ball of chi is an actual structure, even though you cannot see it. It is something you can actually feel and sense, even though you cannot totally describe it. It is so desirable to receive the chi healing, which comes from the life-force energy.

Exercises in Chi Healing

I, Quan Yin, am calling on the forces of the chi to enter this room. We are filling the channel's palms with a great chi life-force field, and as he walks around the room, you can receive the chi. Let your aura receive the powerful chi light, and use this chi as healing energy, allowing it to go wherever it needs to go to give you the spiritual healing, the mental healing, the emotional healing — any healing that you want, that you need. Know that you are replenishing your energy with this chi. Know that you are revitalizing yourself with the chi light. Know that you are calming yourself and going into a deeper state of relaxation so that you can receive even more chi.

[Sings.]

Through the process of spiritual osmosis, let this chi come into your body, into your spine, through your nervous system, and through all your nerve cells. This light, this powerful light force, is filling your energy field. A huge second golden ball of chi enters into the center of this room. Breathe in this light of chi. You are on this beautiful planet known as Mother Earth, but you want to go into your higher fifth-dimensional energy field. Realize this beautiful thought: In order to totally go into your highest fifth-dimensional energy field, you need to be really grounded to Mother Earth, for Mother Earth is the foundation for your ascension.

This is the beautiful thought (though some may see this as a contradiction) and the secret to successful ascension. For on the one hand, as Juliano said, you need to cut your ties to Earth, but you also need the foundation of Earth to provide you with the proper alignments. But now this proper alignment is twofold: Your feet are connected to Earth but your crown chakra is going up out of Earth, out of the solar system, to the higher realms — to Arcturus, to the Pleiades, to the Central Sun, to the fifth-dimensional planet Alano, to the Arcturian crystal temple. Feel your crown chakra opening wide to these galactic energy vibrations coming from these higher sources.

Juliano is fond of saying that the fastest speed possible in the universe is the speed of thought. Know that chi follows this principle of the speed of thought. So the healing chi energy from the crystal temple in Arcturus is now connecting to your crown chakra. The healing light from your guides and teachers, the healing light from the Buddha, the light of the enlightened one, is radiating to each of you now.

[Sounds.]

Please put your palms face-up on your lap as we walk around together.

[Sounds.]

I would like three people who wish to be healed by the group to come to the center of the room. Stand in a line in front of the channel so that you can receive the healing chi from the group. Okay, please face the group. And now, group, your instructions are to send the healing chi to them. This is the undifferentiated chi. They can use this chi for whatever healing they want or need in their bodies. Ready? Now.

[Sounds.]

[*To the group:*] Use your hands to send the chi, and move your hands too.

[Sounds.]

[*To the three volunteers:*] Use this chi however you need it. You can turn around and with your backs to the group.

[*To the group:*] You have so much chi. You can send them more healing chi and send them more healing light.

[*To the three volunteers:*] Okay, you may return to your seats.

Are there three other people who wish to come up? Send them the chi, the healing chi.

[Sounds.]

[*To the three new volunteers:*] You can turn around with your backs to the group so that they can work on your backs now.

[Sounds.]

Use this healing chi light and let it go wherever it needs to in your bodies. It has the wisdom to go into your bodies and create healings for your highest good. You may return to your seats.

[Sounds.]

[*To the group:*] Send them the healing, send them balls of light, balls of golden light.

[Sounds.]

[*To the three new volunteers:*] Feel the healing, especially the strongest light coming out of the palm of your hand, right in the center of the palm. You may turn around, please.

[Sounds.]

You may return to your seats. There is a tremendous amount of healing chi light in this room. You are all emanating it and you are all receiving it. The chi is moving in this room; it generates such powerful healing energy. Feel like you are on a ball — it is the ball of planet Earth. Feel and know that you are connected to the higher realms, to the fifth-dimensional realm. [Sounds.]

Now let this chi healing energy go through your whole body. Let it go through every cell. The beauty of the undifferentiated light, the undifferentiated chi, is that it goes where it needs to go.

The Transformational Quantum Healing Powers of the Omega Light

One of the energies that we work with for higher healing is called the omega light. Now that you have become receptive — of course you were receptive even before you came here, but now you are very receptive to the chi healing energy — you can feel a greater receptivity to the omega light. The omega light is a fifth-dimensional light that has intense powers of transformational quantum healing. When this light is directed toward a specific situation, a specific energy, a specific part of the body that needs to be healed, the doorways are opened to what we call quantum healing.

Quantum healing is the healing energy that transcends the normal third-dimensional space-time continuum. When you came here to the planet, the first energy is contraction. One of the lessons, one of the experiences that you must process, is how to deal with contraction. You also have to learn that contraction is counterbalanced by expansion and that you do not need to stay in a contracted state. Contraction is synonymous with fear; contraction is synonymous with feeling ultimately cut off from the unity that is the Creator light. The omega light is an energy field that transcends contraction and gives you the immediate opportunity to process and experience the quantum energy field within yourself and to even experience the transcendental miracle energy of healing.

I, Quan Yin, call on the omega light to enter and come down in the center of this room.

[Sings.]

Let the omega light fill your aura with the special ray of transcendental quantum light. Know that you are now in a sacred energy field. You are now in a sacred mind. What you think — the thoughts you hold at this moment — can have a powerful effect and manifestation on the third dimension. So choose your affirmation, choose your intention, choose your most perfective thought possible, and hold that thought while I bring down another round of the omega light.

[Sings: *Omega light.*]

You have absorbed a lot of the omega light. You may now come back into your normal state of consciousness. You can come back into your body, if you are feeling you are in a higher body. Readjust yourself to this newer vibration that you are now in, this new frequency that you are now vibrating in. Allow the healings to totally integrate into your fields, and know that a slow process that the guides call spiritual osmosis — the ability to slowly absorb all of this energy into your physical body — is now under way.

I just thought toward the end of the session that it would be actually beautiful to be able to send this energy to the bay to help the ocean. The bay we are near is a nursery for quite a few families of dolphins as well as sharks. Is it possible that we can also send it to the bay where we are?

You have the omega light with you now and you can direct the light to the bay, to the nurseries, to the dolphins, to the whales, and to the sharks. Use the power of your intention. Use the power of the omega light. You can direct as much of this light that you need to from this room, because this room is filled with an abundance of the light-energy field. You can even visualize that you are sending a huge ball of light if you need to focus it more directly. That ball lands right in the center of the bay and is then dispersed and goes where it needs to go.

I, Quan Yin, send you my blessings and the light of the chi and the omega light, dear ones. Good day.

CHAPTER FOUR

Explanation of the Planetary Tree of Life

David Miller

I want to give you a little history of working with the Arcturians over the years. They wanted to establish crystals to hold down the fifth-dimensional energy and anchor it. So the first place they chose for the etheric crystal was Lago Puelo, Argentina. I did not personally go there. I wanted to, but I did not have the means at the time. We organized and directed the downloading of the crystal at Lago Puelo from a workshop in Sedona during a meeting with the Group of Forty. There were 300 people at this lake in Argentina, and they received the downloading of this crystal there. It was really phenomenal. We got many beautiful reports back on the experience from Lago Puelo. On the Tree of Life, this etheric crystal at Lago Puelo is on the bottom sphere.

This Tree of Life is based on the Jewish Kaballistic Tree of Life, but it has been expanded. With Arcturian help, I have updated the Tree of Life. Some people might ask, "Who are you to do that?" I believe that this Tree of Life needs to be updated. I guess the question I have to ask is: Why? The answer is that the earlier Jewish Tree of Life did not conceive of Earth as a planet the way we now see it exactly; it did not conceive of the idea of the galaxy, and it did not conceive of the idea of planetary healing. So this updated Tree of Life is also a configuration of a paradigm that is used in the galaxy and the universe for planetary energy work. The bottom sphere represents manifestation; however, all energy comes from the top of the tree down to the bottom sphere, or manifestation.

The top sphere in our updated version is represented by Mount Fuji in Japan. In the updated Tree of Life, we have assigned sacred areas on the planet to represent the spheres on the tree. Mount Fuji represents undifferentiated energy. What is undifferentiated energy? What would you do to find it? It is energy that is so high that there are no words to describe it. We also have designated it as cosmic light. At the top of the Tree of Life, we put Archangel Metatron as the high ascended master and angel to hold this energy. In the *Kaballah*, Metatron is often considered the highest archangel. So we have Lago Puelo representing manifestation on the bottom sphere, and we have Mount Fuji at the top representing undifferentiated energy.

Wisdom and Understanding

On the first right sphere, we use the famous German lake Bodensee, which is representative of wisdom. Bodensee is in southern Germany on the Austrian and Swiss borders. We designated Chief White Eagle to be the spirit guide of wisdom.

The sphere opposite wisdom is understanding. There is a difference between wisdom and understanding knowledge. You can have understanding of events without wisdom. Wisdom is a higher function that comes from a higher energy. Bodensee is a beautiful area; it is also known as Lake Constance. It is a lake that touches three countries: Germany, Austria, and Switzerland. That is a special connection to central Europe.

Lake Moraine near Banff in Canada is representative of understanding in the updated Tree of Life. You look at one side and the other in terms of the Tree of Life as a balance. If you just have understanding without wisdom, then this is not desirable. So in doing a planetary healing and working with energy, everything in the Tree of Life is about balance. Even now, when we are looking at this planet, we can say that the planet has too much male energy; the planet has too much domination. The whole male approach to the planet is too domineering, and we need more of the feminine. It is also interesting that some of these ideas of the Tree of Life could be related to the concepts of yin and yang in Taoism.

Beneath the sphere represented by the Bodensee and beneath the sphere represented by Lake Moraine is hidden knowledge. The spirit guide for hidden knowledge is the Arcturian teacher Helio-ah. What does hidden knowledge mean? In Hebrew, the term was *data*, which is knowledge that is hidden. In the Hebrew Tree of Life, the connecting lines between the spheres of knowledge and the other spheres were hyphens, or spaced lines, indicating that hidden knowledge is not yet manifested. We are in a condition now where we cannot let esoteric knowledge remain hidden; it needs to come out and be revealed.

I sometimes talk with Native American people, and you hear that they want to hold their secrets, that they cannot reveal them to white people. Every teaching needs to become available now. Even all this hidden information from the *Kaballah* and the hidden information from all these other esoteric religions has come out. This is the time in which hidden knowledge needs to be revealed, because we need to solve this Earth crisis. The sphere for hidden knowledge is represented by the city Istanbul — partly because Istanbul is a secret hidden area that is becoming more known. There are many hidden secrets in Istanbul. It is the seed of many different civilizations.

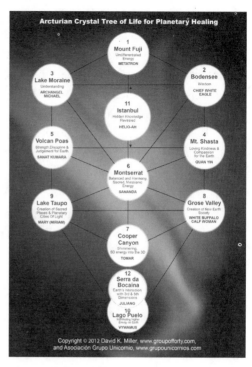

An update to the Tree of Life, which we call the Arcturian Planetary Tree of Life

A Balance of Loving Kindness and Judgment

Mount Shasta is the place representing loving kindness and compassion for Earth. We cannot talk about one side without the other. It is very difficult to talk about compassion and balance without talking about judgment and harshness. Why is that? It is said in the *Kaballah* that God created other worlds. There was a world created that was just a world of judgment and harshness, and that world failed.

On the other hand, if everything is loving kindness in a world, people can get away with murder. The best example is the terrorists. You cannot just say, "Oh, I understand why you feel this way," and give them permission to ruin everything. So you have to have a balance, and in the *Kaballah*, God created this world in the state of loving kindness so that there would be a balance with judgment. We designated Quan Yin for the sphere of loving kindness and Sanat Kumara for judgment toward the Earth. Montserrat is sacred Messianic energy. Now, this sphere in the middle, the center, is the only one that is connected to every other sphere. It is a very sacred area. You can really feel the energy of Jesus there; you can feel the energy of Mary.

There is also a special black Madonna at Montserrat that represents the Messianic energy. We have designated Sananda as the savior energy.

We designated Grose Valley, Australia — two hours from Sydney in the Blue Mountain area — and its crystal as the creation of the new Earth society. In mystical terms, this is the society of the just. What is the society of the just? It means living in a society that takes care of everyone with compassion and justice, a society that is in balance and living in harmony. It is really like a planetary city of light. It has a higher justice, a higher wisdom. We need to not only have the sacredness, but also to live in the sacred energy.

Social Justice and Manifesting the Fifth Dimension in Our World

Lake Taupo represents the creation of sacred places and planetary cities of light. It is a beautiful area. It is very primordial. We designated this as the area of sacred places and planetary cities of light, and one of the big solutions offered by this whole Planetary Tree of Life approach is to make more sacred areas, more planetary cities, so that they will be more protected.

Copper Canyon represents manifesting the fifth dimension in the third dimension. Copper Canyon is holding the energy of shimmering. In Spanish its name is Barranca del Cobre.

Serra da Bocaina is about three or four hours from São Paulo, Brazil. It is in the rainforest of Brazil, and it is called the Atlantic Rainforest. This area represents the interaction between the third and fifth dimensions, and it also represents an alignment with the Arcturian stargate.

We need more planetary cities of light, we need a more just society, and we need Messianic energies. The original Tree of Life in the *Kaballah* has ten spheres. With the help of the Arcturians, we added two new spheres to make it twelve, to correspond to the twelve etheric crystals.

The Arcturian Planetary Tree of Life

Juliano and the Arcturians

Greetings, I am Juliano. We are the Arcturians. The Tree of Life is a model for a way to conceptualize how to heal a planet, and there are many levels to it. The Tree of Life is multidimensional, just like you are multidimensional. There are several ways to look at and interpret the energy of the Tree of Life.

It's Getting Harder for Earth to Keep Herself Healthy

The first and perhaps the most interesting and important way to interpret the tree's energy is to understand the sacred geometry of the relationships between the different crystals and the different spheres. People have asked us, "Well, do these relate to meridians?" They ask this because we have talked about the meridians of Earth and we know that Earth is a living spiritual planet with meridians. Because it is a living planet, Earth has meridian and energy lines, just like a person has energy lines. When the energy lines become blocked in a person, illness happens. In the same way, when a planet's energy lines are blocked, the planet can also become "sick."

Some people have raised the question: "How can a planet become sick? Why would a planet need to be healed? The planet is billions of years old. What difference does it make to the planet whether a river or a ley line is blocked?" This view does not take into consideration the relationship between the spirit of Mother Earth and humankind. It is an honor for a planet to be able to host higher life forms. There are so many planets in the universe and in the galaxy. Yet only a small percentage of the planets actually have life on them. An even smaller percentage of those planets have higher life. So you can see that, from a planetary perspective, it is an honor to have this relationship with humankind. If the planet loses its abilities to sustain higher life, then the planet, as a living spirit, is also going to experience discomfort.

Earth is working to maintain the necessary conditions to sustain higher life. That concept is difficult for humankind to grasp. Let me say it again: The planet is working to maintain certain conditions so that higher life can exist here. If the energies become blocked too strongly, then the planet will fail in its various mechanisms, including the feedback loop systems, and therefore it will no longer have the ability to sustain the life forces.

One of the intriguing things about Biorelativity and the planetary feedback loop system is that there have been numerous changes over the past 2,000 to 3,000 years, particularly over the past 100 years, during which time environmental issues have dramatically shifted. Large amounts of chemicals have emanated to the atmosphere, and large amounts of toxins have been put into the rivers. Yet the delicate balance in the atmosphere, the balance of the oxygen, has been maintained as best as possible.

Over the hundreds of years, there have been natural changes that have occurred in Earth that you would think would upset the balance, yet the balance has been maintained. The feedback loop system within Earth strives to maintain this balance. There is active participation from the spirit of Earth to maintain this feedback system. And Earth is now experiencing a harder time in maintaining the necessary conditions to sustain this system balance.

The Tree of Life tells the planet, "There must be balance; the harshness of the industrial world must be in balance with the softness of nature. If you overindustrialize the planet, then the planet goes out of balance." The lines between the etheric crystals, which are representative of the lines in the Tree of Life, can become new meridians.

How Holographic Energy Applies to Earth

New etheric crystal energy and spheres can create new Earth meridians. You must understand a few of our basic concepts: the holographic world, the nature of the realities, and the holographic nature of a planet. Holographic energy is a concept stating that you can understand the whole from the part; you can understand all the universe from this tiny speck, planet Earth, where you are. This slice of energy that you are living on offers you the ability to holographically understand the whole nature of the universe.

Holographic energy concepts work the same way with Earth. Part of Earth can be used to understand the nature of the whole Earth. There is a healing holographic principle that is tied into the Tree of Life, planetary healing, and Biorelativity, and it states that if you heal and balance one part, the energy from that one part can be projected to the whole energy field.

We talk about spiritual osmosis, which is the process of absorbing spiritual energy downloaded from higher spiritual sources. When you reintegrate those energies into your system, you can allow for a slower integration, because on higher planes, you cannot easily integrate the energies that you are experiencing into the lower and denser third dimension unless you do it more slowly. We use the phrase "spiritual osmosis" for this slower integration of spiritual energy.

We are always asking you to allow time for the spiritual energy you are working with to be slowly integrated. Sometimes it can take several days. In terms of Earth and holographic energy, we can say that the spiritual light and energy of each of the etheric crystals can generate an integrative osmotic process that can expand and be reintegrated into others parts of Earth. One of the proofs and indications of this has been the development of the subcrystals, because people naturally understand that the energy of the crystal areas should be expanded throughout an area. The energy generated in one etheric crystal can be expanded holographically to other areas.

The other aspect of the Tree of Life and the crystals is that they are all anchoring fifth-dimensional energy. In order to bring fifth-dimensional energy down into Earth, there needs to be an anchor, a place where the energy can be sent and stored. If there are no places to send the energy, where is the energy going to be maintained? It is similar to what I have described regarding personal healing and spiritual osmosis. When fifth-dimensional energies are sent to Earth, they have to have time to allow a planetary fifth-dimensional osmotic process. Fifth-dimensional energy that has been sent down needs to be slowly integrated. It is truly important and amazing that fifth-dimensional energy can be stored in Earth, but it has been stored and sent to Earth in many different ways.

You already know that there are sacred energy sites on the planet. This particular Tree of Life configuration and the aspect of designating the sacred areas that we have chosen with you offers a powerful method for bringing in fifth-dimensional light of purity and untainted powers. Each of these sacred places has an energetic purity about it that allows us to work with it and to send the energies directly into Earth, where we know they will be stored and not corrupted or tainted. We also know that these energies can be transmitted freely.

Establishing an Ongoing Relationship with Mother Earth

We have helped to create a newer balance, a newer energetic picture, a fifth-dimensional energy source that can be used for the planet. If there is a certain function that is needed — for example, with the Mount Shasta energy, the energy of understanding and compassion is needed — then that energy of understanding and compassion is stored and resonates particularly at Mount Shasta. When you wish to accelerate the planetary energy of compassion and understanding for Earth as a counterbalance to judgment, you will want to work with that area at Mount Shasta. Send your thoughts and energy there, and ask for this energy of compassion and balance to be sent out to the areas you want to work with. This is a particularly important energy to work with, because there is a lot of judgment energy coming to Earth now needs to be counterbalanced with compassion.

The whole idea of judgment on a planet, and particularly judgment on Earth, can be described in your ideas of the end times, because end-time theorists correctly depict the changes as a clearing, a purification with massive volcanos and hurricanes. We could say that Earth changes are like a judgment against the abuse directed toward the planet. Remember, judgment can include harshness and severity. You have seen already that Earth can easily respond with harshness, judgment, and severity. It is no problem for Earth to reclaim what has been tainted. It has happened repeatedly throughout Earth's history.

How can the energies of compassion and understanding be sent to the spirit of a planet? Would this energy of compassion be strong enough to stop the harshness, severity, and judgment? How to approach planetary work and planetary healing is one of the main reasons why many of you have come to Earth. This is part of your work as planetary healers. You have to understand the process and how to work with it.

Earth, like any planetary system, responds to its inhabitants, but the inhabitants have to have an ongoing relationship with the planet. That is why native people are especially good at working with the planet — because they have an ongoing relationship with Earth. They do not just seek to reaffirm this relationship when there is a crisis, but they continually maintain this relationship with Earth. Part of the core of Biorelativity work is maintaining an ongoing relationship with the planet. Biorelativity and Tree of Life work is more effective when you are in a continual relationship with these Earth forces.

It is not at all an easy task to intervene and try to change the releases of judgment, harshness, and severity from a planet. You have to try to grasp how a planet responds. Does a planet think? Does it think like a human? You can even call it, as native people do, Mother Earth. Is Earth a mother? Does Earth respond as a mother? You can say, "Yes, it does respond as a mother, and a mother is compassionate." But as planetary healers, what words and what energy do you send to Mother Earth to activate her compassion? The answer is in part in the native teachings; the native teachings repeatedly emphasize showing respect for your mother as the basis for establishing the ongoing planetary relationship so that the planet can respond to humanity compassionately.

Medicine Wheels, Crop Circles, and Orbs

One of the most powerful ways to begin instituting and exercising Biorelativity is by performing an action of service that shows respect to Earth. That is one of the reasons why we and the spirit guide Chief White Eagle recently recommended that planetary healers build forty medicine wheels around the planet, representing the forty Groups of Forty. The medicine wheels themselves are a powerful mandala light form in which Earth relates to and receives energy.

I will also add — and this will not be a surprise to many of you — that crop circles are methods of communication with Earth. Some of the fifth-dimensional, higher-dimensional, and extraterrestrial masters and beings who have visited Earth or are working with Earth energies have used the energies and the makings of crop circles to help communicate with the spirit of Earth. These crop circles are representative of language that can be used to communicate with the spirit of Earth.

The paradigm of the Tree of Life can also be built within a crop circle or a medicine wheel, and that paradigm and designation can be used to communicate to Earth that you are aware and working to rebalance the planet. This is a monumental job, and I have always been impressed with the Arcturian starseeds and the Group of Forty members who have devoted themselves so diligently to Biorelativity and creating a balance. Now it is even more important, because there are so many things that are happening on the planet. Earth problems are accelerating and many systems on Earth are out of balance; some of them are becoming more strongly out of balance. The creation of the planetary cities of light and the subcrystals are, actually, a counterbalance to some of the destructive energies and forces that are becoming stronger and more problematic on Earth.

If the crop circles give Earth messages, what about the orbs appearing more and more in the sky over the past few years?

The orbs are an electromagnetic vibration, and they are contributing to the communication with Earth. The orbs are based on general electromagnetic energy fields. Earth is in an electromagnetic energy field, and you are also an electromagnetic energy field. So there is a vibrational resonance between you and the electromagnetic fields. If the electromagnetic fields shift too much — if there is a newer balance and there is depletion or overexaltation of the electromagnetic energies — then it can affect your mental balance.

Please understand that your mental balance and your energetic balance are specifically linked to electromagnetic energies. The orbs are an expression of communication with the electromagnetic vibrations of Earth's atmosphere. The crop circles are based on the concept of the medicine wheels. In our opinion, the medicine wheels came first. But the complexity of the crop circles is at least an indication of the complexity of the communications that are going to be necessary for planet Earth. Being planetary healers is highly technical; it is skillful work. You might think that part of being planetary healers also has to do with being politicians and getting people to change their viewpoints. Of course, there is truth in that as well.

Does it matter if the crop circles are man-made or if people go out and try to make one themselves?

Well, yes, it does matter, because the ones that are man-made do not have the higher-dimensional electromagnetic energy charge. So the answer is yes. The ones that are man-made do not have the intention of helping Earth. They are only made to prove that it can be done. I am totally aware and in agreement that the medicine wheels can be as powerful as the crop circles, but the medicine wheels have to be used. The crop circles are just put on Earth, and they stand alone. The crop circles do not really need the human interaction, whereas a medicine wheel, to be most highly effective, has to be lived in and has to be worked with.

Transmitting Fifth-Dimensional Light and the Energies of Compassion

We recently worked with the energy of Lago Puelo, Argentina, because Lago Puelo is the area where the primary base crystal was downloaded, and we felt that it needed to be reupdated. So we helped to download higher energy there. And it was successful, by the way. Each of these etheric crystals on the Tree of Life represents an area where the higher-dimensional light can be downloaded. It is always important to remember that the Tree of Life and the etheric crystals are all related to what we call the Arcturian crystal temple and the Arcturian crystal lake.

The Arcturian crystal lake is a fifth-dimensional area that holds this beautiful master etheric crystal that we have worked with for Earth healing. It is the primary source for the transmission of fifth-dimensional light to Earth. The fifth-dimensional light is transmitted from crystal to crystal, and the idea is that each etheric crystal was made as an etheric duplicate of the original etheric crystal at the Arcturian crystal lake. All of crystals now have an inherent resonance with each other.

The Planetary Tree of Life relates to planetary healing. It includes the concept of triads and triadic energy. Triadic energy means that three spheres at a time are interacting with each other to create a higher balance. When you are working with Japan, for example, you might find that you are working with the spheres on the Tree of Life represented by Mount Shasta, Volcán Poás, and Mount Fuji. You can work with different configurations that form triads. The triads are very powerful.

What is also said in the traditional Tree of Life is that not one of these spheres stands alone; they can only be understood in their relationships to the others. You cannot make a lot of sense of judgment unless you understand the concepts of balance and compassion. There has not been a great deal of compassion expressed for the state of Earth by humanity. It is generally extremely healing to send the energies of compassion to areas and situations on Earth.

Can miracles still happen?

Yes, they can still happen. That is where the energy of Montserrat, which represents the Messianic light, comes in. This is also referred to as the energy of the savior. We look at it as a miracle but also as transcendental energy. The transcendental energy is the energy that is going beyond space and time. Quan Yin talked about the omega light. The omega light is like quantum healing light; it is light coming from higher sources that does not follow the traditional rule of the space-time continuum of Earth. The space-time continuum of Earth is linear. When we look at the many different issues that are falling out of balance on Earth, we conclude that the current linear energy processes may not be capable of healing Earth in the time that is left.

Remember, we have talked about an Earth crisis. We have talked about the idea that there is an evolutionary urgency calling for a dramatic change in the current situation. A dramatic change is necessary to correct the many imbalances now. You call the answer "miracles"; we can also call them Messianic energy and light. Messianic energy can be shifted, or downloaded, so that it transcends the space-time continuum. Montserrat, the center of the Planetary Tree of Life, also represents Sananda. Sananda will explain more about Messianic energy and light and how to call on it and use it.

The Presence of Extraterrestrials on Earth

How are the more frequent sightings of spaceships in the sky helping Earth? Which extraterrestrial factions are the major parts in those spaceships?

There are different levels of sightings. Some of them are more four-dimensional. The sightings are making people aware of the galactic process and that Earth is part of the galactic system. One of the things that we want to emphasize is the Sacred Triangle. Part of the idea of the Sacred Triangle is represented in the unification force of the three areas that we have repeated often: galactic force, higher mystical force, and native-people force. All three of them. This is the new paradigm for planetary healing. So the sightings confirm the existence of galactic forces and also that galactic forces can and do interact with Earth.

Biorelativity is also based on planetary healing that integrates these three forces. We speak about the native customs, but we also know that parts of the galactic healings come from the awareness and use of the etheric energy fields and the White Brotherhood and Sisterhood, which are helping to raise the vibrational frequency of humanity. I can only say that the extraterrestrial forces that are more effective are those who are following Sananda.

Sananda is generally considered the commander of Earth's ascension process, healing, and transformation. Those beings of light of extraterrestrial nature and higher dimensional nature who are following, using, and acknowledging the light of Sananda are acceptable, and they are helping humanity. There are some extraterrestrials who have ulterior motives and purposes that are not for the overall good or light of humankind. Some of these beings have done some rather bad things, including sharing higher-space technology with Earth governments for military purposes. This is not really an acceptable thing to do because we know that the wisdom of humanity has not kept up with their technological and military achievements. In other words, the wisdom is behind the advancement of technology.

Working with Crystals, Subcrystals, and Planetary Cities of Light

Since we are here in Australia, would it be a time to upgrade the Australian crystal?

We can do that from here. We can do that at this workshop. I think this is an excellent idea. Australia represents a very small fraction of the world population, yet it is playing an increasingly major role. We have spoken about Australia in previous lectures, during which we have said that Australia is like the canary in the cage. What is happening in Australia and how Australia responds are examples of what is going to be happening in the rest of the world.

We are aware of some of the storms and other events that have happened in Australia recently. At the same time, I believe that your work with Biorelativity and anchoring light has been of assistance. Plus, people have a greater awareness of the nature of Earth and their relationship with it. We can work with you, and we think it is an excellent idea to upgrade the crystal of Grose Valley, near the Blue Mountains in the Syndey area. There is a particular energy to the just society that the Grose Valley crystal carries. The Grose Valley crystal is very active, but at the same time it will benefit from an upgrade.

Will the five subcrystals also be updated simultaneously?

They will also be updated simultaneously because they are all connected to the main crystal. That is one of the ideas of the subcrystals. They are support crystals for the main crystal, and the upgrade of the main crystal will automatically be transferred to the subcrystals.

Because we are in such a large continent, would more subcrystals help?

Not necessarily. It is not like this is a race to see how many subcrystals a place can have. The important thing is that there are subcrystals and the main crystal, and they need to be worked with. If they are neglected, they will not be as powerful.

In order for a planetary city of light to be most effective, you have to have people working with the energies there. What does working with the energies mean? It means, for example, forming a relationship with the city and the energetic boundary around the city, doing shimmering around the city, helping to assimilate higher light and energy in the city so that only people who have higher light can come. People should try to work with the energy of the city to beautify it, and they should show respect for it.

There are many things that you can do to work with the energy of the planetary cities of light. They are just not designated as cities of light and that is the end; rather, you also need to work with them on a continual basis. The crystals and the subcrystals are the same. It is a beautiful thought to just say, "We are going to designate a subcrystal for these areas and bring down the energy," but it will not be sustainable unless you are going to work at the subcrystal area. This is why, when we are talking about planetary cities of light, one of our requirements is that there will be people there who can work with the energy.

How is the relationship between the Telos and the Arcturians? When will they surface?

They are not going to be coming up immediately. As you know, it is still quite shocking to the Telos people what is happening on Earth. They are particularly flabbergasted by what has happened with the nuclear energies. Adama, who is one of the leaders of the Telos, is working with us, and the Telos are particularly excited about the activity of the planetary cities of light and the Arcturians, as well as the Tree of Life. They are very proud of the designations of the many planetary cities of light. I am hoping that, in Australia, there will be more planetary cities of light. Even this area here at Nelson Bay has beautiful ingredients for being a planetary city of light.

It helps the spirit of Earth when she knows that these areas are considered sacred. It sets up a geomagnetic vibrational frequency. Naturally, what you are really doing in the planetary city of light is setting up a geomagnetic vibrational frequency around the outskirts of the city. It is like a protected area and the shimmering is to show that you can go in and out of higher light, bringing the city into a higher-dimensional space.

So, yes, there can be more planetary cities of light in Australia. From our perspective, I think that is a higher priority than subcrystals. The planetary cities of light have such a direct influence on the Biorelativity process because they communicate to Earth that you are calling this place sacred and holy, you are working to respect and hold the energy in that place, and you are working to bring fifth-dimensional energy particularly to the area designated as the planetary city of light.

I want to make it clear that the subcrystals are also powerful. But you still have many avenues and possibilities for more planetary cities of light in Australia. I said before that Australia is like a canary in a cage. This goes both ways. It does not mean that there are only going to be bad things — there will be also good things. The higher Biorelativity and planetary city processes that you can engage in can also have a profound effect, not only on Australia but on the rest of the world, because Australia is going to move into a leadership role in the world. I am Juliano. Good day.

CHAPTER SIX

Working with the Holographic Healing Chambers

Helio-ah

Greetings, I am Helio-ah. We are here today to receive instructions and teachings about the holographic healing chambers.

Your Past, Present, and Future Selves Can Interact with Each Other

Our work is both for personal and planetary healing, and we are looking at the whole picture of the self, which includes the past, the present, and the future self. The self appears as a circle. Time in the third dimension as you are experiencing it appears to be linear in nature. That is to say that you have a past, a present, and a future on the horizontal line. The past, present, and future selves do not interact in the linear model.

In our conception of time, the present, the future, and the past interact because time is circular. This changes a great deal the way that you see reality and, in particular, the way that you see yourselves. If it is true that time is interactive in a circular fashion, the future time after you have ascended is interactive with the present time, or now. As your future self, you have made the gains and the necessary growth for your ascension. More importantly, that growth and those gains are available for your access now. To put it another way, your future self is accessible to your present self.

Equally important is the past; since the past is part of the circle, it is also accessible to you. What we find particularly interesting in working with the past is that the past is accessible. Also, the imagery and the recordings of the past and how they affect your present can be altered through certain imagery work in the holographic healing chamber. In our conception, the events of the past are stored in the brain as holographic images. Another way to look at these images is as if they were slides or individual photographs.

Each event, each experience, each trauma, and each joy is stored as an image in your mind. These stored images create and contribute to who you are and how you think. They contribute to your belief system and your basic foundation of self.

This fact is also important when we are talking about certain traumatic events, certain deficiencies that may now be contributing to your self-image, and perhaps even distortions about yourself that are causing limitations and even emotional suffering. That is to say that these events that were unpleasant or traumatic are stored and recorded, and they appear in this image designation that I am describing. We compare this series of images that are part of the storage system within your mind as a deck of cards. The only reason why we are using the term "deck of cards" is because it metaphorically shows you that there are many images stored in your memory. They are all packed in alignment like in a deck of cards in your unconscious.

When you look at a normal deck of cards, you have fifty-two cards, but in this metaphorical description I am offering you, your deck of cards, which represents your experiences in this personal incarnation and lifetime, could have as many as 60,000 or 70,000 cards. Each significant event — especially in your childhood but also including your adolescence, adulthood, and even your most recent events — is stored in this deck of cards.

Events in the beginning of your deck of cards do influence your personal self in the present. If you have certain issues or problems that are perhaps related to self-esteem or limited abilities, it is possible that these are related to traumatic events in your earlier life. The events have actually been recorded in your mind, and your mind is still reacting to the imagery on these cards. If the image shifts in any way, it will influence, appropriately and concurrently, all of the cards after it and all of the issues of self related to that particular image.

Modifying Past Events in the Holographic Healing Chamber

To do a healing using these concepts and tools requires the holographic healing chamber, because it requires a methodology that is able to access the images easily, bring them up, and change them. The holographic healing chamber is a device we have developed that enables us to call up those images and then work with and change them.

If you imagine that the deck of cards holds all the images from your lifetime, we could go back to any period and bring up the card of that experience onto the screen. Once it is on the screen, we can look at it. At this point, after we look at it, we have the ability to modify the image. If the image is modified, we can exert a function that is very similar to what is known in your computer world as the save button. It is very similar to calling on a document and reediting or adding things to the document and then pressing the save button — the modified image is saved, and it replaces the old image that was in there. When you put the image back, the modified version replaces the original.

Once the modified image goes back into its appropriate order in the deck of cards, the effects of the new modified image are felt. All of the cards after the modified card are updated, especially those cards that are related to the situations of the original modified image, so that you get a series of effects that will now affect the current self. This is a description of how the past is used in the holographic healing chamber. The healing in the present takes place when you go back to modify the original incident from the past.

For example, let's talk about an incident in which you were physically abused by someone as a child. It could be physical beating, for example. If that really did happen, then modifying the image does not mean that it never happened. Let's say that you were beaten by your father; now you can modify the image and put an archangel in the picture for healing purposes. As the image of the father beating the child is brought forth, a secondary image of the angel sending light to the child can be shown. The light emanating from the angel fills the aura of the child, and the light becomes so strong that the father stops the physical beating. Maybe the father does not even know why he is stopping. The important thing is that the child has a feeling of being protected by the angelic presence.

There are certain principles that this modification exhibits. Number one: The whole image can be modified, but it has to be modified within a certain range or limit. You cannot just erase the image. That could be possible in special cases, but we are not suggesting that the image should be erased. Rather, we suggest that it should be modified in a way that has a favorable outcome for you and is also within a certain range of limitations and reasonableness.

When you are in the holographic healing chamber, you can go back to any point in your life that contains an unresolved situation that has been particularly painful and that you would like to modify within the limitations that I have described.

That modified image is then placed back into your deck, and it updates all of your files. You then have the ability to experience a powerful healing that you will feel in the present.

Is this something that you can also use for events in the past that were positive and that you would like to bring into the now?
Yes, you could enhance the positivity. This is a perceptive question. You could enhance the positivity so that it becomes more powerful. You could make the colors brighter, and you could cause the event to become more striking. The overall intention is that the card itself becomes more powerful so that it updates all future cards and you become more saturated with the light and energy of that experience. I think that is a reasonable proposition. Again, we would say that such a change is within the acceptable range.

Using the Holographic Healing Chamber to Modify the Future

Let us talk about the future. The future is also a deck of cards, and if we project your timeline and can see your future self six months or a year from now, we can also project whether you have accomplished and completed certain tasks and certain lessons that you have been working on. You can bring the images of that future event into the deck-of-cards imagery in front of the computer screen, and then you can download that image into your current deck of cards so that you can receive the energy from that future work. This might be a way of describing how to access or borrow your future self's energy in the present.

The holographic healing chamber is also calibrated for the future. When we look at the holographic healing chamber, it appears to be the size of a phone booth, but it is curved on the top. Each booth is small. You go in and there is a seat in front of a dashboard with controls, and above the dashboard is the screen. On the dashboard, there is a huge dial that is calibrated and begins at twelve o'clock. There is a special setting in the holographic healing chamber: You press a button and the calibration of the dial shifts so that turning the dial to the left represents your past, or your past lifetimes, and turning the dial to the right represents your future lifetimes. Twelve o'clock represents the now, this moment. Turning the dial to the left, from twelve to six o'clock, represents your past in this lifetime. Going to the right side, from twelve to six o'clock, represents your future in this lifetime.

For our work today, we are going to use just the past in this lifetime and the future in this lifetime. We are not going to work with past lifetimes at this point. In the holographic healing chamber, we are going to work with your energy field and spirit. We will gather the spirits together and travel through the corridors to the Arcturian Starship Athena, and we will enter the lower level of the ship, where we have set up the healing chambers for you. We will direct you individually to a healing chamber, and we will begin the exercise.

When you pick a future benefit and then you bring it into your now life, does that change the future benefit?

It depends on your perspective, because let's say that in the future time you have 100 dollars. You bring the image of you having that money onto the screen. Let's say that having 100 dollars makes you happy and wealthy, but you cannot bring this money into the present. But that feeling, the energy of having that wealth, comes into the present. Having that image downloaded into yourself in the holographic healing chamber gives you the feeling of engendering this future event, and you will start acting accordingly from that feeling. Thus, you could then set in motion energetically the events that will lead to that image. I do not want you to think that this exercise for the future is about the getting material wealth, because it is not really so much about that material wealth anyway; it is about the feeling that you have about yourself that material wealth could bring to you. So the answer to your question is that this would enhance and accelerate the likelihood of that event becoming a reality and bring it closer to you.

The Planetary Holographic Healing Chamber

I want to give you further clarification on using this healing method for the planet. We have the personal holographic healing chamber, and we have the planetary holographic healing chamber. The planetary holographic healing chamber is much larger than the personal holographic healing chamber. The same principles apply, only on a planetary basis; we use the imagery of a large theater for the planetary healing chamber. So instead of a small, computer-like screen, we now have a gigantic theater screen, and the images of the planet are projected onto that screen using exactly the same technique and the same type of calibrated dial. We have used this technique for planetary healing on Earth, but it requires more participation, finer work on the imagery, and a larger healing chamber.

We are tying into the concepts of the collective unconscious in the planetary holographic healing chamber. Remember, there always is a chain of cosmic events that lead to some specific current event. What you are now seeing in your reality is just one aspect of a chain of events. There are other things that happen in other realms before an event occurs on Earth. In the planetary healing holographic chamber, we are beginning to deal with the collective unconscious, and especially the fourth dimension and the imagery of that realm. We can shift the imagery that goes into the wheels of the collective unconscious so that a new image can be downloaded.

The planetary chamber uses the same principles as the personal holographic healing chamber. You can calibrate either chamber to a future event. In the future event, we can use the concepts of the miracle or the omega light. For example, we can look at the nuclear accident in Japan and we can project that the event has been stabilized, cleared up, and that the area has been restored to the normal environmental integrity it had before the accident. We can all work with that image in the future time. Through the techniques that I have described, we would bring the image back into the present and hold that image on the screen with great intensity so that the likelihood of an early resolution of this nuclear problem can become a reality in the present.

The planetary holographic healing chamber is a more advanced and complicated technique for planetary healers. This technique needs to be done on a large scale with many people participating — for example, you might need a thousand people to participate. This would be coordinated with amplifications from etheric crystals.

We want to introduce and practice the planetary healing techniques that I have described using the holographic healing theater. But our first step today is to do a personal holographic healing.

With the planetary healing, what would the minimum number of people be to be helpful?

Well, the minimum number is actually one, but the intensity of the exercise is a factor. The use of arcan energy amplification is a factor. Because we are dealing with a planetary system that has complex interacting variables, the work requires more intensity, more interpretations, and more presentations. It can be done by a minimum of several people, but it would be preferable to have a large group, such as forty to one hundred people.

When we are changing events that affect other people, such as weather or a nuclear accident, should we be asking for guidance in terms of the karma that affects other people?

Yes, that is a good point. You should ask for guidance for the highest good of everybody, for the cleansing, for the clearing, and for the organization of karma. Remember that you are putting the images back into your minds, or in the case of the planet, you are placing images in the planetary unconscious. Let us say, if I can use the computer model again, that you download a new program into the computer. Everything is updated, but it is updated within the ramifications and parameters of that program. The healing chamber will be updated within the parameters that are acceptable and most beneficial for all.

You can even use this method in terms of making the twelve etheric crystals stronger. It was also used in the development of the Group of Forty, so that in the future time there will be 1,600 people. The highest and most effective benefit would be if you had a large theater room on Earth with 1,600 people in it and you did the imagery in that room. That would be the ultimate thing, but we realize that this is something that is very complicated to achieve on the third dimension. The development of the Group of Forty film *The Blue Jewel* is a movement toward that goal.

An Exercise in Personal Holographic Healing of a Past Event
We will now begin the first stage of the personal holographic healing in the holographic healing chamber. Feel the room begin to go around in a circle like a merry-go-round. As the room spins around in a circle, your chair is spinning around in the circle, but you experience no dizziness, and you actually become more relaxed. As you become more relaxed, the room continues to go around in a circle, and your spirit rises very gently out of your crown chakra and goes to the top of the room. I, Helio-ah, send down a golden corridor of light into the center of the room, and you see me there, right above the center of the room. This is a fifth-dimensional corridor, and I am able to appear to you in it.

If you have trouble seeing and experiencing this, just follow and listen to the verbal instructions to the best of your ability, for everybody has different levels of ability. Even listening and following the instructions verbally will have a high benefit for you. We enter the corridor and begin to travel at the speed of thought through the corridor to the entry of Starship Athena, which is now in the Jupiter corridor of your solar system. Let us begin the travel at the speed of thought.

[Sounds.]

We travel through the corridor. It is a wonderful journey, and we come into the doorway of my Starship Athena. Welcome to our ship! As you walk in, you feel a sense of joy and unity with your star brothers and sisters — unity with us, the Arcturians. Looking around the ship, we are gathered in the healing center. We have set up special healing places for you. Look to the left and you will see a series of small phone booth–like chambers that we call the holographic healing chambers. They are attractive booths. Some of them are colored.

I have prepared a booth for each of you. Go into your own personal booth. Follow your intuition and your telepathic nature and you will reach your individual booth. Enter the booth, close the door, and turn on your personal holographic healing booth. As you do that, everything turns on just like a computer. You are in your own personal holographic healing chamber; you are in a chamber that is connecting you with your holographic self. This is an important experience — to be able to contact and connect with your holographic energy field.

We have set the dials at the twelve o'clock position, and I want you to turn the dial back to an experience from your past that you wish to modify. It is up to you when, where, and which experience you choose. You can choose an experience in the immediate past, within the past five or two years, or you can go back to your earliest childhood years. Perhaps you have been in some type of healing therapy experience and you have not been able to resolve this certain issue, even after months or years of therapy. Maybe you will choose something that happened in your adult life — for example, an unhappy ending to a marriage that has greatly affected you. The important thing is that you go back to the event that has the strongest image in the repertoire of your deck of cards.

You turn the dial to the left. Six o'clock is representative of when this life started. You have to turn the dial back appropriately. If you are going back to when you were one year old, it would be going back to one minute after half-past six, approximately. Turn the dial back until it comes to the calibrated approximate area of the event you wish so that the image of the event is now on your holographic screen.

Look at that image and study it. It could be an image in which you were unhappy. Some of you might have decided you wanted to choose an image in which you were happy, but you want it to have a stronger effect — you can do that too. Look at the image, and now modify it so that the change you are going to make will upgrade and enhance your overall functioning and total state of well-being. Even if you had an illness, the effects of that illness can be modified so that you will now be in a greater healing state. Now modify that image in a way that is of the highest benefit to you.

[Sounds.]

Beautiful work on that image! Enhance it, make it brighter, make it stronger, and make it have effects of the highest possible benefit to you. When you are done with that image, press the save button on the right so that that image is saved. Look at the image and place it deep within your inner being. We are now going to put the image back into the deck of cards, in the same place where the original image was.

At the count of three, the image will be reinserted into the deck of cards: one, two, three. As the image is reinserted, you experience a surge of energy of light as you are totally upgraded within your current self. This energy of the modified image has created a chain of enhancement that sends a huge energy flow of light into your current self. You are enjoying the surge of energy and light coming into your current self. Please take the time to correctly finish this part.

Holographic Healing Using Near-Future Events

We will now turn the dial to the future, and I am only going to work with you between now and a future time of your choosing. You can only turn the dial as far to the future as is appropriate for your wishes. You are all working hard on yourselves; you are all working to make great progress in yourselves. Turn the dial to a time in the future.

Turn the dial to that point at which you see yourself with the greatest gains and advancements in the future. Choose that image and bring that image up on the screen. Press the hold button and see the image with as much detail as you can. Make the image as bright as you can. Make that image appear really strong on the screen. As you turn the dial back to the present, you are going to bring that image back into the exact present moment. Now turn the dial very slowly as the image comes through the future back into the present. Now the energy of that future imagery is in your present. Press the save button again, and the energy of that future advancement, that future self, is now downloaded into your current self. You feel a great surge of joy and happiness. All the energy from that future advancement is brought into your present self.

[Sounds.]

You have completed this round of the holographic healing work. Look at everything. We are going to shut your holographic healing chamber off. Stand up and leave the chamber. Come out of the chamber and meet me at the center of the healing platform in the bottom of my ship, where we started. We gather together and we are going to begin the journey back to your Earth body. Follow me through the golden corridor of light, traveling at the speed of thought.

[Sounds.]

We come above the room where we started, and you see your body going around in a circle. Align your spirit body exactly over your physical body, but do not reenter until I tell you. Proceed to an exact perfective alignment. Tell yourself, "Upon Helio-ah's command, I will reenter my body in perfect alignment."

One, two, three. Reenter in perfect alignment now. The room stops turning around. You are back in your original position, and you have reentered your body in perfect alignment. Take some time to reorient yourself, and know that all your inner workings are being updated with this powerful work that you have done. Gently open your eyes as you are back in the room. I am Helio-ah. Good day.

CHAPTER SEVEN

Uncovering the Mystery of the Mental Body

Vywamus

Greetings, I am Vywamus. I am a soul psychologist, and I am here to work with you on your mental body. I know that there are exercises for the physical body in which you build up your muscles, and many of you are worried about your physical bodies and how they look. You want to make sure that they have the right shape and so on. But how many of you are really paying attention to your mental bodies?

Remember that you are not going to be able to take your physical bodies with you. I always try to understand why people are so concerned about their physical bodies when they realize that they cannot take their bodies with them. A part of your mental bodies, on the other hand, will go with you. So wouldn't it make more sense to work with the mental bodies? I have been asked to talk to you about your mental bodies and help you to condition them so that you will be able to use them most effectively throughout the time you are here on Earth. How many people even think about exercising their mental bodies? The answer is not very many people.

The Power of Thoughts and Beliefs

So let us go into the roots of the mental body — how the mental body works — and this is not going to be "sit back and listen to Vywamus" time. I am going to have you participating, and you are going to have to do some work with me so that we can uncover the mystery of the mental body. I think that we can call this lecture "Uncovering the Mystery of the Mental Body by Vywamus." It sounds like a good title for a book, in fact.

The mental body is based on beliefs and thoughts, which are so powerful that they can totally change the person who holds them. For example, there was a man who was told that he had incurable brain cancer and was given an amount of time to live. He believed the doctor who told him his cancer was incurable. He believed he had a limited time to live, and he went out and killed himself. Now, that was a belief. The question is: Was it really true that he had incurable cancer? And how do we know that it would proceed the way that the doctor predicted? Even though everybody might agree that he had cancer, there is no way to know how it would have turned out. But we do know that the beliefs and thoughts that he was given were so powerful that he could not deal with them anymore, and he ended his life.

There are people who believe that they have incurable cancer and that there is no hope for recovery. Imagine one such person consulting a doctor who says, "Well, sir, we have this new pill that has just been discovered based on a plant in the remote part of Tasmania. This plant was recently discovered by an aboriginal research team in a cave, and it has only been used five times, but each time it has cured the cancer of the person who took it. We only have ten tablets left, and we are going to give them to you. Take one of them every month for the next ten months. They are very powerful, so please be careful and do not drive after you take the pill." So the patient takes the pills from the doctor.

The patient comes back a month later, and the tumor has shrunk down. The doctor is totally flabbergasted, and he says, "Okay, we will keep you on the pills." Then, after a period of time, the pills run out, but it does not matter because the tumor is completely gone. The doctor says, "Sorry, that is all the pills that were brought from the Tasmanian trip and the pills have run out, but do not worry, because you are now cured." Then, surprisingly, after the patient has been out of the pills for a short time, the cancer comes back.

This again is another example of the power of the mind. When the doctor talked to the patient, he said, "This is a rare plant based on a pill in Tasmania," and so on. Then the man said, "Oh, this is very rare, from the deep forest." Then the man said, "Oh, this is from the ancient plants." The pills were probably not really anything, but the doctor presented them in a way that was so powerful and so mysterious that the man's belief system accepted the pills as an agent that could produce a powerful cure of his cancer. The doctor even said, "You are very lucky that you were chosen to receive this."

So again, we have the power of the mind. But what is even more mind-boggling is that when the pills ran out, the patient's cancer returned, and that makes you really think about the power of the mind. The mental body can also react by really being sacred. So what is the correct way to treat your mental bodies? We have some ideas about how you treat your mental body, because we know what you are telling yourself. We know what your self-talk is and we know the way many people talk to themselves.

We also know that the current state of the media, TV, and commercials are all based on trying to train you to talk a certain way to yourself. They are trying to corrupt your mind to think that you need to smoke this cigarette so you will be cool and to think that if you drink this soda, you will feel refreshed. It has to do with how your body looks and what you should think.

You Have the Free Will to Reclaim Your Mental Body

The one thing that is totally yours is what you are thinking, yet it is what you are thinking that creates so much of your reality. I have heard people complain. They say, "Why do people come to Earth?" And we say, "Well, it is a freewill system." They ask, "What are you talking about when you say 'free will'?" They believe in predestination and that everything is preprogrammed. You have severe limitations about what you can and cannot do in this reality. But the truth is that you are free to think whatever you want.

I want you to think about that: You are free to think about whatever you want. When people say, "This is a freewill zone," I want you to remember that you have the freedom to think what you want; even in the darkest days of the concentration camps and imprisonment, you could still think what you wanted. In our opinion, one of the greatest tortures is to have someone trying to shape and control your thoughts. And that is exactly what is happening; that is exactly what has been occurring often in many parts of this world during the past fifty to one hundred years. Thought control has been going on for centuries in various civilizations. That is not new. What is new is that the power of the thought control is growing, and the methods of thinking and controlling your mental body are getting more sophisticated and more technical.

So how do you reclaim your mental body? You must ask yourself this question: Are the thoughts and beliefs you are carrying about yourself based on reality, or are they based on information wrongly given to you? Obviously, the earliest authority figures that you had were your parents. Were they enlightened? Were they giving you correct information about yourself?

More importantly, were you giving yourself the correct information about yourself? Do you believe that you are worthy? Do you believe that you are worthy of ascension? Do you believe that you have all the things necessary to complete this life process? What do you believe about yourself? Can we really be honest about that? If we can get in touch with what we call your core belief system about yourself, are you willing to look at it? And how can we change the core belief? Nothing is more powerful than working with your core belief system and accessing the deepest part of that system.

Accessing Your Core Belief System

I love your computers for many reasons, and one of the best of these is the way they can be used as a metaphor for the self. There is a core operating system within a computer, but access to that system is often denied unless you have special privileges to go into the system. You certainly do not want to manipulate certain files in the core of the computer unless you have permission and special knowledge. So the computer is an interesting metaphor for your self. Are your core beliefs about yourself accessible? And if they are accessible and you look at them, do you want to change them, or do you want to allow them to continue to dominate you? Do you want to update your belief systems about yourself?

So, to demonstrate and work with this idea, I would like someone who would like to volunteer to talk to me, Vywamus, about their beliefs systems. Is there someone who would like to do that? Okay, we have a brave soul who is willing to volunteer. Can you come up a little closer so that we can hear you? When you think about your belief system about yourself, do you have a sense of your core belief system about yourself?

I do not think so, because I do not think very well of myself.

I see, so we've got an indication. You say that you do not think very well of yourself, correct?

Yes.

So that is a core belief. But it is not really exactly what you think. Do you know why?

Because it is somebody else's thought.

No, because you said: "I do not think very well of myself," so you are describing your core belief, but you are describing what it is not. So that means that we have to go beneath that layer of "I do not think very well of myself." And I agree that it is probably true, but what is the belief? Can you go beneath that?

Maybe it is: "I am a bad person. I am a confused person. I am whatever."

Or "Oh! I do not think I can." So, this is access denied. This belief is so powerful that even here, with this very bright and determined woman, who is also brave ...

And foolish.

Pardon? No, that is not one of the terms that I would use to describe you, but maybe you would use that term. So, she is trying to get into her belief system, but access is denied. The closest we can come is: "I do not think very well of myself." Is that correct?

Yes.

How does that belief system affect you? Do you remember the case of the man who received the medicine from Tasmania? Imagine that I was able to go back into that Tasmanian jungle or the forest — we can call it the bush — and when I came back I said to you, "I have this pill that I want you to take. And if you take this pill, this feeling you have of not thinking well of yourself will change." Would you take the pill?

I think it would depend on some of the circumstances surrounding me. I would be skeptical.

Of the pill?

Of the statement about the pill.

That it would change you? I would assure you that I had given it to many people and that everyone who had taken the pill had changed their opinions and beliefs about themselves.

Can I have some client numbers?

We have client confidentiality. I cannot reveal the names of the other patients. So access is denied and there is a resistance to change. Would that be correct?

Change can be difficult for me, yes.

Okay. What if I told you that I, Vywamus, took this pill from the Tasmanian bush? How would you feel about that? So the question that we have to ask you is: How does that belief come into and affect your current life? And how are you doing?

It makes it tough. Like I said earlier, I am questioning any decision I make, which I think goes back to my childhood.

I see.

That is one aspect of it.

So we have a little bit more information. We know that the original belief system came somewhere in your childhood. You are willing to admit that, and that is a big step. And we know that one of the effects of your belief system is that it affects your ability to make decisions, so you do not believe that these decisions are right. Is everything I said correct?

Yes.

And you are sure you do not want to try this pill?

I prefer not to take pills unless I really, really have to. I would ask my doctor.

Well, I thought that this was what people were trained to do in this culture — take a pill.

Not this one.

Ah, you do not go along with those thoughts.

No, not necessarily, no.

Ah! How interesting. You go along with the thought: "I do not think very well of myself." You can accept that, but you will not accept the thought: "I have to take a pill," even though it is so ingrained. I believe it is ingrained, but perhaps it is not.

There is quite a strong streak of independence within me.

So what is your belief about this independence? So we already had the primary belief, and now we are getting the secondary belief. You said you have a very strong source of streak of independence.

People call it stubbornness.

Stubbornness? But stubbornness is based on protecting the integrity of the self. So somewhere in this deep belief system, there is another belief, another thought about the protection of the integrity of the self. I hope you do not think that I am going to cure you today. We are just using this as information, as an example of a belief system.

Now I have become very interested in trying to get at the strength that is behind the integrity of the self and protecting that integrity of the self. I have perceived that belief, that core belief she has about herself, and it could be something as simple as: "I have the right to protect myself at all costs, and I will not give up my integrity." I believe that this belief, wherever it came from — maybe from her father — is so strong that it is able to override the other belief. And certainly it is strong enough to provide a strong core of thinking and a strong belief foundation. So here, we are demonstrating that you can have one belief that is maybe a problematic belief, but you can have a secondary belief that is able to override the first belief.

Okay, I appreciate you coming up here and sharing this. I would encourage you to maintain that stubbornness, because it is based on a very strong belief about the fact that you are right. And that is good.

As a youngster, it was the only way to have my say, if you like.

Well, I would just recommend that you modify this. Instead of stubbornness, say, "I have the right, and I am capable of protecting the integrity of myself."

That sounds nice.

And that belief is more effective and more powerful for the development of yourself than "I am stubborn," which has kind of a negative connotation. If you tell yourself, "I have the right to protect to myself," that will override the other belief: "I do not think very well of myself."

So I didn't need the pill, did I?

Well, I guess not. I will have to give it to somebody else. Maybe somebody else needs the pill, and you are saving it for them.

I am very generous.

Good, that is a good belief. You may return.

Thank you, Vywamus.

The Slow Speed of Manifestation on Earth

Earth is a place where one of the lessons is to work with your mental body. Fortunately, everything that you think does not happen immediately. Some of you have very catastrophic thinking, but it does not materialize because things are slowed down on the third dimension. Remember, if you experience sacred energy on a higher plane, then what you are thinking can manifest more quickly.

Generally, your thinking is slower, and that is for your protection. Things are slowed down on the third dimension. There would have to be a series of special thoughts on Earth to make things manifest. This is for your protection.

Accessing Core Beliefs to Help Fix a Memory Problem

Is there someone else who would like to look at their core belief systems with me and who has the courage to come up and sit here? You may be the lucky one who gets that pill from the Tasmanian bush.

[A volunteer comes up.]

Your name, please.

Lisa.

Okay, Lisa. What is your core belief?

I like myself. I have a few issues with a fading memory and not remembering names.

What do you believe about your memory? You said your memory is fading? What do you think that is?

A lot of things that I used to remember, particularly names, I now have trouble remembering.

So what is the self-talk about that?

Being a crystal person, I think I am usually busy looking at people rather than taking in what their names are.

You are critical of yourself for that?

No, I enjoy people's company, but I would like to remember their names.

So that is an observation of an ability; that is not really a belief. In other words, you think that there is some lack of whatever — acetylcholine or some kind of thing like that. But your idea is that your memory is fading and that this is due to some circumstance — possibly biochemical changes in your brain?

I think it is just aging.

And what do you believe about aging?

It is a pleasant state of being. People do not expect as much of you. It has its advantages.
But the basic belief you have stated is: "I like myself."

Exactly.
So does that mean you think you are a good person?

Yes.
So what part of your belief system about yourself needs to be changed? Or is there any part? Is your mental body in a really good shape?

It is just the forgetting thing. That is really the only issue I have, and I do not know if this is physiological or psychological.
What you believe?

I hope it is something I can change.
What do you believe?

I do not know. I think I have been conditioned to believe that it is just my age.
So it is physiological.

Yes.
Do you think you have a disease?

No.
That is good. You did not hesitate one minute. So I do not see a relationship between the fading memory and your belief system. Do you?

No, but then what is the cause?
You have just told me the cause was aging.

Okay, I have said that.
You said aging is a very pleasant experience.

Except for the fact that you lose those bits that you treasure, like remembering people's names. That is one example.
Let's develop a new belief about your memory.

That would be very nice.

Would you be willing to develop a new belief about your memory?

I hope so. Yes, I would.

Well, I would be willing to help you with it. It seems like, as with the last person we worked with, maybe you do not need the pill from the Tasmanian bush either. I suggest you try this affirmation: "I am able to compensate for the loss of any memory I have due to aging."

I like that. That is good.

Do you like those words? Can you say them?

That is the problem, see.

Well, could you try to repeat them?

I would like to believe …

No, no, not with "would like to." That does not go with beliefs. We have to either believe it or not believe it.

Like a statement?

Yes.

I accept that I will have perfect memory without the use of the pill.

Is that what I said? I do not think so.

I cannot remember what you said.

"I am able to compensate for any loss of memory that I may have from aging."

I had forgotten what you had said. I am able to compensate for any loss of memory I may have.

"Due to aging."

I am able to compensate for any loss of memory that I may have due to aging.

Okay, say it again. Let us make sure you have it.

I cannot remember! I am able to compensate for any loss of memory that I may have due to aging.

Could somebody please write it down right now?

This is why I type things.

That is okay. You are under a lot of pressure now. We are putting you on the spot.

No, this is normal.

So, "I am able to compensate any loss of memory that I have due to aging." What does "compensate" mean? That is a big word. Do you know what that means?

It usually means you give something up to allow something else to happen.

You give something up to have something else. That is interesting. I look at compensation as: "I am able to find alternatives to improve." I like that better. Let us remove the word compensate: "I am able to find alternatives, alternative methods. I am able to apply alternative methods to improve my memory due to aging issues." Do we have that down? Can we say that again?

I am able to find alternative methods to improve my memory due to aging issues.

Well, let's just leave out "due to aging issues." Read it without the last part.

I am able to find alternative methods to improve my memory.

Period. I want to change the word "find," because what good is it to find something if you do not use it? "I am able to use" or "I am able to implement." Is that too big of a word for you?

I can remember that.

Do you like the word? Okay, can we remove "find" and replace it with "implement"?

I am able to implement alternative methods to improve my memory.

Period. Now, that is a new belief that I am offering you today. Are you willing to use that belief?

Yes.

It is actually considered an affirmation in your language. One of the things about beliefs is that you can change your belief system by repeating an affirmation, and then eventually it goes into your subconscious. Once it is in the subconscious, it can be implemented. Let's look at that one more time to make sure that it is said in the best way and that you are comfortable with it. Can you read it?

I am able to implement alternative methods to improve my memory.

Notice that we are not saying what these alternative methods are, but what you are telling your subconscious is that you are able to do that. Now you will be attracting, learning, and finding those alternative methods, and then you will be able to implement them. How does that sound?

It sounds very good.

So we are demonstrating several principles. The primary principle is that beliefs must be changed, shortened, and made concise. And then you will begin to download that belief system. What I am most worried about is if you will remember the affirmation. I am glad your friend wrote it down.

I will write it down and repeat it so that I can say it.

I assure you, it will have a dramatic effect on this problem.

I might just add that I have a sister who is only eighteen months older than me and who has Alzheimer's, and my mother has no memory at all. So the problem is probably fear-based.

So we get into another issue, because I asked you earlier if you thought you had a disease, and you said no.

I do not think I have one, but I can see that there is a pattern that might be repeated.

So do we need to create another belief to deal with this fear?

No, I can now see that it is fear-based.

But fear is based also on perception. So if you just say, "It is fear-based," that does not really heal the energy. You have some reasons for having that fear, correct? Because you said your sister has some issues?

Yes, she has Alzheimer's. It is actually worse than that, but it is something like Alzheimer's.

And you said your mother does too?

Yes.

But you believe that you do not have it.

Yes.

Okay, I appreciate very much that you have been honest and shared this information with us.

You are welcome.

And please use this affirmation.

I will certainly do that. Thank you so much for it.

Well, she is very amenable to working with the affirmation. Can you say the affirmation again, my friend?

I am able to use or implement alternative methods to improve my memory.

That is a beautiful affirmation. The core message I want to say to you is: These belief systems are usually quite simple statements. Notice that the first person said: "I do not think very well of myself." It was pretty simple. Then the second belief system was: "I am very stubborn." Belief systems are quite simple, but their power lies in their simplicity. When you want to change and work with your core system, it is much better to create simple new beliefs. We also demonstrated that some new beliefs can override earlier beliefs and that even though one belief might be a core belief, a secondary belief sometimes can overcome the first one.

I am Vywamus. Good day.

CHAPTER EIGHT

Just Societies and the Etheric Crystal of Grose Valley

Sanat Kumara

Greetings, I am Sanat Kumara. I am working in many capacities for the overall benefit and development of Earth at this precious time in the development and evolution of humankind. We are also in a period of evolution for Earth. In order for a planet to evolve to the fifth dimension, advanced spiritual beings like yourselves must inhabit the planet and work with the planet. So in truth, the ascension of Earth is interactive with humankind's ascension.

I know that Juliano and others have spoken about the rather startling conclusion that the fate of all the species on Earth is dependent on what humankind does and how humankind acts. Will humankind be a protector or a destroyer of the biosphere? This observation must also include the fact that Earth's ascension into the fifth dimension is also dependent on how humankind acts. As I said, a planet cannot ascend into the fifth dimension unless there are interactive spiritual beings like yourselves who are working. So it is a joint interactive process.

Challenges to the Balance of Earth's Biosphere

Now, this is a challenging time for Earth because of the many biospheric problems that have been created, which are now affecting Earth's meridians. These meridians are like breathing pathways or energy pathways; they are also called ley lines. Many of these ley lines have become clogged. Earth has had to adapt, and it is working hard to monitor and regulate its biosphere. Earth is seeking to maintain a stable environment so that humankind can continue to exist and maintain its presence here.

There have been several incidences — some even in recent times — in which it seemed entirely possible that the feedback loop system was not going to be able to sustain and maintain the conditions necessary for human life to continue. More directly, it looked like the biosphere might not be able to continue to remain stabilized. Several noteworthy observations would relate to the ozone level and weather issues. The current situation with the nuclear power plant in Japan represents another severe challenge for Earth. And the global implications of this nuclear disaster are far greater than what people suspect and what people are talking about. The issues of radiation and contamination of the biosphere are major challenges to Earth's feedback loop system.

Currently, Earth's feedback loop system does not have the resiliency to absorb all the damage that humankind is inflicting on her and still return back to balance. For quite a long period of time, it has been true that Earth's feedback loop system has been able to rebalance itself from biosphere problems, but now the time required to return to balance is very long. It is also possible that humankind could adapt to some of the changes. But that adaptation is also quite an elongated process. For example, Earth has been dealing with these radiation issues since the Second World War, so it is not a new issue for the feedback loop system and Mother Earth.

Repeated nuclear testing has been done before — including tests aboveground, underground, and even in the oceans — resulting in Earth learning how to rebalance energies from this whole process. Remember that Earth is an entirely self-regulating planetary system, and therefore what happens in one part of the system affects the other parts of the system. So what is going on in Japan can affect Australia, can affect Russia, and can affect America.

The Power of Etheric Crystals

I am happy to observe and oversee the downloading of these etheric crystals that the Group of Forty has worked on, because these crystals anchor and stabilize fifth-dimensional energy. There has been an anchoring and stabilization of fifth-dimensional energies that would not have been possible without the crystals. Yes, we — the ascended masters, guides, and teachers — are all excited about the interaction of the fifth dimension with the third dimension, or this intersection of dimensions, as it is sometimes called. I want to clarify that even when the intersection of dimensions occurs, you do not have to ascend. And even though you might choose not to ascend, you will still receive a great benefit to your spiritual light quotient by being here on Earth at the time when this intersection occurs.

Now, the particular etheric crystal that we are focusing on at this time is the Grose Valley crystal, which is in the Blue Mountains near Sydney, Australia. This crystal has a tremendous energy and beauty and relationship to Earth and to myself. I know that there are ancient, primordial energies of the highest caliber in Grose Valley — ancient energies that must go back to the basic formulation of the birth of Earth, the birth of life forms here, and the birth of the fifth-dimensional connection of Earth to the fifth level. So humankind is programmed genetically to ascend and to deal with the issues related to the ascension.

In the same way, Grose Valley was genetically configured from its birth to hold fifth-dimensional energies and to work as a transmitter of these energies to Australia and to other places on the planet. In fact, the work of the Group of Forty has helped to broaden the knowledge and fame of Grose Valley, and this has been a wonderful boost to the energy of this area because sacred spaces attract fifth-dimensional interaction. This sacred place now holds etheric crystals, and these crystals are thriving on the intense interaction available through your work. They are like other crystals that perform better when they are played with, when they are meditated with, when they are held, and when they are visited. It becomes an interaction with the mental energy of people and their meditative abilities.

Grose Valley has volunteered to hold the Planetary Tree of Life's energy for the creation of the new Earth societies. I also call these the just societies, the heavenly just societies. What this energy entails is an important further explanation of the power of the fifth dimension and how the fifth dimension is concurrently going to change the way Earth's societies are established and set up. This is an important foundational energy for both the transition into the fifth dimension and the planetary cities of light.

The Just Society and the Planetary Cities of Light Are Vital to One Another

If you look at the Tree of Life, you will notice that the energy of the Planetary Tree of Life and the energy of the creation of the just society are represented in two spheres opposite one another. This demonstrates that they are contiguous and they are almost like a binary star system in the way they interact with each other. That means you are really not going to create a just society without having it be a part of the planetary cities of light. At the same time, in creating a planetary city of light, you are setting the groundwork and the foundation for the just society, or "The New Earth society."

So what does a New Earth society look like? To understand the just society better, we can talk about some of the planetary cities of light on other planets. Even the name "planetary city of light" has an implication that the city has an awareness, a cognizance of its relationship to other planetary cities outside of Earth. A just society is set up on the moon-planet Alano, for example. That society on Alano has a strong foundational structure directly interacting with fifth-dimensional ascended masters. You would strongly desire to live in such a society.

We will mention this just society in relationship to the songwriter John Lennon, who wrote a song called "Imagine." He was a starseed and he connected with the higher starseed energy when he wrote that song about what a just society would look like. I would encourage you at some point to get the lyrics of that song and read them over. The just society is a world without war, without conflict, without money, and without greed. It is a world of social justice where there is an equal distribution of goods and there is no poverty. Yet there is nothing negative about this equal distribution. The just society is not a dictatorship; it is not something that would take away individuality.

There is a particular balance in the just society that is uniquely tied into Biorelativity. The just society holds the balance of the relationships between itself and Earth. This relationship is honored foremost, and the inhabitants continually strive to update their relationship to the area they are living in. There is a powerful spiritual bond between the inhabitants of the city and the place of the city, the location of the city on Earth. In the just society, people are interested in what we call the relationship of this city — and of the society as a whole — to the fifth-dimensional energy that it is tied to on Earth and in the galaxy. This is another way of saying that there is a sister city of the just society in the planetary city, and that sister city is often located on another fifth-dimensional planet.

The just society devotes itself particularly to the spiritual development of its members. There are ascended masters or aspiring ascended masters living in the city, and they follow certain guidelines about how to work to create the thought-structures of the society, the city. And perhaps most interesting for you is the fact that they develop imaginative and creative ways of dealing with discord. They can deal comfortably and compassionately with people who do not seem to be able to conform to the fifth-dimensional energies. That means that they give these people education; they work with their energy. There is no violence — there is no need for violence. The stress and tension so common in life in your cities is not present. So, generally, the just cities and the newer societies are based on unity. This unity is expressed in certain spiritual concepts of the Native American tribes. They say: We are all family, we are all one, and we are all brothers and sisters. What a powerful foundation for a society to have, thinking that all of its members are part of a family and are all brothers and sisters to each other.

The Grose Valley crystal holds this energy and this description of this kind of society. This information needs to be disseminated throughout the world. This foundational structure can be integrated into the planetary cities of light, because these cities are going to develop their cities into the just societies. You might be interested to know that, in the fifth dimension, there are societies, cities of light, and planetary cities of light. In the fifth dimension, you are not just living alone. Many people have asked me, "What do we do in the fifth dimension? Do we just sit in the garden, meditate, and enjoy the flowers? Or is there actual work to do? Are there things to happen?"

The answer is that there are communities of higher soul-beings in the fifth dimension. There are chambers; there are palaces. For example, some of the ancient rabbis continue their study of the Torah, the books of Ala, which is the galactic name for the Creator's light teachings. They continue to study in the fifth dimension. There are heavenly temples, heavenly synagogues, heavenly churches, and heavenly mosques. There are groups of people who are connected to soul groups and soul families, so there is interaction in the fifth dimension just like there is in the third dimension. Fifth-dimension interaction is based on the principles of the just society. There is beautiful work to do, and there are beautiful interactions in the fifth-dimensional societies. So you are not going to be alone.

Propagating Brotherhood and Sisterhood

One of Sananda's great gifts to Earth was to teach some of the principles by which the just society is to operate: to treat each other as brothers and sisters, to treat each other the way you want to be treated. This is not the usual foundational structure of the way societies are set up in the world now. Cities now are not particularly built or structured to propagate the ideals of brotherhood and sisterhood. But the idea of how a just city is to be founded and what principles are to be enacted is beautiful. I believe that the just society has been discussed in terms of the energy of Shamballa, also called Shangri-la, which is essentially a spiritual community that also has its foundation in service.

Let me speak about service. We know that service is a great tool for being closer to the Creator. We know that service comes from a higher calling. We know that service is a giving of yourself and, through that giving, a beautiful energy returns to you. The just society is also based on service. So there will always be people who are of lesser spiritual development; there will always be people who are needier. But that is part of the upliftment that is the overall goal of the just society: to lift up all who need to be lifted, to help raise all who need to be raised, to teach all who need to be taught.

When the Group of Forty was developed, the idea was that it was going to be a network of individuals who would work with all of the participants to ensure that everyone would have equal access to knowledge, that everyone would have equal access to information, and that those who had higher evolvement would help those who are not as evolved. The Group of Forty itself was just meant to be one foundational piece in the just society. The Group of Forty could present an idea of service as the basis of the teachings about fifth-dimensional energy for group members. The Group of Forty could allow people to come into a group where there was no competition, where everyone was working for everyone else's benefit, and where there would be a general spiritual upliftment. The just society will encourage people to come together in soul groups and soul families.

With the Australian meditation in which I have been involved in the past two months, we are now bringing all of the crystals — including the crystal lake crystal — and then connecting them all to the Grose Valley crystal. When we have done all of the work with Australia, we will then send all the energy out through the Grose Valley crystal to all the other crystals. Are we doing the right thing?

Well, yes, you are doing the right thing. I would like to add that the teachings of the just society will begin to be transmitted through your work. It is the just society principles that are going to be transformers for the planet. It is the creation of the planetary cities of light that is going to be the foundational interactive web that is going to make this shift happen more quickly. People are going to have to realize that there is going to be a whole rethinking of the foundation of how we are living with each other.

True societal protection is going to be guaranteed by societal evolvement to a higher fifth-dimensional modality. That will be based on the coupling of the planetary cities of light with the just society. So I would like you to suggest that, in your meditations, you pick one aspect of the just society that really resonates with you. It could be, for example, the fact that the just society is a society in which we all are brothers and sisters, we are all part of a family. But when people hear the word "family," they think of their biological family, which is often filled with a lot of conflict. This is a different family; this is a soul family.

I thank you for your work in spreading that light and the fact that the energy of Grose Valley has volunteered to accept the energy for that teaching, among the other things. This is not the only energy that the Grose Valley crystal is holding, but it is a significant piece. So promote the just society within this planetary city of light.

Do I need to bring the idea of the just society when we do the exercises for the city of light?

Yes, remember that these spheres on the Planetary Tree of Life are in pairs, as Juliano explained. It is hard to talk about harshness and justness without talking about compassion and mercy. It is hard to talk about the planetary cities of light without talking about the justice and the evolvement of the New Earth society, and the fact that the New Earth society is fifth-dimensional. Wouldn't you want to live in a fifth-dimensional society? Wouldn't you want to live in a community that is based on more highly evolved principles? Think about such a community and how it would approach its roles as the protector of the part of Earth that its members are living on and the holder of the sanctuaries, or the land, that its city is occupying.

Beginning the Creation of the Just Society

I have a property just north of Nelson Bay, Australia, and I would like to create a just society there. Does it need a city of light as well?

Let me say that the two energies are connected. The energy for the just society will attract the energy of the planetary cities of light. So maybe your area now is not a planetary city of light, but I guarantee you that it will become a planetary city of light as you work with these energies of the just society. Your work will attract people to you, to that area — that is, assuming that you want other people to come to the area, correct?

This raises a good point: You can set the energetic vibrational frequency to attract those people who want to live in the higher light, who want to live in a society that is maintaining that higher light, and who want to live based on these principles. So I bless your land and I bless your intention. It is a beautiful service to hold land now and begin the process of attracting people to it who want to live in this higher energy.

Now, keep in mind that there have been many other people throughout the history of civilization who have tried to set up these places based on higher principles. Many of them failed. So I do not want to minimize the difficulty of setting it up, but there is a new Earth energy now. There is a new golden light creating higher opportunities. The crisis of the evolutionary cycle is moving people to make changes, to stretch their boundaries, and to incorporate these changes into a newer Earth justice, a newer just society.

My recommendation is to create a call of energy from your beautiful land saying that you are now setting up and you are ready to invite and assimilate those who wish to live in this just-society energy. I also want to emphasize that you describe this energy as evolving. You may not all live together right now. You might not immediately experience this just society, but working toward it now would begin the process of evolvement toward this energy.

As Earth's situation seems to accelerate, you will find that people will be more open to making the necessary changes, because it will be part of survival to be able to live in a just community. I want to say that this is another important issue about the just society. Sure, it's nice and lovely to live with these principles, but it's also going to be necessary for survival to be able to live in this type of society.

You mentioned the concept of Native American tribes giving brotherhood and sisterhood. In New Zealand, we know that some aspects of the Australian indigenous peoples who live here are inviting and could also be worth teaching, because they could be incorporated in a just society.

Yes, of course, because they have centuries of experience in that, so that would be appropriate. There are probably conflicts among some of the aboriginals. It is more of a challenge now to live in just societies than it was for the earlier aboriginal peoples. Third-dimensional modern technologies, overpopulation, and the other side effects of living in this technological world are stressful.

Would a good preparation for the just society be A Course in Miracles?

Well, I think that is one basis, but it is not the only basis. Remember, there is a long history on this planet of different groups coming forth with these ideas. In one sense, living in a just society is not a new idea at all. Yes, of course, miracles have foundational energies in the aboriginal teachings. There are foundational energies in the native teachings. In coordination with Juliano, we are saying that this is a society based on a spirituality that is called the Sacred Triangle energy, which is the integration of the galactic, the mystical, and the native peoples. It is interactive with the concept of the planetary cities of light, but it is also interacting with the existing Earth crisis and the need to do this for survival. So, yes, I think that *A Course in Miracles* provides a good foundation as well.

People, once they commit to living in a just society, will evolve. They will find the means. Again, I return to the idea that was the basis of the original conception of the Group of Forty, in which you have a group of people interacting with each other in higher principles. Maybe you are not in the situation now to move into a just society, but you can begin to interact with people in groups exhibiting the principles you want to evolve toward in the setting up of the just society.

I am not asking anyone to make radical shifts. We are not asking you to move into a commune — nothing like that. The just society is within the planetary city of light. It is in the city, and the city is set up on higher fifth-dimensional energies. We are not suggesting that the structure of the city changes. We are not suggesting anything like communal living, but rather a city where a fifth-dimensional basis can be adhered to. This could come in stages. And, most importantly, it is the just society that is going to hold the energy to keep Earth in balance and work with the preservation of the biosphere. You cannot have a movement of preserving the biosphere without people being willing to live in a certain balance, a certain higher energy.

Preparing for the Ascension

You said that once we reach an ascension stage, we do not necessarily need to leave the planet. How long after the planet and everyone reaches that stage we will still need to stay?

At that point, even if you chose not to ascend, you would still benefit from a higher spiritual vibrational energy. This is because of the fact that you are aware of the ascension. There are going to be waves of ascension. So you might not choose to leave in the first wave, but you might go in the second wave.

I know that many starseeds like you are concerned about staying for the foundational benefit of other people. The work you are doing now is setting up a foundation, and the whole work of the Arcturians and the Group of Forty is a powerful foundation that will be implemented fully even after you all leave the planet. You are setting the groundwork. Just consider that you have particular work to do here. As you are working to your fullest capacity, there will be a point at which you will have done what you came here to do. You might decide to stay longer after that. That is your personal choice. But just remember that it is of greatest benefit that you do ascend when the time comes, when your job is completed.

I would like to recommend that instead of worrying and saying, "Well, I am going to stay, and I do not want to ascend right away" and so forth, you now focus as much as possible on putting all your efforts on completing the mission. You are doing the work you are supposed to do and performing that work with the fullest integrity, the fullest intent, and the fullest devotion. That is the greatest preparation for the ascension. Once you are satisfied with your work, you will be in a whole different state of mind about your ascension.

One of the interesting effects from the many workshops is that the energy of the just society is permeating the groups. So if you notice this group energy during the time of these meetings, there has been no conflict within the group. It is almost like those who have the energy of conflict or vibrational energies of discord do not wind up in the workshop group anymore. Have you noticed the calmness and the brotherhood and sisterhood energies here? You might even feel like you are all a family already. I know that some of you know each other from before, but even among those of you who did not already know one another, there is an ease and comfort among you within the group. This is the energy that is present in the just societies.

It feels wonderful.

When you are setting up a workshop, you might think about all the different levels and possibilities for people who can come to a workshop. All of you have had experiences of people in workshops who were very antisocial. But it does not happen here. People who have those kinds of energies are not able to come through and be here. The vibrational threshold of light that has been set up around this meeting is such that those who have a lower energy cannot and will not come into the group. That is again how a city of light works.

When we are working with our crystal here in Grose Valley and the subcrystals elsewhere, should we invoke your energy in calling forth the work?

Yes, I have been designated as one of the overseers of the crystal. I am not the only one, but I am one of them for the Planetary Tree of Life. The mission has been to work with the just city of light. Yes, invoke my name, Sanat Kumara. Thank you. Also, the teaching is that the preservation of the ecological balance of the biosphere is directly linked to the just city, to the development of that city, because the people living in the just city will naturally gravitate toward protection of the biosphere. I know that we also want to set up global healings, and we will continue to do that. The other idea is that the just city of light will be able to emanate and transform larger healing energies. Remember the principle of holographic energy that Juliano and Helio-ah have spoken of: With just one spot that is holographic, the rest of the planet can feel the healing effects. I am Sanat Kumara. Blessings to you all. Good day.

CHAPTER NINE

The *Kaballah* and Receptivity

Metatron

Greetings, I am Archangel Metatron. I have many functions and many roles to play in the ascension, and I am also working with the Arcturians at the Arcturian stargate. But I am also offering guidance and teachings on the inner light, on the inner mystical thoughts, and how to raise your vibrational frequency using tones and sounds.

You Must Empty Yourself to Receive the Highest Truths

The *Kaballah* is a body of knowledge that is passed on from generation to generation. Moses received the *Kaballah* information at Mount Sinai. The word "*Kaballah*" in Hebrew means "to receive." There is a powerful meaning in this word. Part of the idea of receiving is that you have to be receptive. To be receptive, you must empty yourself in order to have the space to receive. You understand this perhaps in your spiritual terminology as the emptying of the ego. If you think that you know everything and then somebody presents you a new truth, there is no room to receive that new truth because you are already full.

There is a paradox in the fact that to receive the highest information and knowledge, you have to be empty. There is a great emphasis in the *Kaballah* on humbleness and lack of ego. This is partially a spiritual skill, but it has to be sincere. Many people are confronted with their egos in many different ways, and it becomes necessary to resolve some of the problems that result. There are many cases of people who incarnate in order to resolve problems of ego. Ego is a big issue on this planet now. Part of that is because the ego of humankind has led to the desire to dominate Earth and to be in control.

On the Arcturian Planetary Tree of Life, I have been designated as the explainer of the cosmic undifferentiated light. To understand the cosmic light, I like to use the energy metaphor of electricity. Electrical power coming from the main station is at a very high voltage, but you cannot use it unless it is stepped down to an electrical voltage that is appropriate for your home. It is not good to have 1,000 volts — even if that is a lot of power — if your home is only able to process 110 or 220 volts.

In many ways, the top of the Planetary Tree of Life and the cosmic light represent this higher voltage. It is a power that is extremely high and indescribable, but it needs to be stepped down. There are two ways of looking at this. One way is to step the power down, and the other way is that you increase your capacity to receive so that you can process a higher light. Part of the teachings of the *Kaballah* is working with both sides. On the one hand, we work to bring your vibration up, and on the other hand, we work to bring the light into a form that you can work with and perhaps step down.

Unlocking the Codes of Ascension Held in Your Genetic Structure

There are many stories and much information about Adam. It is interesting that Adam is also the Hebrew word for "earth." When you are saying the word "Adam," you are saying "earth," even if it does not sound the same as "Adam" to you. Adam had the power and the vibrational frequencies to see the highest undifferentiated light, and it is said that his abilities were so strong that he was able to see the light across the universe, the unending light. It is also said that all of the genetic codes and seeds for all of humanity were contained in Adam's originals genes and genetic structure.

When you say that we are all related, you are really speaking a truth. It is also known among the spirit guides and teachers that, over periods of time, there has been interference in Earth's genetic codes. However, the original genetic codes that came from Adam are still intact and in place within you. In some people, the purity has been lost and corrupted by downloading things through alien or extraterrestrial sources that were not of the highest intention. But the predominant genetic structure within you is still directly linked to Adam.

The genetic codes that you hold also contain the programs for your ascension. You have the ability, the structure, and the inner knowledge to ascend. It is similar to when you speak about dying. We note that many of you, at an unconscious level, know how to die. You go to sleep every night, and that is a type of dying in a way because you end reality for a period of time. Also when you reach a certain level of sickness and you become unconscious, your body knows what to do, and it has a certain procedure that it goes through. You may not know consciously what that procedure is unless you have studied it and observed it, but your body knows how to respond and heal itself. Sometimes the process of the soul leaving the body is interfered with, but overall the body knows how to die. As an ego, you might not know how to die or want to die, but it is natural for your body.

It is the same with ascension. The body knows how to ascend. The only difference is that there are certain inner codes that have to be opened, and one way that they can be opened is with a vibrational tone or sound. It is like an awakening. In order to ascend, you have to be vibrating at a certain level. If you cannot vibrate at that level, you are not able to ascend.

In the *Kaballah*, we teach that the vibrational frequencies and the activational tones required are contained in the sacred Hebrew chants. There is a particular chant or sound that can be used for ascension. You have to understand that, in the *Kaballah*, what is important is not only the vocalizing of the chant, but also the intention, the emptying of the self, and the preparation required through meditation to receive higher energy. Some may need to sing sacred chants over and over again before the chants have an effect. You can practice these chants. Have the intention to prepare and open up for ascension, and the chanting will have a powerful effect for you.

We are going to have the channel sing tones that are a special chant — an activation for unlocking the codes of ascension. Your job is only to listen and allow the tones and frequencies of the chant to set up and open vibrational frequencies within your inner soul and mind that will help you to open and unlock the codes of ascension. In many ways, the codes of ascension are already partially opened for you, but this will bring you into a higher vibrational activation. After that, I will speak about the activation and the special calling of the tone that will be used for the ascension. This is the activation sound or chant in preparation for unlocking the sounds of ascension.

[Chants and tones in Hebrew: *Kadosh, Kadosh, Kadosh, Adonai Tzevaoth.*]

Try to sing it together with me. Let the codes of ascension inside of you be unlocked. Let the vibrational frequencies that are necessary for you to experience your ascension now be activated.

[Chants again: *Kadosh, Kadosh, Kadosh, Adonai Tzevaoth.*]

The Power of Names

In the *Kaballah*, names and the sounds of names are understood to have special powers. There is much discussed and written about the name of God, known as *Adonai Tzevaoth*. The exact translation is: "my lord of hosts." The word "hosts" here is used in the sense of an army, so "my lord" here is the lord over the army of angelic hosts in the angelic realm. So *Adonai Tzevaoth* is one powerful name of God.

There is a vibrational frequency in every name. I believe you can feel the vibrational frequency of the powerful name of God. If you know the name of someone, you are able to experience their vibrational frequency and you are able to have a closeness to them. You have experienced that yourself. When someone who does not know you very well — or does not know you at all — calls you by your name, you are going to at least stop, listen, and open up to them somewhat.

One of the goals in the Kaballistic world is to achieve a closeness to the Creator. Ultimately, when you talk about your mission on Earth — soul development and evolution — you can generalize and say that the overall goal of the evolution of the soul is tied directly to experiencing more closeness with the Creator. The divine will of the Creator is such that you are here on Earth to do this service for the starseeds, for the ascension, and for the planetary healing. All is directed toward this closeness. The fact that you know or can experience the name of God is another indicator of your ability to be close to him/her.

You can achieve a greater closeness with the Creator, which is the greatest joy in creation, by being of service to the Creator and by doing your mission here. That is part of your service. There is a special compensation and experience awaiting those who incarnate in the third dimension and do service. A special closeness becomes available to them. It is interesting that this closeness is only made possible through an experience. You enter the third dimension in a contracted way. You come into the third dimension and experience contraction. Then you expand and return home. The service you do helps you to expand, especially as you are doing the will of the Creator during your short experience on the third dimension.

Some of you have asked: "Why do I have to come to the third dimension, especially if I have been in higher realms before?" This whole process of experiencing the third dimension with its contractedness and expansion will ultimately lead to a greater closeness to the Creator. It is a great gift to be able to know and speak the name of the Creator, because then you are able to have a closeness to the Creator. That is beautiful.

There are many other names in the *Kaballah* for the Creator. *Adonai* is one and *Adonai Tzevaoth* is another, but there is also the name *Elohim*. This name is so sacred. Often we are not able to speak or write the name *Elohim*, except in cases when we have to honor his name during a sacred time. We have to say, "Are we pure enough in vibration to experience the light and energy that the saying of the name will engender and activate?" The vibrational frequencies of the name, when enunciated directly and correctly, can put us in a state of profound consciousness. We must be sure that we are pure enough energetically to hold the energy and light of the frequency and vibration of the name.

[Chants the name of God, followed by silence.]

The vibrational frequency activated by that name allows your energy field to go to a higher level. The enunciation of the name with the proper intention can bring you into higher energy states. Let us look at the name of Jesus. Jesus/Sananda is at the center of the Arcturian Planetary Tree of Life. He is the center and the holder of Messianic light. In the Hebrew *Kaballah*, his name can be stated as "he who saves, son of David." The Kaballistic enunciation of his name in Hebrew is Yeshua Ben David. You may also hear his name as Yeshua. It is translated as "he who saves." The enunciation of his name in this way can bring you an energetic closeness to him.

[Chants: *Yeshua Ben David.*]

Let the light, the energy, and the love of Yeshua Ben David fill your heart and this room.

[Silence.]

Yeshua Ben David holds a special place on the Tree of Life because he is in the center and he is able to download the higher frequencies of undifferentiated cosmic light into an energy form that can be used and activated by everyone. He does this as a service on Earth for humanity. Remember, it is not useful to have a higher spiritual voltage than what your "house" is able to process. Sananda is able to help step down this light. What is this light? This light is a vibrational frequency that comes from a higher source, and we call this higher light "holy light." Holy light comes from a higher source, and we experience an activation within ourselves when we receive holy light. The name for the holy light in the *Kaballah* is *Aur HaKadosh*.

[Chants: *Aur HaKadosh.*]

Another name for God is "The Holy One, Blessed is He."

Some of you have had the experience in this lifetime and incarnation of feeling like you wanted to change your name. I encourage you to follow that intuition, because changing your name is an indication of the need for a vibrational energy frequency, an activation, and a shift that is necessary. Your intuition for the need to change your name is good.

With the very little study of the Kaballah *I have done, I know that it explains that the two* A's *in* Adam *have to do with the masculine and feminine energy. The* D *is in the middle, and it grounds the two energies on Earth, like the tree going down. Do you agree with that?*

I agree with that interpretation. The different letters and aspects of the name represent different forces. I think that the male, the female, and the grounding is a reasonable interpretation. The energies of the letters represent forces that are coming together in a name. I also like to point out to people that the original Adam was a hermaphrodite. In other words, Adam was a being who had male and female attributes manifested physically together. The separation of Adam was separating the male and the female so that Adam was no longer a hermaphrodite. There exist other beings in the galaxy who are hermaphrodites.

Vibrations and names — could you elaborate a little on them?

Everything in the universe is a vibration. The existence that you have is a unique, individual vibration. It is like a snowflake. No two snowflakes are exactly the same. So the sound of your name has a resonance relationship to your unique, individual vibration. When we speak of names, we want to say that your names can also change from one incarnation to the next. You do not necessarily have the same name in each incarnation. Your name and your vibrational frequency could activate to a higher level. This is why you could find the need to change your name — so that it will record a higher vibration. It is the sound and the vibration.

This is why it is a great discovery in the spiritual world to have the name of God. Michael means "he who is like God." Raphael means "he who heals like God." That would be a general interpretation. Your name has a vibrational relationship to your energy field. Know that each of you has a unique vibration. Each of you is carrying a unique energy field. It is not a matter of anyone being higher or lower, but each of you is fulfilling and expressing your energy and the vibration that you carry, the energy that you is permitted to express and to heal.

Unification Serves the Divine Will

This brings me to the point of unification, which is one of the key contributions of the *Kaballah*. Unification is bringing together in unity the discordant part of this creation and world. Anything that you do to bring together a unity is serving the divine will and helping to heal this dimension. On a greater level, the Sacred Triangle is bringing together galactic spirituality with native teachings and with mystical teachings. It is teaching unity.

The unity is also in your daily life and in your personal work world. You may be doing work as a healer and helping people to unite with their greater selves so that they become better healed. Each of you has a unique set of parameters to work with to achieve this unification and healing, and each of you has a unique group of people who you can work with and do healings with. This is all part of the vibrational energies you are carrying, and people will be attracted to you according to that. In some cases, you can expand the range of people you can work with. I can say that the author/channel David expanded his boundaries when he began to travel, even though it was a great stretch for him and he did not want to travel. But his higher guides prevailed and assured him that he would be safe, well taken care of, and so on.

It is a great gift of service to be able to expand the number of people you can reach. We are not saying that each of you has to travel. In your current life, you have a range of people you are able to heal and bring the message of unity to. You can help them to unify, and ultimately you are unifying with your fifth-dimensional higher self. This teaching of unification is also with you. You are unifying your lower third-dimensional self with your higher fifth-dimensional self. And your name is part of the vibrational energy. It can indicate teachings about what you need to do. If you feel moved to change your name in any way, do so. You can be totally happy with your name, it can carry enough vibration, and you can be comfortable with it.

El Shadai Ji, the living almighty God, is another very powerful name. Or you can also say *El Shadai*, God almighty. *El Shadai*. *El Shadai*. People ask, "Why do you need to say it in Hebrew, and what is the exact pronunciation?" I refer back to the original concept. You hear the name "Earth" and then the name "Adam." Which carries the vibrational frequency for you? The name "God almighty" also has a frequency, though. Some English words do carry a frequency; some words do not. Some of the words in Sanskrit carry a powerful frequency that cannot be replicated in other languages. What sound can come close to "om," for example? It is a unique sound. Having said that, we can also say the word "shalom," and we can find the word "om" in "shalom." There are certain sacred languages on the planet, like Hebrew and Sanskrit, that are able to carry a lot of frequency light.

I am Archangel Metatron. Good day.

CHAPTER TEN

Deepening Arcturian Spiritual Technology on Earth

Juliano and the Arcturians

Greetings, I am Juliano. We are the Arcturians. There is a new spiritual technology that is being offered to the starseeds. It is based on fifth-dimensional interaction. We know that the fifth-dimensional sphere is coming closer to Earth and to the point of interaction. Already we can feel the energies of the future interaction and, in order for the interaction to occur, there must be anchor points that can attract and hold the fifth dimension. This means that Earth has to be prepared for the transformation.

More than even before, Earth now has powerful anchor points that are receiving areas for the fifth dimension. It does not help to bring down fifth-dimensional light unless there are ways of receiving and holding that light. The light of the fifth dimension is actually a light of unity and quantum energy. By that, I mean that the fifth-dimensional process and energy transcends logic, the space-time continuum, and cause and effect. Everything that occurs here looks something like A equals B, and therefore C happens; A hits B, and then B hits C. That is the linear process. But the reception of greater quantum light says that many things are possible, even things beyond your imagination. Many healings are possible, but it is about your field of perception.

Opening Up the Human Perceptual Range

We have talked about the assemblage point. This term is especially used by shamans to describe a gateway in the human aura that can be opened or activated so that the doors of perception open and what is normally not perceivable can be perceived. To clarify this, we look at the normal hearing range of the human ear. We all know that there are sounds and vibrations that exist beyond the normal thresholds of the human range. This is proved by the fact that your pet dogs can hear things that you cannot hear. The same applies to the vision. There are wavelengths that are beyond your eyes' ability to see, but there are telescopes and other means used that can perceive and record these.

The whole universe is a vibrational energy field, and you are now trained to see, feel, and touch things with a certain range of perceptions. If you were activated more and your perceptual doorways were opened, you might see the table as moving lines of energy, and you might even want to put your hand through the table thinking that it was that way; you might be surprised if you did that and your hand stopped. The issue is that the real reality is that everything is a vibration. Opening up the assemblage point gives you the ability to see that. But that level of perception has dangers. For example, if you had such heightened perception in the quest for survival in the forest or in the bush, you would not pay attention to certain details. You would not be able to focus on what the dangers were because you would be bombarded with all of this perceptional energy.

On the other hand, when you are in a safe position and environment, opening up the assemblage point brings to you a truer picture of things, and the truer picture is who you are. Your aura can be described as a luminous ball of light. Instead of seeing different people and the shapes and bodies that you normally see, you might see energy fields and some people giving off more light than others. Luminosity is a measurement of the magnitude of light that is being emitted. If I say that you are a highly luminous being, that means you are giving off a lot of light.

In the experience of opening your assemblage point, you would actually see light being given off by somebody who is very luminous. You would see that light as energy waves. I know that in modern physics, there is a debate over whether light is a wave or a packet. There are different discussions about the exact quality. The important thing is that you would see either packets or you would see waves coming into this person's energy field, and he or she would be absorbing them, and then his or her luminosity would be raised.

This is an interesting configuration, because you are also aware that when there is enlightenment and higher thinking, the luminosity of a person actually shifts, and he or she is holding more light particles. We are talking about light particles that are far beyond the range of light as you know it. We are talking about a spiritual light.

We talk also about thought waves. Thought waves themselves are visible when your assemblage point is opened. In terms of Biorelativity, we are talking about sending telepathic communications to Earth, and with the opening of the assemblage point, you would actually see waves of thought being sent into Earth. It is hard for you to visualize where the spirit of Earth is. Where do you send it? One of the ideas is that you actually send thought waves to the crystals within Earth, because the etheric crystals are already in Earth and they can receive the energy waves that you are sending.

Measuring the Power of Thought

We have previously explained that there is an intensity, an amplitude, and a measurement of thought. We use watts for measuring electrical power. For example, you have 100 watts and 1,000 watts; these are measurements of the strength of electrical power. Certain light bulbs can receive, or use, 100 watts. There are certain appliances that need a certain amount of voltage to run effectively. In our new spiritual technology for Earth, we offered the arcan as a unit of measurement to describe the intensity of thought.

We have referred to a famous psychic — at least he was famous twenty years ago. His name is Uri Geller. He said that he was able to bend spoons with his mind. If you were to bend a spoon with your thoughts, you would need a certain power — you might need 500 arcans of thought wave to bend the spoon. It is helpful to have a measurement.

It is also known, in the fifth-dimensional world, that interdimensional space travel must be coordinated with thought. The antigravity transportation devices of the starships can bring them to a point close to the speed of light. According to the laws of dynamics and physics, no objects are able to travel faster than the speed of light. Laws are made to be broken, so there are circumstances where objects can travel faster than the speed of light. Even if they are traveling at twice the speed of light, it would still take eons to travel across the galaxy. So there is another methodology that combines the starship with an antigravity/antimatter engine with a certain level of thought power.

When a certain speed is reached, a certain level of thinking combines with the functioning of the ship, and you travel at the speed of thought to where you want to go in the galaxy or in the universe. The beings operating this ship must be trained to reach a certain arcan-thought threshold, because if they are unable to exert the right power of thought — and let us say that they may need 38,000 arcans of thought to interact with the spaceship — then the ship will not travel at the speed of thought. Even though the ship is going almost at the speed of light, those on the ship will not be able to transport themselves at a faster speed.

It so happens that when you come down to Earth, into the third dimension, the arcan ability of your thinking is lowered. Some of you may have crashed on Earth or may have otherwise come to Earth and found yourselves unable to return home. You frequently hear stories of crashes — "this person came from the higher realms but could not go back and then was forced to become involved in Earth's reincarnational process." Some of this is true, but in other cases, when such beings appeared in the third dimension, they lost some of their arcan abilities, and they were thus unable to reintegrate their powers to develop the intensity to travel at the speeds necessary to return home. They were stuck here on Earth.

There is another reason why we have to be careful not to appear in the third dimension. Although we are higher beings from the fifth dimension, remember that even we are subject to your laws of karma, or cause and effect, when we appear in your reality, and it therefore weakens our arcan abilities. We want to discuss and work with the arcan light, because a certain level of thought powers are necessary to create certain activations when doing Biorelativity exercises.

Amplifying and Working with Arcan Light

When you are doing Biorelativity exercises — when you are using the Tree of Life for planetary healing — you really want to visualize the packets of thoughts you are sending into the crystal. How would you envision and see an increase in thought power? If I am telling you that you want to come to five or ten arcans, there are several descriptive ways of looking at this. One is to look at a thought as a wave. For example, if you think about sending compassion to the crystal, you would see the thought coming in as a wave. When it is a higher wave, it is going faster, and when it is a slower wave, it is more elongated.

We know that your ability to send certain high-powered arcan thoughts is limited. For most lightworkers, twenty or twenty-five light arcans is very high. Remember when I was talking about changing a spaceship's configuration? Working with an antimatter gravity engine would take 3,800 arcans of light, and sometimes even more. So twenty-five is not a great amount compared to that, and in some cases, it might even require 30,000 to 38,000 arcans. That would be a good range for somebody to be considered an expert in sending arcan energy, arcan light. We have people trained to do that.

In your situation, the highest thought you can send is, let's say, twenty-five arcans. That thought energy would go into the crystal, which has the ability to amplify the thoughts. What is an amplifier in the electromagnetic world of radios and electronics? An amplifier is a special device that receives a certain amount of wattage; let's say it receives seventy or eighty watts. Using its tubes, which have a special arrangement, an amplifier can produce up to 1,000 or 1,500 watts. But it has to have an input of energy to drive it; it cannot produce the 1,500 watts by itself without a small input of radio waves. There must be an input frequency first, which can then be amplified.

What is interesting is that with special devices of amplification — I am talking about radio devices — no more than 10 percent of the desired output needs to go in. So to get 1,500 watts, you might only need to put eighty watts in. It is the same with arcan energy and the etheric crystals. You do not need to put in a great deal, because if you have many people simultaneously sending the highest arcan thoughts possible into the crystal, the possibility of amplification increases.

So we have thought waves going into the crystal and then thoughts emanating outward from the crystal. If you think thoughts of compassion, they can be sent from the crystal directly into Earth. This energy of Biorelativity, calmness, and deintensification can be directed to an area. If you have a cyclone-like energy in northwestern Australia and you want to deintensify it, you can send energies to the crystal and think about deintensification. But you can also send your energy directly to the area without the crystals. It could be both. I am suggesting to you that the etheric crystals themselves can be used as amplifiers. In some cases you need more intensity, more arcan power, to affect a situation.

Remember that everything is a vibration, even a storm. A vibration can respond to a certain intensity or level of thinking. When you are talking about volcanic and plate interactions for earthquakes, it is a different process, but that is also a vibration. A vibration is a good description for an earthquake, because it is a vibration of the most literal kind.

Dangerous Human Technologies Are Causing Serious Earth Distortions
There are even people who believe that HAARP, the High-Frequency Active Auroral Research Program, can send high frequencies into the aura to set in motion disruptive vibrations that can in turn set off an earthquake. That is a frightening

thought, but we are convinced that the world governments own these types of devices. Some of these ideas were given to the governments by other dimensional beings, and there is no effective counterbalance to this.

These types of high-frequency auroral propagation devices can also send vibrational frequency waves into other dimensions. These vibrations can travel through the dimensions. From the Arcturians' perspective on Earth, I want to point out that some of the technologies that humankind has developed do have implications in the dimensional worlds. That is to say that the introduction of nuclear devices, wave distortions, and so forth can affect other dimensions.

It became clear from the callings that we received that there must be some containment. It will not be allowed for these technologies to be transported outside of Earth. At the same time, because of the holographic principles of your world, what is happening on Earth can be felt and experienced in other areas, in other dimensions, and in others parts of the galaxy. But matters become more urgent when things can be transported off of your planet. This is another way of telling you that some of the technologies available on this planet are much closer to dimensional travel than you could ever imagine.

I have a question about the devices you were talking about. Which countries possess that knowledge at the moment?

The United States of America and Israel.

Would the Illuminati that we heard about earlier be using the same kind of technologies?

They have access to them, yes. They do not personally have these technologies, but they have ways of getting to them. The idea of changing dimensional energies has been used in several of the wars that have gone on recently. Waves of energy, or high-frequency energy distortion patterns, are created when there is an attack. It is not just bombs that create destructions, but also frequency distortions emissions can harm people. These do not shift the dimension, but when they approach a certain frequency, they create a type of temporal insanity because you have no defenses against this frequency shift. There are special devices that can be worn like spacesuits for protection against frequency distortions. These were described in the Tesla experiments that occurred in the forties, I believe, when they were doing the Philadelphia Experiment, as I believe they called it. They were working with high-frequency radar, moving objects, and time distortions, and they moved events in reality. Some of the world events that have now unfolded are related to events that may have happened in earlier times, when people were playing with time distortions.

The events that you see unfolding now are related not only to immediate events — in other words, the recent tsunami and earthquake in Japan — but also to other events that you do not know of, events that took place beforehand and contributed to current events. No event exists in total isolation. The issue is that this also distorts Earth's aura. You can imagine when there are such high frequencies that the entire Earth becomes distorted, and it takes a while to reshape itself and to recover itself.

Would working with the crystals and calling on them to raise the light quotient in groups or individually, for example, help to lessen some of these distortions?

Yes, it can help, but you have to send thought patterns to stabilize the energy field. That would also be an appropriate exercise for Japan now, because the whole energy field in that area is greatly distorted. The etheric temperatures of the area are very hot. Yes, you can work to stabilize an area after a catastrophic event, trying to decrease the temperature with a nondistortion thought pattern.

The Ring of Ascension and the Iskalia Mirror

I also want to emphasize the ring of ascension. We have talked about this ring for many years. The idea of the ring of ascension, which is part of the new spiritual fifth-dimensional technology, is that all of these different issues and distortions that we are talking about are often incomprehensible and difficult to reintegrate and stabilize.

One of the great gifts that came to the new spiritual technology table was the idea that a ring much like the ring of Saturn, Uranus, or Neptune would be placed around Earth. This is more a ring of fifth-dimensional energy and light. This ring would also be a participatory ring. By that, we mean that fifth-dimensional guides and teachers like myself, Sananda, and others will also be working and sending energy to the ring. Remember that this whole process of ascension helping Earth in this transition is being assisted by many guides and teachers, not just the Arcturians. Many guides and teachers are working on this. It is a group effort. The ring of ascension goes around the entire planet. By sending the arcan energy from the crystal to the ring, the ring can stabilize itself and send, direct, and balance the energy field of Earth in an effective way, because the ring is already in place around Earth.

The second energy related to this new technology is the Iskalia mirror. This mirror is based on what we consider to be the crown chakra of Earth, which is in the North Pole. There is something about the North Pole that is more representative of the direct reception of the higher light. Do not feel slighted in any way because you are closer to the South Pole.

Anyway, the Iskalia mirror is actually an etheric mirror that has phenomenal powers of receiving. When I say "phenomenal," I have to add that there is a great healing, a powerful new arcan energy coming from the Central Sun to Earth. But that energy needs to be intensified. Just like the crystals intensify your thoughts, we want to intensify the thought energy, the healing energy, the new energy that is coming from the Central Sun.

We have helped to place the Iskalia mirror into the etheric energy field. Imagine a mirror as big as the North Pole — it would cover a substantial distance, but it would still be very minute compared to the Central Sun. Yet it would be able to receive light energy, amplify it, and then redirect it back into the ring of ascension or into any of the twelve etheric crystals.

Serious Problems with Nuclear Technology

We are talking about disturbances in Earth's energy field caused by technology that humankind does not totally understand and does not know how to repair, just like humankind does not know how to sufficiently repair the damage from nuclear energy and does not know how to act when nuclear energy gets out of control. Most of these technologies and the things that have been done with them are creating problems that are beyond humanity's control to repair. So we are calling on energies and technologies like the ring of ascension, the etheric crystals, and the Iskalia mirror to bring light force fields capable of handling and repairing these problems.

If the nuclear reactors are running well, are they still affecting the aura?

Yes, they are — not as harshly, but they are still creating an energy vibration. Remember that everything is a vibration. The nuclear reactors are creating an unnatural energy vibration. There has to be a certain counterbalance. An effective way to use nuclear energy that has been done on other planets is to create a counterbalance, a countervibrational field, that can neutralize the effect. So you could take the fuel rods, for example, and put them in a container that would then weaken them. For every nuclear reactor, there has to be a counterbalancing energy force field, and it is just not the fuel rods that can be done. The creation of the counterbalancing energy force is beyond even the thought ideas of anyone on this planet. Remember that, as we said with the Tree of Life, there must be a balance. If there is, you are exerting a very yang energy, and there must be a counterbalance of the energy of yin.

With nuclear energy, you are just building the reactors, but you do not have a counterbalance for it. Even with such a counterbalance, it still becomes a complicated issue, but it would definitely be safer. There is still a possibility of another nuclear accident within the near future because nothing is really being corrected. There has been no movement toward creating a better balance. People say, "Well, we are making it more safe, and we are doing this and that procedure," but that is like putting a Band-Aid on an earthquake crack or trying to put cement in a crack in an earthquake. It does not work because it does not deal with the core issues of the energy field.

Nuclear energy is creating distortion energy waves. I know that many people say, "Well, a lot of it is contained in the reactor core and there is concrete" and so on. That is true. This does minimize the effect, but it is all accumulative. Even a minimal distortion is still a distorted energy field. Would you want to live close to a nuclear reactor? It is the same thing with electromagnetic radiation from power lines. Basically, they create distortions in the energy field and this affects those of you who are living close to them, because you are an electromagnetic energy being. If your electromagnetic energy gets distorted, you can get into neurological problems and mental problems; you can have difficulty thinking. You are very delicate devices. You are luminous, electromagnetic beings of light. It is a very delicate balance.

I have talked to you in earlier lectures about the null zone. When the planet enters an electromagnetic null-zone area, you need what we have called spiritual batteries in an earlier lecture. These spiritual batteries are a way of restoring your electromagnetic spiritual energy. So when there is a cutoff of the charge, temporarily, you still can recharge yourself from your reserve capacity. You must have a spiritual reserve capacity, because there will be periods in which the electromagnetic light and energy that normally come to you from guides, teachers, and even the ring of ascension will temporarily be null. When it is null, you will have to rely on your spiritual light capacity.

I checked my emails at home this morning, and one of them said that the HAARP was part of the reason for the earthquake in Japan.

I would say that it is an accumulation of factors. In other words, there are many energy distortions in the planet. If you are asking whether there was direct HAARP activity in Japan on the day of that earthquake, I would say probably not. I would say to you that there are continued electromagnetic wave distortions going on around the planet. Some of the electromagnetic distortions are coming from outside sources. The Sun has been active lately, and there has been more electromagnetic energy coming from it than usual.

Again, I keep on using this term "accumulation." Maybe twenty years ago, HAARP would have been one thing, and it would not have been too accumulative, but everything is accumulating now. So HAARP could be one factor, but it is not the only factor now. There is a combination of factors. You might want to use the HAARP energy when there is a certain level of solar activity, when there is a geo-electromagnetic storm, for example. But you also have to take into account the electromagnetic energy currents and waves coming from outside of the solar system, because Earth is in a different position in the Milky Way than it was ten years ago. Earth is going around the Milky Way, even if it may take a million years.

Past Karma at Play in the Recent Tragedies in Japan

It was suggested yesterday that the nuclear problems in Japan might be a karmic reaction to the nuclear bomb in the Second World War. Is that true?

Well, I would say that the people of Japan have a problem with nuclear energy. This nuclear energy is something that is related to previous karmic activities in the earlier histories of other civilizations, like Mu, Atlantis, and other civilizations in which many of your current leaders and scientists participated in earlier incarnations. I would say that it is incorrect to assume this recent accident happened because the bomb was dropped there previously. That is not a cause and effect.

There are brilliant people, brilliant scientists, and brilliant technologies in that country; you all know that they have led the way in so many different revolutions in the computer age. It is a case of people who were involved in other technologies in other civilizations and other times coming back now and attracting that energy that was there. One of the factors in attracting the energy of nuclear technologies is that when you attract it, you do not know if you are going to attract the good or bad side of it — you just attract it.

Remember I talked about cosmic karma in my earlier lecture. I would look at it this way: Some of the karma that these people in Japan have brought to their country is the karmic lessons from other planetary experiences. That is to say, we know that other planets have participated in the development of their sciences that use nuclear energy. Remember that we have said that we have visited many planets, and we do not endorse the use of nuclear energy at all, because we have not seen anyone on other planets successfully using it, and there are other technologies that can be developed that are actually better. Developing any reliance on nuclear energy is only slowing down your need to change, because once you develop these plants, you will want to use them to their fullest for financial reasons.

There is also cosmic karma involved. People who used this kind of energy on other planets have now come to Earth, attracting that kind of energy and using it again. Maybe now they will learn the lesson. That would be another aspect.

Remember to try to be broad. There are so many things that have happened that are not explainable. There is no way to explain the deaths of the Holocaust. There is no logical explanation. You can never come up with karma for six million people, for example. There are planets that have been destroyed with millions and millions of people on them. There are cosmic events that are contributing factors to many of these unimaginable, incalculable, and unexplainable events happening on Earth now. Planets have been totally destroyed by nuclear energy. There have been planets on which certain light technology was used, and they were destroyed as a result. Even here on Earth, you know about Atlantis being destroyed.

So the short answer to the question is that it is a combination of Atlantian and Lemurian energies with cosmic karma that attracts this type of energy. From that perspective, yes, the nuclear bombs that were dropped there and the nuclear event now are related because they are both attracting the karmic energy. When you attract the karmic energy, sometimes you do not know how to differentiate it. You are attracting a force that is uncontrollable. Remember, no matter what they tell you, there is an aspect of nuclear energy that is uncontrollable, and humankind does not have the scientific knowledge to control all aspects of it. They have some ability to contain it, or at least they think they do, but it is obvious that they are limited even in that, as has been shown in this accident. I am Juliano. Good day.

CHAPTER ELEVEN

Current Feminine Power and Allusions to Mayan Prophecy

Chief White Eagle

Greetings, I am Chief White Eagle. I am an ascended master, and I am working with other ascended masters. I am happy to report that there are many native ascended masters working on healing Earth and bringing forth the fifth-dimensional energy and light to this planet at a time of great need.

The Sacred Triangle is dear to us. We are happy to be part of the Sacred Triangle. We are happy to receive the acknowledgment that our special gifts are welcomed and needed in this unity and this effort to move Earth to its next evolution, its next stage of development. Equally important is the effort to move humankind into the next level.

I know that the past years on this planet, Mother Earth, have been filled with great polarizations, great conflicts. Some of the acts of warfare have been painful and very traumatic. Mother Earth has been a kind mother to humankind with all of the different events — wars, pollution, and now even nuclear pollution. Mother Earth still has been able to hold and maintain the life-force energy for the biosphere.

'We, the native peoples, always feel a special energy and connection to Earth. This comes naturally to us, for we have all lived and been raised to connect with our ancestors, our grandmothers and grandfathers, and to follow the ancient teachings. These ancient teachings from our grandmothers and grandfathers contain deep wisdom and deep knowledge about Earth and how to relate to Earth. For us, it is natural to listen to and perform the Biorelativity exercises.

We do these exercises through ceremonies. Our way is to work on developing techniques using the medicine wheel, sacred dance, drumming, and gathering people in huge circles.

We have received instructions from our star brothers and sisters. We know that we are part of the star family. We have known this throughout the generations; it is not a new discovery for us. Also, we are happy that others are becoming aware of their starseed heritage and star-family connection. We believe that becoming aware of the star-family connection will create a sacred energy, because it will be revolutionary to the entire thought system, the entire social structure, and the entire religious structure of this planet when it is irrefutably shown that we are all related. We come from a deep bond, a deep connection with our star brothers and star sisters. When we say that we are all brothers and sisters, we include the fact that we are brothers and sisters to the star families as well.

The Wisdom and Limitations of the Ancient Prophecies

I want to speak about the Maya and the end-times prophecies. I also want to speak about our view of this. Prophecy comes from many of our ancient grandmothers and grandfathers. Our Hopi brothers and sisters, as well our Mayan brothers and sisters, have lengthy, elaborate, and precise predictions about this time. From our personal observations as well as from our study of the Hopi and the Maya, we know that we are witnessing a time of great change and unprecedented shifts at all levels. We are witnessing shifts at an institutional level, at a religious level, at a financial level, at a geopolitical level, but also within Earth herself. We have just begun to see some great, dramatic changes caused by earthquakes, tsunamis, windstorms, and flooding. It is predicted that this will continue.

What you have recently seen is the first part of a continued series of major disruptions. We know that these events will create disharmony and disruption on one level. But on another level, they will force many of the great powers to seek union and work together to alleviate the great damage and suffering that potentially can come to pass. I want to emphasize the word "potentially," because our teachers — our grandmothers and grandfathers — continually say that those of you in these times must change your ways so there can be an amelioration of the upheavals. This is written in some of the ancient texts: Those in power must learn to change their ways.

We view this as a positive sign among the prophetic visions, because a prophecy is a look into the future based on present events and the assumption that present events will continue in the same direction without any major shift. Prophecy does not totally take into consideration the work of those who are seeking, through their new powers of spiritual strength, to exert an influence on events and to exert their energetic, perceptive, and spiritual powers.

I want to say that the coming events and coming times will not be the end of this Earth. We are all clear that Earth is not going to end, but in our readings of future times, we are also all clear that there are going to be major changes. We are all clear that these changes are going to come in a way that is going to be painful to many people. But we all know — and you know from your personal experience — that when you have to change, you experience this as a personal disruption and as a possibility of some suffering and pain.

One of the circumstances of change is that there is always a resistance to the change. There is always a will to hang on to the older ways. When our ancestors and the Maya did the prophecies, they knew of this resistance. In some ways, they dramatically emphasized the worst outcomes and possibilities. They knew these prophecies would be received and heard. When the worst of our prophecies are made public, there is a possibility of greater change among those who are able to listen to the prophecies and exert change. Those powers become more focused and more listened to.

As a series of disruptive events occur, more people become open to newer ideas, look for newer spiritual answers, and even look to the native peoples. I say this half jokingly and half seriously. Jokingly, I say that things have to get pretty bad for the general world to look to the native peoples for answers. And seriously, I say that those in power do not generally seek the spiritual advice of the native peoples; they do not wait to hear what the native peoples have to say. Yet it is you, the starseeds participating as our star brothers and sisters, who want to see, hear, and know what we, the native peoples, think about what is occurring and what we think needs to be done. What we think needs to be done has been very clear in the teachings of the Sacred Triangle and in the teachings of Biorelativity: There has to be a new balance.

The Purifying Power of the White Buffalo Calf Woman

In our teachings of the Native American way, we see that our savior — our indicator of the newest changes that have to come and will come — is represented by the arrival of the White Buffalo Calf Woman. It is predicted that the White Buffalo Calf Woman, a female prophet, is going to return to our lands, bringing new wisdom and new teachings, and she is going to be received by many peoples around the world. The White Buffalo Calf Woman is not just for North America, but for the globe, the whole planet.

The forerunner of her coming is going to be the birth of the white buffalo. This is a sacred symbol to our people. The white buffalo is a sign of purity, a sign of fecundity, and a sign of a great joy to know that through genetic codes, a newer evolutionary purification energy can and will emerge. Just think that a newer and more purified energy in humankind's genetic code is about to be birthed and brought in to stabilize this Earth situation. The White Buffalo Calf Woman, a powerful female energy, is bringing these new evolutionary genetic codes for the upgrade of humanity and humanity's links to its own evolution.

The White Buffalo Calf Woman, of course, is a female power. This is a time in which the male energies are going to shift; they are going to have to become subordinated to the female light, the female energies. The male energies are often described as holding the energy of control, domination, and power. Yet that attitude is not going to work anymore. In our cosmology, Earth is a feminine spirit, and her healing is coming through the new feminine light, the new feminine power. This feminine power is different. It is not the female acting like a male and being dominant; it is the female following the light of the White Buffalo Calf Woman, who is a very powerful energy. Make no mistake — she has powers of healing and powers of manifesting the purifications that are necessary.

I want to speak also about the Galactic Kachina. The Galactic Kachina is known as a new intermediary kachina that is ushering in the White Buffalo Calf Woman. But more importantly, the Galactic Kachina is the intermediary between the energy of the Central Sun and the light forces that are coming to Earth and culminating at their peak on December 21, 2012. This alignment represents the peak of the higher light that is coming to Earth. But this peak means that the energies needed to make the shift are going to be at their fullest intensity at that point. This means that those things that are holding on to the darkness and the old ways will burst, will not be able to hold on. It also means that those same powers, those same energies, will be entering a higher energetic balance if they make the changes and adapt to the newer light, the newer ways.

[Chants.]

I ask that you chant with me. And while you chant with me, I will be saying a prayer. In the background, you will continue chanting.

[Chants.]

White Buffalo Calf Woman, we are gathered today to call on you, to tell you that we are ready for the new light that you can bring. We are also ready to receive your new powers, which will help us to overcome the old ways that are proving destructive to Earth and the biosphere. We see that we are helping to pave the way for the entrance of this new light, this new power that is coming with your arrival. It is prophesied that a new time is coming. It is prophesied that a new energy will bring a light to humankind that will help usher in a new revolutionary stage in our development. So we are humbled in accepting your light, but we are also eager and enthusiastic to assist in this new way of finally living in balance with Earth and with the cosmos.

We stand ready to welcome the White Buffalo Calf Woman. There are many starseeds here, many lightworkers who understand the native ways, the native traditions, and the powers of that. These are star-family members who are working with their opened hearts to bring the highest evolutionary changes possible so that Earth, the biosphere, and all of humankind can come into a new balance.

This is a beautiful land filled with beautiful people, and they are advanced in their understanding of welcoming higher-dimensional light to their country. You will find your energy and your work well received and greatly welcomed in this beautiful land known as Australia. We are praying and asking that you show the way and allow these lightworkers in Australia to be leaders in the spiritual development of the evolution of humankind. They are ready and eager to do their part. We receive your blessings at this time. We are honored, White Buffalo Calf Woman, that your spirit has come to Australia so that we can connect with your energy and light. All my words are sacred. I am Chief White Eagle. Thank you.

-

CHAPTER TWELVE

Unlocking the Energy of Your Heart for Changes

Chief Buffalo Heart

Greetings, I am Chief Buffalo Heart. All my words are sacred.

The buffalo is a sacred animal to my people, but we also know that the buffalo is a great teacher to us. She is not only a provider of shelter from her skins and a provider of food, but she is a teacher of the heart energy. Her energy is so powerful because she has a big heart, a buffalo heart, and that is where my name comes from. I am here to speak about heart energy and the buffalo heart. This is a time of great need for the buffalo heart; this is the time on Earth when the opening of your heart is of paramount importance.

White Buffalo Calf Woman Will Bring Down a Great Heart Opening

The return of White Buffalo Calf Woman is a fulfillment of a prophecy, but it is also a time when the heart energies will become stronger, more recognized, more accepted, and more influential. The time of the mind ruling — the time of this logic ruling the planet through calculations, investments, and other methods — is falling away to make way for this new time, when the White Buffalo Calf Woman will return, acknowledge the heart opening, and bring it down. But you already are feeling this heart opening, and you may even already know that it is necessary to open your heart.

You may already notice that many of the tragedies and many of the upheavals that have occurred are touching your heart deeply, and you may feel your heart opening more when you see many species of plant and animal life becoming extinct. This is not an easy event to witness. We witnessed the destruction of our sacred buffalo. It was painful; it was our way of life to follow the buffalo. Yet the buffalo endured and accepted what was happening, for in some ways, this is the way of nature. The buffalo was ready to leave the planet, just like many of the species — some of whom you dearly love — are ready to leave Earth.

Yes, there is some pain involved for the animals and the plants, and this includes the fish dying and many species leaving. But it is a painful event that affects the heart. And these animals and plants becoming extinct now appreciate and receive your love and energies, and those who are close to extinction but still can be saved appreciate your love and energy, and they especially appreciate your heart energies. Yes, Earth has a spirit, and the spirit can be communicated with. But also from our perspective, the animals, plants, fish, and forests are also spirits that can be talked to. They can be influenced, and they respond to the heart openings that you are now sending to them.

So the Biorelativity process includes sending your emotional heart energy to Earth and to the plants, animals, and oceans. It is well known now that the ocean is in danger of totally collapsing as a life force. If this collapse occurs, it will be a huge loss to this planet, even if pockets of life forms will remain in certain areas in the oceans. The openings of your heart to the life forms and to the biosphere are needed now, but we experienced a great sadness and pain when we saw our buffalo needlessly assassinated. It was something that was not easy to witness.

I know that, in your heart, it is not easy to witness what it is occurring on Earth. But at the same time, know that your heart energies and the newer openings of your heart are helping to ensure a better, safer, and more spiritual transition, because all of this destruction will stop when the hearts of the many are opened. And part of the evolutionary change that the masters have talked about — including the abilities to be more spiritual and to use Biorelativity — is that a new heart opening, a new heart energy, is coming as part of the next evolutionary step for humankind.

Yes, when we heard the discussions of the ancient Neanderthal man, for example, many people said that it was the intelligence in the Cro-Magnon man that allowed him to adapt. So it was something in the thinking power. Well, now the next evolutionary step includes the energy of your hearts opening to Earth. Those who cannot open their hearts will not be able to sustain their positions of power over the planet.

Carrying the Light of the Buffalo Heart

Become aware of your heart energy. Also become aware of the pains, disruptions, and even the hurts and trials you have undergone. Become aware of all these things you have endured in this lifetime, some of which you may never even be able to resolve — they are just the pain you carry with you. And now feel how these take up so much space in your heart. But with the buffalo heart, you can make your heart larger. And the solution to many of the pains that you may experience really lies in the ability to enlarge your heart energy, to make your heart like a buffalo heart.

It is hard to have heart-opening energy toward those who are leading the destruction of things, corrupting the planet, misusing the planet's resources, and creating the circumstances leading to further extinctions and further misuse of resources. In many ways, they cannot be forgiven; but on the other hand, they need to be shown their ways are not working anymore. They need to be shown that the old ways are not good, and therefore their hearts have to be opened so they can feel the pain that they are causing to this planet and to its biological inhabitants, including its human inhabitants. So pray and send the opening of light and energy to all those in power. All of their hearts may open.

Earth needs to become a heart-based planet, and the leaders and others in power will have to understand the new light, the new energy, the new evolutionary step of heart energy. For the energy that we are all one, we are all brothers and sisters, means that our hearts remain open and we accept our responsibilities for being here and carrying the light of the buffalo heart. I know that with your wider heart openings you will become better planetary healers, and you also will heal yourselves quickly of any other issues that confront your own personal development and evolution. And with your heart opening, you will be able to attract more lightworkers and more seekers of spiritual light to your work. It is a great time to be on this planet, for there is so much service awaiting you and so many who will respond to your calling.

I am Chief Buffalo Heart. You are all brothers and sisters. All my words are sacred. Ho.

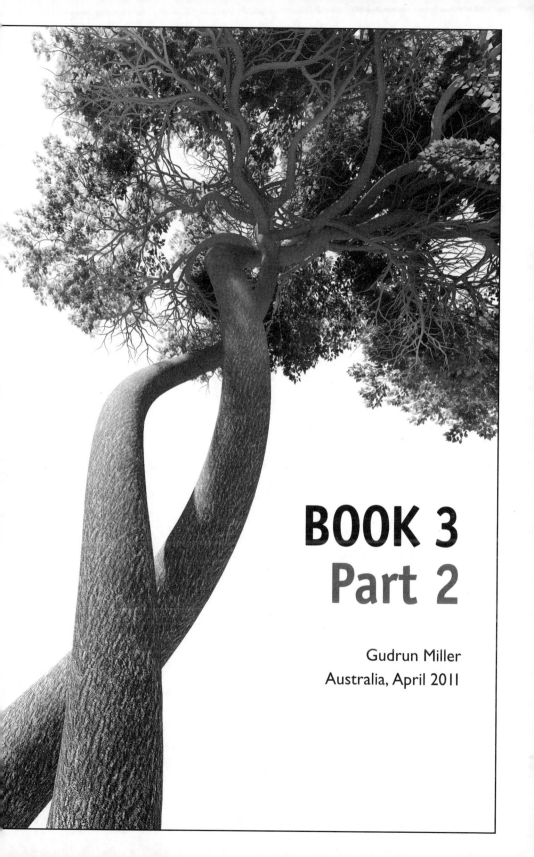

BOOK 3
Part 2

Gudrun Miller
Australia, April 2011

CHAPTER ONE

Trauma and Ascension, Part 1

Gudrun Miller

I am going to speak to you about the emotional body and the mental body in conjunction with the clearing for the ascension. Over the years that the Arcturians have asked me to give talks about the emotional body, they always prepare me before I speak and they give me some guidelines, something to focus on so that I do not get stuck. They always have interesting topics for me and things that I am very happy to talk about.

This is the first time that I have been very precisely asked to talk about the ascensions connected to emotional clearing and mental balance. So I am pretty excited about that. The Arcturians have talked about the emotional, mental, and biochemical component of the ascension process, which they say is all part of something that is coded in us and already there, waiting to be activated. I think it is very critical that we really attend to our emotional and mental processes, have as much information as we can get, and really begin to take our emotional healing very seriously.

Coping with Exquisite Sensitivity in the Third Dimension

Some of you have heard me talk about the emotional body before, but when we — starseeds — are born into a physical body, we bring with us highly evolved spiritual bodies. We come into our physical bodies highly evolved spiritually, but we also come in with exquisitely sensitive emotional bodies. That is all beautiful, but then here we are in the third dimension. Some of us come into families that are very damaging to us and difficult for us to manage. We come to a third-dimensional planet that maybe causes us grief and pain, and we are perplexed. Our sensitivity can work against us, because we want to shut down, close off, and develop addictions so that we do not feel anything. Then our sensitivity becomes a handicap.

The title of this lecture today is "Trauma and the Ascension" or "Stress and the Ascension." Juliano introduced me to this concept of starseeds being trauma survivors or survivors of severe stress. I had not put things together quite this way before. After I thought about this, I concluded, "Well, that makes a lot of sense." Again, going back to our exquisite sensitivity, how many of you felt traumatized when you heard about the tsunami, the earthquake, and the ongoing nuclear disaster that is occurring presently in Japan? With your sensitivity, it seems like every day there is more and more stuff to integrate. For us, as starseeds, it is hard to turn that off. Some of us end up maybe traumatized too.

We have to be careful not to get absorbed and involved in the happenings that have been predicted. I think we all know this. For me, it is like I knew it but I did not think it was going to happen this way, with this much devastation and this much impact on the planet. But we all know it, and we have to find a way to integrate these experiences without damaging our emotional bodies, without slowing or preventing our ascension process. So it is quite challenging.

Choosing an Earth Family

In terms of the earlier comment about trauma survivors, most of you — but not all of you — have had many lifetimes, and some of those lifetimes have involved trauma. Some of you who know some of your past lives know about that. It has not been a pretty ride. Even though we have agreed to come here and we are honored to be here, especially at this time, this has been a painful journey for some of us; our emotional bodies have been severely traumatized in other lifetimes, and for some of us, even in this lifetime. Some of us have karma to pay, so we may end up having to do that, or some of us have just been born into families in which there was a baby or a physical body present for us and we took it, because we needed to be here at a certain time. That is like a roll of the dice. It can be a good thing or maybe not.

Let me share this with you. I did a regression with David, and he had two physical bodies that he could choose from in the precise time of the star alignment that he had to come into for this incarnation. So there was a family in India, and there was a family in Cleveland, Ohio. His higher self and his soul family decided that the family in Cleveland, Ohio, would be the more appropriate one because it would give him the right opportunity. Plus it was a Jewish family, and he had some prior experiences being Jewish in other lifetimes, so that was very familiar to him.

On the other hand, this family was dysfunctional, and he was not at all karmically connected to it. He had no prior ties to this family, and he waited until the moment of birth to actually join with the fetus, because he really did not want to be in that family. That was a difficult childhood for him. But, again, when we come into a physical body and our perspective is from the astral fourth-dimensional plane, it looks like a piece of cake. It looks easy, like: "Oh, I can do anything, no problem! A little abuse, a little neglect — so what? I have had worse." But then, when we are in the third dimension experiencing these things, we get traumatized. And as children, most of us do not necessarily have access to an understanding of who we are. We do not have the spiritual guidance to help us integrate these experiences so that they do not traumatize us.

The Hidden Strength of Trauma Survivors

Let's talk about the concept of trauma survivors. I work a lot with trauma survivors in my practice, and I love working with them because, by the time they get to my office, even though they have so many wounds and they are struggling so much in their lives, they are very strong. They are strong to even make it to adulthood, to know they need help, and then to find help. Most trauma survivors are stronger than anyone normally would want to be in a lifetime, because they experience things that most people do not.

Trauma is an extraordinary experience that does not normally happen to you in a lifetime. We can have an ongoing childhood trauma, severe abuse and neglect of many different variations. And then we can have, of course, trauma as adults from relationships and disasters. Again, if you are able to heal yourself from these traumas, you end up being a magnificently strong person, and things just do not rock you very much when they happen.

I encourage all of you to see yourselves as survivors — maybe not survivors of trauma, because Vywamus suggested that was too strong of a word, even though I kind of like it because it is dramatic. Maybe instead try to see yourselves as survivors of stress, and see your own strength. You would not be in this room today if you did not have much strength. You would be hiding out somewhere saying, "I cannot wait to get out of this body. This lifetime really stinks. I hope it is over soon."

One of my patients came to my mind. She is a starseed, and she is unawakened. I want to use her treatment as an example of what can happen in the healing and recovery process, and maybe you can relate to that in your own healing and integration. She came to me about two years ago. In the United States, if you are mentally disabled, you can go on a pension. This woman had a long list of diagnoses. Everyone had diagnosed her with different things over the years and she had received much treatment. She was on disability. She was cutting herself, and she was taking many different medications. But still she had clarity of focus and the desire to heal, which I was very impressed by.

She had experienced severe trauma throughout her childhood from both of her parents, and then she had married a man who was an alcoholic and physically, mentally, and emotionally abusive toward her. She had two children. She raised them as well as she could, given all of her obstacles. She divorced her husband and then got a master's degree. This was amazing. Then she had a total breakdown when she was working with some children and flashbacks started to come to her from her own abuse. She could not neglect it anymore, and that was when she was diagnosed with severe mental illness. She has a different therapist than me for private therapy, but I have a group for trauma survivors, which is a really fun group. So I put her in that group, and she has actually thrived in that group. She gave up being on disability and found a very good job. Her whole identity has changed — she does not harm herself anymore, and her medications are down.

Learning to Look at Ourselves in a Whole New Way

Now she is facing something that is totally perplexing her, and this is where I think we can all can find a parallel: She has to change her identity as a human being and look at herself in a wholly different way. She actually was, on some level, comfortable with being a victim, seeing herself as someone who is a barely functioning trauma survivor with all the syndromes that go with that. She had identified with that so deeply that it was hard for her to let that go. If she let that go, who would she be?

She has to form a new sense for herself, a new thought structure about who she is. What is happening for her with the group now, after two years — and she is moving very rapidly — is that she is beginning to trust the group members, form connections with them, and let what the group is telling her about who she is penetrate her defenses somewhat. Several weeks ago, she came to the group and she was totally withdrawn. She said, "I do not know what is wrong with me. I do not want to be here today. I just want to flee. I like all of you, but I do not feel I fit in. I do not belong here."

I responded, "That is great. I am glad you are facing this now." She looked at me. She gets really angry with me because I always interpret her issues with a positive twist. Instead of making a horrible thing from the fact that she was ready to flee, I had to help her see that it was very good, because she was letting her guard down, she was beginning to open up. It was a whole new experience for her, and she did not know what to do with that. It scared her almost more than being abused. She changed.

So that is part of being human beings. Even though starseeds have these magnificently advanced spiritual bodies, we are still humans. And guess what? We do not like to change and give up all thought constructs, acknowledge that we might be somebody more powerful than who we believe we are. We do not like to give up all of the things that give us comfort, all the beliefs about ourselves that we think are so true that we are so attached to. What if you had to give them all up? Would you not be scared? I would be. I get scared. I have been scared over the years doing this work, because I certainly had to give up a lot of my old ideas of who I am in order to accommodate and do this work.

Someone asked me, "If I had told you twenty years ago that you would be doing this work, would you have believed that?" And I would not have. I would have thought you were crazy if you had suggested I would be doing this. My client is courageous, and she perseveres because she understands that this is a positive process, even though she is in a lot of pain with her growth. So growth causes pain and change causes pain. But there is growing pain and there is trauma pain, so maybe part of what all of us are going through at this point may be growing pain. As Juliano said, ascension is about leaving the third dimension — leaving our pets, leaving our loves ones, leaving our identities — and stepping into something much greater than maybe we believe ourselves to be. What does that mean about this life and all of our work to achieve and attain success? What does that mean about our relationships?

You said that she is an unawakened starseed. What signs make you think this?

I can usually tell when they walk into my office. There is a certain energy. All of you carry certain light. My starseed sensor goes right off and I get so excited. I cannot say, "Oh! Another starseed!" — they are going to think that I am really loony and walk out the door. But I can tell right away. Plus, her magnificent perseverance and strength in spite of all of her hard times in this life is an indicator. My clients know I do these workshops, and some of them are brave enough to ask, "What is it that you do exactly?" Of course, I tell them. She is really interested in that; the majority of my clients are. I do not push their awakening process; I just invite it. I encourage people to think in broader concepts about themselves and to explore spiritual questions and issues. That is a very good question, yes.

Would you believe that certain people have only incarnated on Earth? Have we not all been in different planetary systems? Would we not all at one level qualify as starseeds? Everybody has been on other planets, so we are all starseeds, as opposed to some people having just been on this one planet.

The definition of a starseed, according to Juliano, is that our first and primary soul evolution was done in another star system — so not here. When we come to Earth, we bring that awareness, that knowledge, that wisdom, and that energy with us.

Why We Are Challenged with Emotional Bodies

Could it be, then, that we can have many lifetimes of trauma?

Yes. Certainly, some of us have. A Kaballistic teacher who David and I know said, "Well, some of you know you are old souls and you are quite proud of that. Maybe it is possible that being an old soul is just another way of saying that you are a slow learner." I thought, "That makes a lot of sense. How much pain and trauma do we have to have before we finally get it?" The drama of the third dimension is very attractive. It is just so interesting to get all wrapped up in that. Our emotional bodies are so captivating, and we can get so stuck in our emotions.

One of the most challenging things that we actually come to this Earth and into these bodies for is to deal with our emotional bodies. Juliano stated over and over again that this is one of the primary lessons we came to master: regulating our emotional bodies. If you think about the emotions and how difficult they are, especially in relationships ... Some relationships are just horrible at times, because it is just so easy to get emotional, misinterpret, take things personally, project all of your unresolved issues onto the other person, and see the situation in black and white: This person is bad and that person is good. You never get to the core of the matter. You can get so lost in your emotional self.

I shared this with some of you earlier: I had to ask Juliano, "Why do we have the emotional body if it is such a pain to regulate, understand, and master?" And he said, "Well, given the wide range of the emotions — the lowest of that range being guilt, shame, grief, jealousy, fear, anger, and all of that, with the higher range being acceptance, understanding, forgiveness, love, and lack of judgment — the answer is that our emotional bodies let us experience joy."

This is why we are challenged with emotional bodies. Joy in this body in the third dimension is apparently the closest we can come to experiencing the Creator's light and energy third-dimensionally. That is why we are challenged with our emotional bodies, and that is what we have to discover. How can we experience joy when people are dying in Japan, our food is being radiated, all these beautiful animals are dying all over this planet, and flora and fauna are being extinguished as we speak? How can we experience joy? Does anyone have an answer?

Because it is all part of the life cycle.

Right. We all know that it is part of what is to happen. That is hard knowledge. You need detachment.

When I counsel my trauma survivor clients, I work a lot with detachment. Detachment means that you do not deny your emotions. You accept all of your emotions, but you do not attach to them, to what has happened to you in your life. You do not personalize; you accept your feelings about it. If you know that a species is going to become extinct and it brings up grief in you, you accept that. As you accept it, this actually releases it from you.

Is this neutrality?

It is not neutrality. All of you are exquisitely sensitive human beings. If you see something traumatic happening, you have an empathetic and compassionate response to that, correct?

Do you then try to maintain neutrality of that?

You do not put the cart before the horse. As human beings, we have emotions and we have to experience them. Allowing yourself to have the emotion and express it also allows you to release it. Juliano gave me this concept, which now I am using a lot, and I think it is perfect.

"Accept and Expand" Instead of "Fight or Flight"

We have a primitive animal response in the limbic system of our brains that allows for our survival as an animal species. Our limbic system is based on adrenaline — fight or flight. If we are threatened, we either run away from it or we fight it. This does not work for us as starseeds, nor does it work for the ascension process.

Juliano suggested this approach: "Accept and expand." Why are you accepting what is going on on the planet? Because you understand that you have been given a lot of information indicating that this is going to happen, and you accept it as best you can. And then you expand your awareness and your consciousness. Accept and expand instead of fight or flight. I really love that.

Accept all of your feelings. Feelings are a natural part of our process. If you ever watch children and how they deal with their feelings — if they have not been traumatized or damaged — you have seen how they go through the process of overriding their emotions in a ten-minute span. They do this and then they are okay. They can move from extreme anger to joy and laughter in ten minutes.

I have noticed that the new babies and the new children who come in have much less of that anger and those negative emotions. They are much more sunshine babies. Is that what is going to happen with the newly activated DNA and our emotional bodies?

Probably. I would think so. I think Juliano addressed that also, and he talked about a biochemical shift that is a natural process in our bodies. If you experience trauma and adrenaline, then you move to love and acceptance. That actually creates a biochemical shift in us that opens up our DNA to the ascension process. Most of us are older and we came into this life pretty veiled. We did not have that many memories of who we were and who we are, and we agreed to that beforehand. So this life has been an interesting challenge for many of us. I know it has been for me!

Do you come across starseeds who feel that they were forced here to do service, penance, or whatever? I recently met a beautiful healer who felt that she was forced here.

I suppose that can happen. Accidents do happen. When we did the regression with David, we learned that he was requested to come here. He really did not necessarily welcome it, but he agreed to do it. So here he is.

Thank you for coming. So David was requested to come here. Does that create trauma for him?

I do not think so. I think that, on a higher level, we do not experience trauma the way we do here in the third dimension. If you think of the third dimension as a horizontal way of looking at things, then if you are just wrapped up in that horizontal plane and you have no awareness of your higher self on the vertical plane, life will be quite challenging. But with the understanding of the vertical plane, I think it helps.

I do hypnotic regressions through which most of my subjects are able to access their higher selves or their soul families, guides, and teachers. My subjects enter a supraconscious state. All of them report that this is the reality, this is who they are, and they do not ever want to leave it again. They are very sad. Some cry when they have to come back into their physical structure. They complain about being so dense, and they are unhappy about it. But when they are in that level of awareness, they are in bliss. It is a wonderful, liberating place.

I do not think that we are traumatized with the idea of coming. When I think back on my time right before this incarnation, I do not know whether or not it was arrogance, but I thought, "No problem, great life — this is going to be interesting." Well, it is interesting, but I had to go through a lot of things that were quite challenging for me to get to this point. But from a higher perspective, I could not see that. I was not traumatized by that.

I remember a story in which someone said that he didn't need to come back, but that if he did return, he would have a very blissful life. Is this fact or fiction? And do many of us choose to do that?

I think it is a fact. Some do choose to come back. I have not encountered that many clients who I have regressed who have told me about that, but those of us who achieve that high mastery can come back maybe out of pure love or just for the joy of being here. It is a blissful existence.

Changes and Continuities from One Life to the Next

I've got another question about the emotional body. According to the Arcturian perspective, when we pass over, is there a total clearing of the emotional body in the places we go between lifetimes or not?

No, especially if we have unresolved issues. We actually take baggage with us from other lifetimes.

But could there be opportunities to clear a lot of this baggage in schools of learning between lives?

Yes, it is like going to class. You get all the ideas. It is like learning to fly a plane, for example: When you get on the actual plane and you actually have to fly it, it might be a wholly different thing. When we get back into our bodies, we get caught up in the horizontal plane. We lose our awareness and maybe the gains we had made. But we can also have such severe trauma in one lifetime that the emotional body carries that into the next lifetime to an excessive degree, and we are given this next lifetime to actually heal that.

In the case of a friend of mine, she was very traumatized as a child, but on one level, she came to understand that she had actually been one of the perpetuators of her own trauma. Now that she has done both sides, what are possible scenarios for her?

I think it is just wisdom, compassion, and forgiveness. With my trauma survivor clients, what happens when they actually come out of their trauma constructs is that they are able to look at all the perpetrators and at themselves with compassion. Most of my trauma survivors are highly critical of themselves; they are perfectionists and they have a lot of high expectations of themselves. It is like forcing them to go beyond their own traumas, to go beyond wanting to be traumatized people. They try to be perfect.

Is that like putting them in their mental bodies?

Yes, and they have to learn how to correct their thinking about themselves, and then that eases them up emotionally. If we, as starseeds, can look at our past traumas in other lifetimes and see them as experiences that cause soul growth and evolution, that is a wholly different perspective than feeling sorry for ourselves, for example. This is a good group. You have good questions.

Is there a tendency for people to want to stay in the victim role?

Yes, because it is the known thing. If you give up that identity as a victim, who are you? The female client I was describing earlier is beginning to understand that she is an interesting and likable person who has many strengths and attributes. The group is pointing these positive things out to her, and she is beginning to integrate a little bit of them into her idea of herself, but it is not easy. She fights it all the way because her deep belief of seeing herself as a victim is hard to dislodge. I think that some of us, as starseeds, maybe have that too. Maybe it is hard for us to see that we can ascend and that we are beings of light, glorious in who we are and the energy that we bring. It is hard for us to see how precious we are.

Moving beyond Judgment and Obsessive Behaviors

My question is really that I sometimes find this issue of guidance personally challenging. Somehow it has become quite difficult for me to work through. That is triggered by my own issues as well.

You have to find a place of detachment. I look at some of the drama going on on this planet, and a part of me wants to move in with judgment and react, wants to be angry — "These people are so stupid and bad!" And then I think, "That is not useful because it is necessary. These people are going through their own evolutionary processes. They need to do this. It is a freewill planet. People get to experiment with all levels of evolution on this planet, and it is not my place to judge. Although, sometimes when I am tired or distracted or whatever, I am just really involved in the drama of the horizontal plane. I can get judgmental and I can get angry, but it really does not solve anything.

My question has to do with obsessive-compulsive thought-forms coming through from experiences in past lives. For example, regarding a fear of something — how can you let go of excessive thoughts or excessive behavior? How can you escape from a thought construct that repeats itself and underlies a whole set of emotions?

That is a complicated question. In order to answer that fully, we would have to go into a lot of detail, and we have no time for that. The obsessive-compulsive disorder is especially a fear disorder. The person is stuck, and there is probably a deeper reason for it. The hardest thing to let go of is the fear, whatever the fear is. A person who has that disorder is attached to that fear; he or she believes it is very real.

I council the people I work with to accept their fear and to accept that they have a problem. I urge them not to fight against it so much. We try to move to a more vertical understanding, a higher self-understanding, and have compassion. That can sometimes dislodge a bit of the blockage, because most people who have this disorder have some shame and self-judgment. And shame, self-criticism, and self-hatred impede the healing process.

What I do in treatment is help my clients to remove all the blocks that they have erected to their own healing. They might be emotional blocks or mental blocks, and in those cases, the healing process is very natural. If someone who has this kind of disorder can accept that they have fear, that is really helpful. In our culture in the United States — and maybe here in Australia also — we are embarrassed of the so-called negative emotions. We are taught that those emotions mean that we are "less than" and that we are not perfect. Most are not taught to accept these emotions and be curious about them; we are taught to medicate them or hide them with compensatory activities, like perfectionism, more extreme behavior, success, or whatever else it takes so that we do not have to deal with the underlying feelings inside, these so-called "negative emotions."

Free Will, Soul Advancement, and the Choice to Return to Earth

Why would we choose to come back on Earth?

I wonder that too. In the case of David, it was requested of him and so he agreed. Our Kaballistic teacher has told us that, in the oral tradition of Jewish mysticism and the *Kaballah*, there are many stories of old masters who have ascended and perfected their incarnation but chose to come back out of love for Earth. Oftentimes they come back as handicapped people with limited abilities, because with that physical limitation, they can just focus on love energy.

David Miller: We each have a higher self, and that higher self is operating according to totally different thinking and principles than those we use in this realm. Your higher self is not even affected by your death, nor by things like the fact that you just lost your job or you just lost this or that. The higher self does not have an ego as we do, so there is the possibility of advancement and soul work, and from its own perspective, the higher self will choose this path.

I have been struggling for a long time with the whole issue of soul advancement. Why would the soul have to advance? And is there something about being in the third dimension that helps the soul to advance? The answers came through a channeling. In order to totally understand the experience of being in the fifth dimension, you have to understand polarity. But you cannot understand polarity in the fifth dimension because there is no polarity there, so you come to the third dimension to understand polarity. But then you have to reunite with unity, so it is a very circular process.

The answer is that there is third-dimensional work that advances our soul. Also, people may be asking themselves the question, "Why do people volunteer?" The reason why people volunteer to come to Earth is because Earth is a freewill zone, and you have the opportunity to learn and achieve higher development in this type of situation. This is the greater opportunity for our higher selves, though maybe not for us.

What it would be like to have a world that is not a freewill zone and very regulated?

David: You could be talking about the Grays. Have you ever seen the newer *Star Trek* TV series? The Borg are beings on this show who all function in group consciousness, like ants. They are all just functioning for group survival. They do not have individuality or heart energy. In some of the channeling that I have done, people would ask, "Why would these other lower extraterrestrial beings come to

Earth?" The answer is that their race was coming close to extinction and they felt that they had no heart energy; they had no emotions of love. They wanted to incorporate that into their genetic structure, because there is something about the heart energy that is very human that was missing for them.

This confirms what Juliano has said. One of our major purposes for being on Earth in this third-dimensional existence is to master the emotional body, and it is not an easy thing. The beauty of a balanced emotional body and a healed emotional body, as some of you know, is that you have such an exquisite ability to see beauty and to be sensitive to the energy of love and have it affect you deeply. That is what the Grays want.

CHAPTER TWO

Trauma and Ascension, Part 2

Gudrun Miller

Several years ago, when we went to Istanbul, several of us took a big van and went to the Black Sea. It has fabulous energy. David speaks Turkish because he was in Turkey for a couple of years as a young man in the American Peace Corps. He was chattering away with the taxi driver, and the taxi driver kept calling him Baba. I asked, "What is this Baba business?" David explained, "Well, this is the word you use to be respectful to an older man." The driver was respecting David by calling him Baba. As a group, we thought that was interesting, so we started calling him Baba. If you hear me calling him Baba, that is what it's about.

Later on that year, I did a regression with one of my patients. She is a very unassuming, quiet, petite, and lovely human being. She asked for this regression, not really knowing much about herself at a soul level. As it turns out, she is from Andromeda. She is seventh-dimensional in origin. We were four-and-a-half hours deep in trance. At that point, her higher self–energy was present, and she was channeling an energy from Andromeda. Because of the difficulty of translating seventh-dimensional concepts into words, she was speaking very simply. I asked her quite a few things, and I was getting pretty punchy and tired. Through her, I asked her guide, "Could I ask you a personal question?"

She said, "Yes."

I responded, "My husband David channels Gurhan from the seventh dimension. Are you acquainted with him?"

She started to grin and said, "David, your husband?" She grinned really wide. Of course, this was not my client, but the being she was channeling. "Your husband, David, is a beam transmitter," she said, then grinned really wide again and added, "and he is very good at it." At that point, my mind was pretty fluid and creative, and I pictured David as a Jewish action figure: Baba, the beam transmitter. When he does his work, that is who I picture.

At breakfast this morning, we were talking about the ratio of women to men doing this work. I may have shared this with some of you before, but as I do these regressions between lifetimes, I find that when people go to that place where they choose their next life, their guidance often chooses the body of a woman, even though most often they themselves would prefer to choose the body of a man. The reason they are encouraged to choose a woman's body is because, in the culture that they are going to be born into, it is much easier to access the spiritual light and energy as a woman.

It is much more challenging as a man. Men have a lot more inhibitions and restrictions on their emotional and spiritual bodies, and their mental bodies too. It is much more difficult to come to the place of awakening in the form of a man. So it is wonderful that you see men here. It is a blessing, and it is a miracle. For most cultures, it is still easier for a woman to access this awakening. We are allowed to be a little emotional, and we are allowed to be a little flaky spiritually. Men have to fit into a certain contracted state.

Our Emotional and Mental Bodies Have Much Work to Do

In review, yesterday I talked about trauma, the ascension, and the concept of starseeds. We talked about all of us being trauma survivors or survivors of extreme stress and how hard it is for the emotional body to keep up with the spiritual awareness, growth, and acceleration that are happening. It is imperative that our emotional bodies keep up with our spiritual acceleration, spiritual growth, and awareness. Our mental bodies also have to accommodate all the changes that are happening almost every day on this planet. It is a phenomenal amount of work that our emotional and mental bodies have to do. Through David, the guides have recommended the concept of "accept and expand." I use the letters *A* and *E*. In the United States, that is a television channel: Arts and Entertainment. So A and E, accept and expand.

In Australia, that stands for "accident and emergency."

"Accident and emergency," okay. That will work for you. When you perhaps find yourself in a contracting or fearful state, or one of these tragedies happens on the planet again — apparently they will happen more and more — instead of going into fear and contraction, remember A and E, accept and expand. How does one emotionally accept something that is so awesomely traumatizing? You use your mind, you use correct thinking, you help yourself, and you talk to yourself. You also accept the feelings. It is not that you should avoid your feelings; your feelings are very important, and they are not necessarily to be viewed as burdensome, an annoyance, or a nuisance.

I think feelings are a barometer. They tell you how things impact you. They give you a good overview of how things impact you in every moment. You want to accept your feelings, but you do not want to hold on to them and get stuck with them. Feelings are energy. If you allow the energy to pass, it passes, and then you move on to the next thing. If you are willing to accept your feelings — even the trauma, shock, and horror of what you might see — you might feel a lot of grief, sadness, and anger. Again, accept it and find the way to express it.

People have different ways of expressing emotion. You can talk about it, write about it, do physical activities, dance, sing, call your friends, or even work with someone to help you release the emotion, because you do not want to go into contraction. At this point in your evolution as a starseed, you want to go into expansion. Actually, if the emotional energy is not expressed and we hold on to it, we can begin to get blockages in our emotional bodies and they can be present throughout all of our lifetimes. You can actually be blocked in your emotional body due to events in other lifetimes, and this might lead to you coming into this life with only a percentage of your emotional body active or present, because some of it is stuck in time somewhere else.

The shamanistic concept of soul retrieval is about releasing these blockages. It is about going back to retrieve those lost aspects of yourself that have been stuck in time so that you can be fully present. I think, with the accelerated energy present now, it might not be as difficult to unlock those traumas as it used to be. I think we can access them a little more readily and release them. I think that has to do with your activation, your awakened mind, and your mental-body knowledge about this process. When you sense in yourself that there is a blocked emotion, go into meditation and ask your higher self to show you what that is about. When you find out, you might be able to release it yourself. If you need help, go to a practitioner or someone who can help you to release it. How I do regressions is interesting, because with the starseeds who come to me, I might have an intention: "This is how we are going to do it; this is what we are going to get." But then the soul teachers and the higher self comes into that session and essentially take over and say, "Well, this is what we are doing." And I say, "Okay."

Overcoming Past-Life Trauma to Succeed Emotionally in the Present

Last fall, a Group of Forty female member named L gave me permission to talk about her regression. I honor her and the work that we did together. L is around sixty, and she just recently retired. She lived in Europe for many years. She had been a teacher, and she raised four children primarily by herself because her husband was not very supportive. When L and her husband divorced, she stayed in Europe. She is an American woman from the Chicago area. She decided to come back to the United States. All of her children are back in the States. L had a major shift: She sold her home and retired. Her children were all adults, and she moved back to the States.

L wanted to have a regression to access her soul family and her guidance. She also wanted a sense of the direction that she should take now, because she had total freedom. This was sort of profound for her, because she is a capable, responsible person who took all of her life responsibilities very seriously and fulfilled all of them — and then suddenly she did not have any. In a way, L was a little unanchored. When we started the regression, she had a whole list of questions.

We went through L's life, and she had actually had a pretty decent life. There were many challenges and obstacles that she overcame, especially in her marriage, but her childhood was pretty decent. She came into a family who wanted her. I regress my patients through this life and back into the womb. L was fine with all of this. She was pretty happy to be in her mother's womb. She was able to help her mother with her anxiety as a spirit energy entering the womb. Then we went to a past life. L wanted to go to the past life that was most helpful to her current questions and situation. That leaves it wide open. In order to access the between lifetime, it is best to go to the most immediate past life, because it is most fresh in that person's subconscious. But L wanted to go to the lifetime that was most helpful for her search and her questions.

So she came into a lifetime in which she was a young man in the Civil War in the United States. L was a confederate soldier from the South, and she was around twenty. When we entered into that life, she was a courier, a messenger, so she was not actually a combat soldier. She was quite conflicted because she did not think war was very good. Her starseed-self was somewhat aware in that lifetime. In many of these past lives, there was little information — unlike today, when we have so much. It was probably hard for L to have known that she was a starseed and to cope with the fact that her ambivalence about this war had to do with her higher spiritual awareness.

She was deeply traumatized by this process of war, and she wanted to do something to alleviate the war or help it go in another direction. As a young courier, L thought she could meet both sides of the war. She could meet the important people in the battle and maybe convince them that this war was a useless and terrible event. Instead, she got shot. She was shot by accident, and she ended up in a field hospital. She was dying.

Now L is a highly verbal person. When you meet her, it is hard not to notice that she is very intelligent, verbal, and engaged. As I was working with her, she got less and less and less verbal, so much so that I had to pump her for information; I had to pull words out of her. All L wanted was to go silent and dormant. I asked her, "What is happening?" She could not answer me. Reliving this past life, she was dying and she felt great despair at that point. It was a great despair about the fact that she had failed her own purpose. She had failed it. She carried this huge shame, guilt, and despair because her life now was over and wasted.

The emotion was so tense and thick that I attempted to move out of that life so that we could maybe talk about it and integrate it, but she would not leave the body. No matter what I said or did, she kept staying in that body; she kept lingering around it. Even after she died, she did not want to leave. This was in part due to her sense of failure, grief, and despair. I had to bribe, manipulate, and push her, and I finally called on her higher self to help, because I was not getting anywhere.

L's higher self came in. As she came into contact with her higher self, there was a lightening of energy. Her higher self began speaking through her, and that was delightful. L's higher self answered most of her questions. I think what we integrated about her life during the Civil War was that, in her current life, Linda did not want to be in that same place where she was not achieving a greater purpose. She felt that now that she was free, she should have some sort of magnificent purpose. She had very high expectations of herself to do profound work for Earth. She actually does this just in her presence, but she wanted to do more.

L wanted to open a healing center; she wanted to go and learn special techniques of healing. She wanted to do something big to give her life purpose and meaning. In some ways, she may have recalled her life during the Civil War because she was possibly still reacting to having felt and experienced herself as such a failure in that lifetime.

L's higher self instructed her to have faith in her process. We did a lot of work on her emotional body at that point, because she was grieving forward the pain that she had inflicted on herself through her own high expectations. Due to these high expectations, she also had not acknowledged all that she had already done in her current life. L had raised four beautiful children. I met one of them — her oldest daughter is in the Group of Forty. All of her students loved her because she is a wonderful light presence. If you met her, you would love her too, guaranteed.

L was able to release a lot of that pressure she put on herself to achieve and perform, enough that she overcame that Civil War lifetime in which she had seen herself as such a failure. Her higher self encouraged and instructed her to trust the process. Everything that she would need to learn and do would be presented to her in a timely way. She needed to have faith in her life process.

A Time for Acceptance and Expansion

I took this advice in for myself, for the people I work with, and for all of us. I think it is very timely. It is not a time to push, push, push. It is a time to accept and expand, to trust and have faith, to know that you are here for a divine purpose. It is not the time to ask these questions: "Am I doing enough? Should I be doing more? Am I living up to my potential?" It is wonderful that you are here and that you are able to work with this light and energy. Think about that, what a miracle it is.

I would think that every one of you would have an interesting story of your own personal awakening, and it would be interesting for all of us to hear how you achieved that. For some of you there were more obstacles to that than for others, but here you are. So, any questions? What is the new paradigm? Instead of fight or flight, it is ...

A and E, accept and expand.

So when you witness these new traumas, accept and expand. Accept and expand your own process and accept and expand into that. Have compassion for yourself rather than demanding perfection. A lot of starseeds, including myself, have had the disease of perfectionism. I do not know how many of you can say that ...

And addictions.

Yes, all kinds of addictions in order to deal with the emotional body.

Perfectionism is horrible disease because it is a black-or-white way of thinking. It is you are either 100 percent perfect or you are a failure. In these groups, I have encouraged those of you who are still challenged with perfectionism to make at least one mistake a day on purpose and be very proud of it. Say, "I did it. Look at that," without being ashamed of yourself. If you make a mistake accidentally, that is even better — you get points. When you make a mistake without trying, you get extra points.

Working with the Subpersonalities

Vywamus, a spiritual guide who David channels, has a technique where he separates the emotional, mental, and physical bodies and even talks to them. I sometimes find that if you talk to them and you praise them, they seem to respond really well.

They do. One of the therapeutic techniques I use, and I am sure this is not new to any of you, is to work with the subpersonalities. This does not mean that we have multiple personality disorders; it just means that we all have different aspects of ourselves that form the whole of who we are as a combined personality. Some of the subpersonalities are the inner child, the inner parent, the healthy parent, and the critical parent. Part of working with our emotional bodies is working with the inner child, which carries our emotions. If you had trauma as a child in this lifetime, your inner child is a wounded inner child. We can carry trauma from any age. We might have a wounded young adult, a wounded teenager, or a wounded middle-aged adult. You can work with those aspects. But perfectionism usually steps in very early. It is usually a much, much younger part of us, because children think in terms of black or white, right or wrong, good or bad. There is no in between; it is polarized.

The healthy parent, the awakened starseed, and the higher self in you can begin to educate that child to relieve the pressure of your emotional body by saying things like, "It's okay if you make a mistake. It's only human. That was an interesting mistake. What did you learn for that?" instead of "How could you! You embarrass me! How dare you!" or whatever else we might say. Hopefully not all of you do that, but if you do, you might be horrified by some of the things you still say to yourself when you pay attention to your inner dialogue. You cannot imagine yourself ever saying such things to your children, to other people's children, or even to your dog or your plants. But you might say these kinds of negative things to yourself.

Working with the subpersonalities is also a way to work with the emotional body. When a child is frightened and he trusts his caregivers, he goes to his them for comfort. With our inner children, we can do the same. You can comfort your inner child; you can talk to her, and it doesn't mean you are crazy. It actually works well. It is a powerful technique, and it provides a lot of healing. It has to be done with the best intention, compassion, and kindness that you can master. Think of the compassion, kindness, and love that you have for each other, for your families, for the pets and plants in your life, and even for the rocks and crystals. Show at least that much compassion for yourself. The emotional body responds well when you do that.

For me, it is when I make a decision that I talk to myself: "Is it right or is it wrong?" When I do that, I give some more time for myself, although I do not think I figure out what is right or wrong.

If you think about the overall concept of your decisions and you look back at them, have they been mostly right or mostly wrong?

I think it is a good mixture of both, but I ask the question to everybody else around me when I am stuck. There are some things I have no doubt about.

I think part of that is natural when you are doing something entirely new. You need a lot of input and reassurance.

Asking for Help Is a Necessary Step

Part of perfectionism is that you are not allowed to ask for help. You are supposed to know everything and do it perfectly. It is actually a good thing when you say, "Help! I need help. I cannot figure this out. Can you help me?" That is actually really good. If you think about it, we all need help from each other. We need so much help right now — not because we are not beautiful, complete beings, but because this life is hard. It is good to have help; it is good to have a lot of support.

A precious client of mine is around thirteen, and she is a starseed. It is not something I can tell her; I just know it. She is gifted emotionally, very highly sensitive. She was rejected by her biological mother. Her biological mother is very shut off. At the time that I was working with this girl, she had not seen her mother for five years. She was living with her father and stepmother who were highly supportive and loved her, but she was carrying the grief of her mother. She kept waiting for her birthday calls and Christmas calls. The mother would call intermittently and tell her daughter about her own life without asking any questions about the girl's life. So this girl never got to say: "Mum, I am on this swimming team. I do this and I do that, and my grades are so and so."

This girl carried a lot of grief. She drew a picture of her heart, and it was broken. There was a big glob of grief in it for her mother, and she was very contemplative as she drew this. She looked at me and she said, "Gudrun, this is really hard."

I replied, "Yes, it is. It is hard." This is not self-pity; it is challenging. We have a lot to learn, and now we actually have to do it in an accelerated time. If you need help, by all means, ask for help. If you need help clearing yourselves emotionally, ask for help. If you need help physically, ask for help. We can help each other so much.

Masters beyond the Fifth Dimension

You mentioned the Andromedans, and we do not seem to have heard about them publicly for a while. Is there a reason for that?

David Miller: I am willing to, though. The other thing is that my connections with them are such that they are talking about their incarnations who are beyond actual bodies. I find that hard to relate to. How can you have an incarnation and not have a body? Even in the fifth dimension, there is a body form, but my understanding of the Andromedans is that they are beyond even that.

So the difference between the fifth and seventh dimensions is that they do not have bodies, but they could step down into lower vibrations and get a body again?

David: I do not know. I really have not studied that or worked with that energy very much.

Gudrun: There are Andromedan starseeds. I have worked with several now.

David: There might be different levels in the Andromeda galaxy. I do not know.

So those masters that we talked about, like Quan Yin or Jesus, at what level would they be?

David: They are fifth-dimensional ascended masters.

But in all his lifetimes starting 2,000 years ago — although there is no time — hasn't Jesus evolved onto other levels?

David: Jesus is multidimensional in all dimensions, including those beyond the fifth.

Is he stuck there?

David: I cannot think of him being stuck.

Gudrun: He has accessed the Creator's light, so obviously he is multidimensional and aware of it.

David: You are multidimensional from the third to fifth dimensions, but the masters are multidimensional the fifth to seventh dimensions and beyond.

Gudrun: Our soul energy is multidimensional at all levels, even here. Even though we may not know about it, it is multidimensional. I like how the *Kaballah* explains a way to understand our multidimensional selves: "Think of your physical body as your soul body. The crown chakra is connected to the Creator's light and energy, and it steps on down to your feet. The feet are in the third dimension, but in order to manifest in the third dimension, you have to have shoes; the shoes are your body. This becomes the third-dimensional vehicle that you put your soul into, and that is how you experience the third dimension. But as you know your whole body is connected."

About the time when Moses was at the burning bush at Mount Sinai, talking to the Creator's light, he was requested to remove his shoes from his feet. Now you might know the symbolism of what he was being asked to do. When you take your body, you step out of your third-dimensional consciousness and you move into your divine light, your higher self–soul.

In the meditation group I belong to, every week they bring through masters like Sanat Kumara. When these masters come through, the channels say, "I am coming through as a higher version of myself." I find that quite fascinating. They are coming through as a greater aspect of themselves.

Gudrun: We all have that access to the greater aspects of ourselves too. We take our shoes off, and we are able to connect with our higher selves and bring that energy through. Now is the perfect time to foster that in yourself, because your higher self has so much information and guidance. When my clients are in trance and they are bringing through their higher selves, the energy is always delightful. As I said yesterday, my subjects do not wish to come out of that energy because it is so expansive, so loving, and so peaceful. There is no judgment, no ego. It is a lovely energy, and we all have access to that part of us.

Do our higher selves gradually make the connection, or how does it work?

Gudrun: I do not think that the higher self has judgment or can be disappointed. Like David said yesterday, the higher self is primarily focused on our soul evolution. There is no attachment to anything we necessarily do right or wrong. I would say there is only a focus on spiritual evolution, whatever gets us there. This focus is without judgment, criticism, or any human emotion.

David: But I would say that the other part that would be true is that the lower-middle selves are happy when you connect with your higher self.

Gudrun: I am happy when I connect with mine.

So the connection gets stronger?

Gudrun: Yes, it is much like channeling. The more you practice it, the easier it gets and the more facility you have to do it. You can just go into a light meditation and access your higher self. You will get a lot more answers for yourself, and they will come from a non-ego place.

When these masters are channeled, we feel a lot of compassion coming through. Would they still have feelings of anger or sorrow?

Gudrun: No.

Just compassion?

Gudrun: Some of them have experienced incarnation, so they understand. They might have empathy, but they are not attached like we are to right and wrong and all the drama that we have in the third dimension, such as good and bad. That does not mean that they do not make an effort to help us; they do make such efforts through David and others. That also advances their soul journeys, and when we are fifth-dimensional and doing the work that they are doing now, that is going to be a boon for us. I guess in the higher realms, service to others is the most important work to do.

CHAPTER THREE

Changes in Your Belief System

Gudrun Miller

Some of you probably are like me in that you hear all this new information and it slips somewhere into the cracks of your mind, and then you think, "What was that?" So I will review very briefly the concepts that the Arcturians asked me to bring to you: accept and expand. We talked about that as the new paradigm for dealing with your feelings related to Earth changes, the traumas that are happening, and the changes within each one of you individually.

Acceptance, Expansion, Adrenaline, and Love

"Accept" means that you accept all of your feelings. You do not shame yourself, deny yourself, or judge yourself for having whatever feelings you do. For example: "I should be more spiritual. I should not have these kinds of feelings." This is part of the human condition, and the best way to deal with any feelings that you have — even the ones that are uncomfortable for you — is to accept them. In the United States, they have a saying within Alcoholic Anonymous that they probably have here too: "What you resist, persists." I am sure you have heard of that. If you resist your feelings, they do not go away. They stick around, and if you resist them further, they actually build up to a point at which they might even overtake you every now and then. If you try to push away your negative feelings, they do not actually go away. It is important to accept your feelings.

"Expand" means that you need to use your mental body to understand exactly what is happening now within yourself and on the planet. You expand by understanding, by using your mind, and by tapping into your wisdom. Accept and expand.

The other concept is the biochemical change that helps us with our ascension process. It also has to do with the trauma response involving adrenaline. Again, we transform our response with adrenaline and then move into love and acceptance. So remember: adrenaline, love, and acceptance. Use the energy that comes from your adrenaline to feel your love and acceptance rather than to move into fear.

Fear is a contracted energy. Fear does not allow for any learning; it only allows for defensive postures. When you move into fear and defense, your mind and your emotional body have shut down. You are not learning, and you can move into stagnation. Stagnation leads to death and a lack of soul connection in this life. You do not want that, I do not want that, and I do not think anyone wants that. Again: adrenaline, love, and acceptance.

Where Your Core Beliefs Come From

Vywamus brought up the concept of core beliefs. I have been a counselor for thirty years now, and I know that this is a profound concept to work with and that it can lead to profound healing, as Vywamus said. He wants you to understand how to do this. He covered some of it, but I would like to expand on it a little further, because I think it is so important.

When you were an infant in your family of origin, you were impressionable and you lived with gods and goddesses. Your family — your mom, your dad, the other grownups around you, and even little children — were gods. You look at them to help you understand who you are.

Imagine every member of your social group as an infant, maybe three years old, holding up a mirror. When you looked in that mirror, you got a reflection of who you were. There can be a problem when the person holding the mirror is off balance. The mirror can be off balance too; it can be distorted far beyond belief. The child looks in the mirror and gets a distorted perception of himself or herself. Where does that distorted perception come from? It comes from the person holding the mirror. It is not about the child, but the child does not know that. You do not know that as a child. You get that distorted perception.

Where does that distorted perception go? It goes into your core beliefs. This is where core beliefs come from. They are what has been reflected to you when you look at the people around you. It can be how they treat you, how they talk to you, how they do not talk to you, and so on. All of you are highly sensitive, so you absorb these things. They are core beliefs because they form before the age of three — very early on, oftentimes proverbially — and they are simple. Like Vywamus said, they are not intellectually complicated; they are usually one, two, or three words.

If you grow up in a balanced and healthy family, your core beliefs will actually be congruent with who you truly are. Your family members will look at you, see who you are, and then reflect it back to you. They might say, "You are a lovely child. You are a healer. You are an angel. You are gifted in these areas." And that would be true. It would not be overpraise; it would be done accurately. If you have a family that overly praises you, that is a reflection of their needs, and it is not about you.

If you have correct core beliefs, you are in congruency, and your life and personality unfold on a balanced foundation. It does not mean that you do not have conflicts, but your core does not disrupt your growth, and you are not fighting against negative core beliefs in order to continue your growth. If you have negative core beliefs instilled within you, you have to compensate for that. It is like building a house on a foundation that is not solid. You have to keep compensating for the shifts in that house: The walls crack, the doors do not close, the floor is crooked, the roof starts to leak, and so on.

Negative Core Beliefs Are Like Cancers in Your Belief System

You always have to maintain some of sort of stability if you have a negative core belief. There are two ways to go with a negative core belief. The first is you can work extra hard to counteract that core belief. Even if you know what your core belief is, remember that it is unconscious for most people. They do not even know about core beliefs. They do not understand that they have them. Or you can give in to your core belief. You can just say, "Well, they are right. I am useless. I am worthless. I am stupid. I am ugly. I am a burden. I am a wreck. I am a mess. I am unlovable. I am bad. I am inadequate. I am incompetent." Those are some of the common negative core beliefs.

If you have a negative core belief, how do you know what it is? And how do you know if you have one? I think you would know because you might work hard to compensate for it, but no matter how hard you try, you can never achieve that sense of thinking, "Okay, I have achieved this knowledge." It is an ongoing struggle to achieve that peace and serenity, because your core belief is corrupt. Your house does not have a solid foundation. I think that if you think about that, it makes sense. You can never stop trying to counteract the negativity of your core belief. It is like a cancer in your belief system.

If you have negative core beliefs, it is important to see if you can uncover them. How do you uncover them? It does not have to be so complicated. You can maybe think back to the child you were in the family that you grew up in. Think about how the members of your family treated you, how they talked to you, and how you felt as a child. Think about the struggles you have had in your life. Do your struggles continue to repeat themselves? Maybe you have an inner dialogue that says, "Oh God, I keep screwing up all the time. I really am ..." What follows that? Or if you do not do well in relationships, do you say, "I am really not lovable"?

The issues that happen in your life kind of validate your core beliefs. The core beliefs are actually like fundamentalist religions. This is what I teach my patients. It is not open to logical intervention. It is the truth because gods and goddesses told you so, so there is no logic or reason that can counterbalance those core beliefs. Core beliefs are rigid, and they are hard to crack. Once you find what they are, you cannot just say, "Oh, yes. Those are my core beliefs. Well, I do not believe in them anymore." That is not how you do it; it does not work that way.

Cracking Your Negative Core Beliefs

I will tell you a story of my core beliefs and how they began to shift for me. In my family of origin, I was treated poorly by my mother, and the rest of the family colluded with her in that respect. I have to exclude my older brother, though, because he was sort of helpless in this process. The message I got clearly from my mother was that I was bad, and this was not counteracted by my father. (There were some other people in the family, but they were not available to me much.)

In order to compensate for that belief that I was bad, I decided that I should be extra good. That process exhausted me so much that I developed a depression in my adolescence. I almost felt defeated by the burden of trying to do something that I felt I was just going to fail at anyway, because the truth is that the gods and goddesses had told me that I was bad. "I should go and hide out in the woods somewhere," I told myself. "And when I pass from this Earth it will be a blessing to me and to everyone else, because I do not want to contaminate anyone." So you can see how it was, but in spite of that, I persevered.

In my midtwenties, I was taking a course in art at a community college in the city where we were living, and I had created an organic batik sculpture. It was actually quite lovely. The teachers arranged for the students to have an art display and an art sale, and they asked me to be there, but I was very reluctant and extremely, painfully shy. So I said, "All right, I will set up a table and then hide." I had my paintings and my sculptures and all the things that I had created on display, and I hid from everyone.

There was a woman who came up to my table, and she was looking around, trying to figure out who had done these works. I thought I had better go up, and I did. This is one of those special moments. We were outdoors and a light from the afternoon sun was shining over on this woman's face. Her eyes were beautiful. She looked at the sculpture that I had created, and I could see that she loved it. There was no denial. She was not faking it. She was not doing it to please me or to be nice to me in any way, shape, or form. She was a stranger and she loved my sculpture. She fell in love with it.

That look on her face pierced my heart and my core belief that I was bad. I did not understand about core beliefs then. I did not even know what had happened to me. We lived quite a distance from that college, and on the way home, I started to weep in my car. "What is wrong with me? What is going on?" I asked myself. What came to me were these questions: "How can I be so bad when someone can love something that I have created? How can I be so bad?"

This is a clue about how to change those rigid and hard fundamentalist religious beliefs with no cracks. You have to have something that you cannot deny, that goes against your core beliefs and tells you that they are no longer the truth. It is like when it was believed that Earth was flat and people were killed for questioning that belief — that lasted until there was absolute, ultimate proof that Earth was not flat, and then people finally had to give up on their previous ideas.

Well, that kind woman's response to my sculpture cracked my core beliefs. I started to challenge my core beliefs, and that is how it happened. You have to have emotion with this, not just intellect. Your heart has to be involved with shifting your core beliefs. Compassion and love are also important. I somewhat understood the process I was going through, and it felt like such a relief. So that hopefully helps you to understand what it is that you are looking at with core beliefs. If you have healthy core beliefs, that is a blessing.

Replacing Your Cracked Core Beliefs with Correct New Ideas

The other part of shifting your core beliefs is that once you start to open and release the negative core beliefs, you have to replace them with something. You cannot just leave a vacuum. You have to have a foundation for your personality — you have to. It cannot just be, "I am nothing." The correct core beliefs have to come in. Up to that point, when my core belief was cracked, I had encountered many people outside of my family who liked me and who gave me positive feedback. But guess what my core belief said about that? "Oh, they do not know me," it told me. "They are just being nice because they are scared of me, and they know I am bad." I found one way or another to minimize, deny, or reject what was being given to me from so many of the people around me.

At that point, I began to challenge myself to accept what these people told me. I began to fill the vacuum with new feedback from people I trusted — not everybody, but the people whose mirrors I thought were balanced and healthy. So when I looked in and they said, "You are a pretty good artist," I would thank them instead of responding, "That is nothing." Or if they said, "That is a nice dress," I would say, "Thank you," rather than "this old thing?" Or if they said, "You look really pretty today," I wouldn't ask "Me?" No, I would say, "Thank you." So you can begin to take in the positive comments and begin to loosen up the knots. these things can be changed. Are there any questions about that?

How did your family react when you first began to make this change?

That was an interesting process. I had to detach from my family for quite a while in order to work on myself because they were still toxic to me, although they were unconscious about it. Especially when David and I moved from Ohio to Arizona, I did not see my family for over twenty years, with the exception of my brother. I needed that time for healing because I knew that I was still somewhat susceptible and vulnerable to their projections on me. I understood at this point that it had nothing to do with me, but it still hurt, so I needed that distance and that separation, because David and I had a lot of work we had to do. About four years after moving to Arizona, as I was still processing on my own personal issues, I had this transcendent moment when I truly understood how it was that my family of origin came to be the way they were. With that understanding came a lot of forgiveness and compassion for them. I did not trust them, but I felt overwhelming compassion and understanding.

My parents were adolescents in Germany during World War II. Someone arranged the marriage of my grandmother when she was young. This was my mother's mother. She had to marry the man her family chose for her instead of the one she had chosen. Women were not considered of much value, or at least it was not appreciated that they could be powerful, especially not in my family.

My mother was a sensitive and talented woman growing up in World War II-era Germany. She was in eastern Germany when the Russians invaded. She was a teenager, and my grandparents put her up in the attic so that she would not be raped. She was up there for six months. I think that affected her brain.

She had this female child — me — who did not have any of these experiences. I had a lot of liberty and freedom, and she was jealous. I could see all that; it was just all so clear to me. I forgave her. It was a burden lifted from me. When you truly forgive someone, it heals you. I do not know what it does to the people you are forgiving, if it can be powerful for them or not, but it is powerful for you personally.

After that experience — and again I had a lot of emotions that went with that — I felt very at peace. My parents at that point had become frightened of me because I had become too assertive and outspoken. I did not put up with garbage from them anymore. When they abused me, I said, "Do not do that. I do not like that. Stop it." They did not even talk to me, because they did not know what to say. If it was not abuse, what could they say? So they did not call me. I would send them Christmas cards and birthday cards, and that is about the level of connection we had.

All of a sudden, two weeks after that forgiveness and compassion episode, I got a call from my parents. David answered the phone and said, "Your mum and dad are on the phone."

I asked, "Did somebody die?"

He said, "I don't think so."

I got on the line and heard the oddest thing. My father and mother said, "We are so sorry. We were wrong about you. You are really a good person."

I thought, "Oh, my God! This forgiveness stuff really works." It shifted the energy. Whatever issues we had were completely redone. I was ready to receive their apology, and I said, "Thank you for that." Before, I would have still been angry with them. If they had said, "We are sorry," at any earlier point, I would have said: "Screw you. You messed up. Forget it. I have nothing to do with you." But now I had shifted, and I said, "Thank you. I appreciate that."

My mother died several years ago. Very shortly before her death, pushy Vywamus told me, "I think you should go visit your family."

I said, "Why? Why should I go?" It scared me a little bit, because even though they had apologized, I still did not trust them. I felt vulnerable that they might still attack me, and I did not want to go through that. Vywamus encouraged me and David encouraged me, so we took a road trip from Arizona to Ohio and went to visit them. Of course, after twenty years, my mother was very frail; she was very ill at that time. She was not that mean, snotty, bitchy woman she had been. She was just a frail old lady.

We walked in and right away she said, "Gudrun, I would like to speak with you." I think the whole family was tense because they kept trying to avoid a conversation happening between us. David intervened and said, "Let them talk." My mother took me in the kitchen, sat down, and told me the story of her life. She said, "I am asking you to forgive me because I could not love you."

I told her, "I have already forgiven you." She visibly slumped. I think she had love for me, but it was still a challenge for her.

Were you the only daughter?

I have a younger sister. I was eighteen when my sister was born.

Did your mum have a different reaction to her?

Yes, that was a wholly different scenario. My sister was overindulged, and she turned into a drug addict. When my mother passed away, my sister went into recovery, and she has been clean and doing very well ever since. My father and my sister are very open to the work that David and I are doing; my brother is not. My father has read all of our books. He is very interested in what we are doing. I think he asks himself, "Who is this child I raised?" because he had no clue during my childhood. He was never there with me, he did not protect me, and he did not know who I was. It is an interesting process. He is also respectful of David. When I first met and married David, even though they did not care about me, they did not want me to marry a Jewish man. Of course, that has all changed. Do you have any questions about core beliefs for yourself, or is there any way that I can help you personally?

I want to thank you very much for saying this.

You are welcome. It takes courage to look at your core beliefs. It is like digging in your sewer. You do not want anybody to know about that. You do not want to look at that.

We have to look at these things.

This is our inner sewer. I think some of the new spiritual technologies can be used to uncover your core beliefs, shine light on them, and heal them or crack them open. Take your core beliefs into a healing chamber on the Athena starship like we did. I think all of you probably have a sense of what your core beliefs are. If you have a positive core belief, that is wonderful. I was thinking last night about the question, "What is my core belief at this point?" And it is something like: "I am important" or "I am precious." Certainly, it is a lot different than "I am bad, evil bad." That is what I believed.

Working with Your Inner Child

I do artwork with my left hand. I drew a picture of myself as a girl smiling, with a huge Sun in one corner and many rays coming down. It was a profound moment.

Should you still be struggling with negative core beliefs, one of the things you can do to help this process is to find a picture of yourself as a youngster — a picture that you have a connection with, that you resonate with, that you feel touched by. Put that picture up in your house, and then talk to it kindly. Those of you who have children or have been around children know that most children are so precious, so beautiful, and so dear. When you look at yourself, look for that beauty and begin to see the precious child that you were. Begin to send that compassion through time.

As you know, time is irrelevant to love. Love goes through all things. Your love can touch that wounded child who you were, that child you are still carrying inside. I have a picture of myself as a child in my office. I am very cute in this picture, but I look worried. There are days I do not want to work, and I know that my inner child wants to stay home to play. When I go to work, I thank her and say, "We are going to have some fun today because we are going to see so and so." I can just feel myself being lifted up. "Oh, yes. I like that person a lot, okay," my inner child responds. Your work with your drawing of your inner child is interesting. And you are working more from the right side of your brain, which does not have words.

David: I want to say one thing about ascension work. Gudrun was talking about the core beliefs in her journey. We both feel it is important for lightworkers to clear their inner issues. Over the years, we have seen many people who have done lightwork with Juliano and others but did not do this other work, and they still have major issues of self. We both feel that this work is important. That is why we include it in the workshops, because we want to encourage people to finish their life lessons.

Gudrun: There are spiritual leaders in this time who have not done this work, and they tend to get lost in their egos. You can see that. It is a sad thing. I think that this still has to do with the messages in our culture about the emotional body. It is like a weakness to have "negative emotions." Our culture says that you should be this evolved being, and you should overcome all of your emotional issues just by intent. The child within you has a different agenda. "Hang on. I am hurt," it says. "I need someone to pay attention to me. Do not push me aside." When you attend to that wounded self, you begin to come into balance, and you actually do heal. The child within you can begin to become joyful and anticipate wonderful things. Even in this time, on this planet, we can have fun.

The inner child needs to speak, needs to say something.

Those of you who have children or have been around children know that if they need your attention and you do not give it to them, what do they do? They insist and they get louder and louder and louder. And if you still don't pay attention to them, they sometimes act out — or like some of you, they get depressed and withdrawn.

I have realized that on many occasions. And adults sometimes react in the same way.

Those of us with exquisite sensitivity tend not to want to burden other people with our emotions. We think that they cannot cope with these feelings, so we internalize them. We have panic attacks, depression, anxiety, and all kinds of things.

CHAPTER FOUR

Hypnotic Regression: An Explanation of Life between Lives in a State of Trance

Gudrun Miller

Those of you who have heard me speak before know that I do hypnotic regressions, and I would like to explain a little bit about that and about past lives and the time in between lives. The transition is not that long. It has only been in the past twenty years or so that people have realized that you can regress someone into the astral plane, into the in-between-lives time, and into the fourth dimension, where you can actually meet your guides, your soul family, and the council of wise beings that evaluates your life and makes recommendations for a future life.

Visiting the In-Between-Lives Time

When you are in the in-between-lives time state, you can go into a chamber of review for your next incarnation, where you can look at several possibilities of lifetimes and then choose the one that is more appropriate for you. Apparently that experience can be quite vivid; you can actually feel as you were living through these possible liftetimes. I think that is where déjà vu comes in a lot, because when we have the experience of choosing our lifetimes, we have already seen some of the events and experiences that we will have.

In the fourth dimension, when you access that state in that way, you also get to look at what you do when you are in the fourth dimension. Apparently we do many things in the in-between-lives time, and we do not always reincarnate right away. We may travel to other star systems, we may teach, or we may just kind of languish for a while because we are tired. So there are any number of things we may do. We may have recreation; we may do fun things.

How does the hypnotic regression work that I do evolve? I offer to do that work with my subjects. I offer to take them through this lifetime, to regress into the womb, to go to the most immediate past life, and then to go into the fourth dimension. But I think because I work primarily with starseeds it does not always turn out that way.

Many of my subjects choose an alternative. They say, "Let's go to the lifetime that provides me the most healing in this life. Let's go to the lifetime that might be causing a blockage or an obstacle in my current life that I am struggling with and am not aware of." If we do that, we usually do not go to the most immediate past life. We may go very far away; we may end up in a lifetime thousands of years ago. And from that place, it is much harder to access the in-between-lives time state, because it is pretty remote.

You remember this time even though you were in your subconscious state and approaching the supraconscious state while you were there. It is not as relevant at that point, but many other issues come up, such as your soul journey, the lessons that you have been challenged with throughout your incarnations, and possibly even the lesson that you are dealing with now and the reason why you came to Earth. My understanding of doing this work is that I am not in charge; my subject's higher self is in charge and so are my subject's guides and teachers. I just happen to be the facilitator of whatever process has to happen.

Integrating Lessons from Previous Lifetimes

A Group of Forty member came to me, and she had a couple of problems. One she described in this way: "I feel that a part of me is numb, and no matter what work I have done in this life, I have not been able to find out what it is that makes me feel dull." She could not get through that. There was another issue, but I cannot think of what it was. Anyway, my subject said, "Let's go to the lifetime that is causing my block."

In regressing through her present life, what this woman came up with was that she grew up in a ranching family. They had raised cattle for slaughter in the Midwest, in the central part of the United States, and it was quite a conservative and fundamentalist Christian area. She was a very gifted starseed looking around at her situation. When she went to first grade as a seven-year-old, she realized that she had to dull herself, that she had to dumb herself down so that she would not be the object of ridicule and could survive her childhood in the school. So that is what she did. In the regression I did with her, she found that out and she was able to shift that around. She also remembered that she used to build spaceships out of tractor tires and old tractor parts, and she would spend hours doing this. She crawled down inside the tires and spent hours traveling the galaxies in her spacecraft. That was interesting for her.

When she went to a past life, she was a person who was in the Civil War in the United States. I think that must have been pretty traumatic. She was a young man who witnessed his family being slaughtered by the Union, the North, and it caused such rage that he lost his soul connection and was killed pretty much immediately afterward. The lesson for him here was that by not regulating his emotions, by giving into that extreme rage, he was ready to go shoot all the soldiers he found; he was ready to kill even though he did not want to kill. But he was shot before he could kill anybody, and he would have had a lot of karma, so he realized something: "Well, I have to regulate my emotional body." When we pulled my subject out of that life, she was able to integrate that lifetime and understand what the lesson in it was.

Immediately following this, one of her main guides came and took her to more of a fifth-dimensional healing facility where she was to undergo an implant of higher-dimensional energy. This was the other issue: She was doing massage and healing work, and she felt blocked in her ability to go much further. Her teacher said that, in the physical structure she had moved into, she was not able to accelerate the energy of that structure at that point in her life. And that is why she had told me three years prior to the regression, "I want to do this with you." And she kept waiting, waiting, and waiting, until all of a sudden she called me and she told me, "I am ready." And so she came to my town and we did this.

Her guides said that she had to wait until that point to activate her system to receive higher light. Her structure was not ready, and we had talked about her physical structure needing to be able to vibrate at a higher rate to hold more light. So she was ready for that, and then they told her it would take from six months to a year to integrate that. So she spent a lot of time having that done, and I was just sitting there with her silently. It was clear that she was busy in her deep trance, and I was checking with her and making sure it was still working.

So that is what can happen. It is an interesting process. It seems to be another way to do some very profound healing. Most of my clients, my subjects, are able to connect with their higher selves when they have these experiences, and then their higher selves speak through them. And I find it fascinating, because I can get so much information from them. That is the brief version of my long lecture.

Do you do shorter sessions?

I have done that. It is hard on me because it is intense. I must shift into a very high frequency to do it, and there can be some profound information that comes through that I have to work with. I work with you on balancing your spiritual experience, your emotional body, and your mental body. I am not that worried about your physical body if you are comfortable. But I have done that — not for the in-between-lives time but to connect with my clients' higher selves. I can do that within an hour or so.

So the longer sessions are better?

There is much more opportunity in longer sessions to do whatever has to be done and, again, I have no clue sometimes about what has to be done.

Extreme Trauma in a Previous Lifetime

One of my subjects was talking about a nuclear disaster, and it turned out she had been killed in Hiroshima. She had lost her husband, and she wanted to have a regression. She wanted to speak with him. She had some very profound spiritual experiences, but they were not all integrated for her. She could not make sense of why she would suddenly see Sanskrit written in the sky. "What is that?" she asked herself. And other things would seemingly just happen to her with no reason that she could figure out. So we did a regression through her lives.

She had a nice life actually, except for losing her husband early in her life. He had just recently died when she came to the regression. So we got into one of her past lives, and she found that although she was alive, she had no ability to see, move, or feel. She also had no memory of anything. She could not go backward or forward in that life. She was still just barely alive in her body after the bomb exploded in Hiroshima. All she could experience was a sort of a blue haze, and she got more and more distressed. I asked her move out of the body, and she did.

Then she immediately said that there were two "doctors" who came and wrapped her in a blanket to integrate all of her pieces. I thought, "Oh my gosh." I did not know at that time that she had been in a nuclear blast. "What possibly could have happened?" I wondered. She was distraught at that time, and she was getting more and more anxious, so I asked her to let me speak to one of the doctors and she agreed. I asked, "Did she die in a nuclear incident?" And she said immediately, "Hiroshima." So I pulled her out of that session pretty quickly because it was clear that it was just causing more and more stress.

I asked permission of her teacher to ask Vywamus, through David, what had happened. And later on, Vywamus said that she chose to have that experience because she is a highly advanced spiritual being here on Earth, and she was involved in Atlantis. She was a scientist in Atlantis and, out of naïveté, she had contributed her gifts and intelligence to the destruction of Atlantis. She had enough soul advancement and soul knowledge to know that she had to agree to be involved in Hiroshima to balance that karma. And she could manage that because she was such an advanced soul being that it would not cause soul destruction for her, so she would still have aspects of herself. That is why she had those strange spiritual experiences.

She actually learned Sanskrit. She said, "I have no clue why I needed to do that," but she knows how to read, speak, and write Sanskrit. We did a couple more sessions in which we regressed to her very, very early experiences as an incarnated being. She was actually a tree once. She came in very, very early as a being in a tree, and she enjoyed that very much. She has an affinity for trees to this day. She came in as a reptile — that was interesting! Then she was a highly advanced medicine woman. It almost sounded like she was living in the fifth and third dimensions together. She was taught by an old medicine woman who was a weaver, and what they wove was the fabric of reality of the third dimension. So it kind of reminds me of the Hopi. She is a weaver now.

She is a very interesting person. She is still working to fill in that gap that the nuclear devastation caused for her. There is nothing there; it is gone. She got some information from David that she had been a man in that life, a weaver who had two children, and that is all she knows. She is attempting to integrate all of that and become healed and whole again.

Planetary Healing

Juliano and the Arcturians

Greetings, I am Juliano. We are the Arcturians. The first principal of planetary healing I want to talk about has to do with the concept of the work that you are doing using the etheric crystals, which is based on principles of remote healing. Remote healing is based on the concept that you can access universal energy and universal light and bring them from a distance into a healing experience for the participant. The idea of remote healing also has to do with the receptivity of the subject and the ability of the healer to send powerful thought energy to that person.

The Energies of the Etheric Crystals and the Omega Light

Now, in the method we are using and suggesting, the thought energy has to be amplified. I think that you are all clear on the idea that the arcan energy, which is the measurement of the thought power, is amplified through the etheric crystals. So the principal of amplification of thought is an important one, but let's be clear that we are talking about a remote healing accessing universal energies that are very powerful. And when you are using the etheric crystals, I think that it's always important to realize you are connecting with the Arcturian etheric crystal in the crystal lake, and that this crystal has the ability to access universal light and universal healing powers that are quite extensive.

The original etheric crystal in the crystal lake is the base of the power of all twelve of the etheric crystals. Remember that we have said that each of the twelve etheric crystals is an etheric duplicate of the main crystal. Etheric duplicates are almost 99 percent pure copies of the original. But even in the computer world, you know that when you make a disk, and then make another copy and another copy, sometimes there is a lessening of the power. This lessening of power is perhaps insignificant for the purposes that you are putting it to in healing, but I want to point out that the original etheric crystal in the crystal lake is able to gather an energy that it is quite extensive and quite broad — perhaps even more broad than the energies and light of the twelve etheric crystals we have downloaded on Earth. So sometimes, in particularly difficult situations, it is helpful to bring down and connect with the first etheric crystal — by that, I mean the Arcturian etheric crystal — and use it as one of three or four crystals, or at least find ways of connecting with it, because you want to bring down fifth-dimensional energy.

The other important point that I want to mention is the fact that this energy you are seeking in remote healing is an omega-type energy; it is a quantum-type energy. And let us just say a little bit more about the omega light and quantum energy, because quantum energy and quantum healing are based on concepts that transcend the third dimension.

The third dimension is a system based on Newtonian logic, for the most part. And when I say "Newtonian logic," I mean the system of energy, the thought processes, and the logic that are all now being used for the culture of the third dimension. So when you are doing quantum healing and when you are doing etheric remote healing, you are looking for energy and light that transcend regular logic, because regular logic will say that you have this tumor or that you have this condition and that you must follow this protocol in order for this to work. But many times that protocol does not work; many times that protocol is not powerful enough to create the energy necessary for transcendent healing.

I want you to understand that what you are working with here in doing this type of healing is transcending energy, energy that transcends logic and the normal protocol that you see in the third dimension. This is why I often say that when you are doing this remote healing and using the etheric crystals, you are calling on the omega light. The omega light a fifth-dimensional light; it is a light that comes from beyond the confines of the third dimension, and it is a light that can be accelerated even more through the etheric crystals.

Earth's Response to the Dangers of Nuclear Energy

I want to point out that the twelve etheric crystals we have downloaded on Earth are creating a new web, a new meridian system, if you will. So what is the best way for you to communicate with Earth and the Inner Earth so that the feedback loop system can be brought into a somewhat better balance? I would say that we should also look at the interaction of the Planetary Tree of Life as a representation of the energy communication systems of Earth and the feedback loop system. The feedback loop system is pictured in the Planetary Tree of Life. The Planetary Tree of Life and the Tree of Life itself are such complicated glyphs, which is a fancy word for paradigms, which are metaphorical symbols.

Earth is able to tolerate a certain amount of nuclear energy. Earth is able to tolerate certain overstimulation brought on by nuclear energy, even though this nuclear energy itself is life-killing and the resulting radiation is also life-killing. From that aspect, we can say that Earth is very compassionate, and if you look at the Planetary Tree of Life, you will see that there is a special sphere for compassion and understanding. And you can say, "Well, okay, Earth understands that humankind wants to play with native forces that are interdimensional, forces that unlock this powerful thing called the nuclear energy." So we will accept that.

But then Earth, the Inner Earth, and the feedback loop system have a limit. For example, the limit could be expressed like this: "You have continued and there is no movement toward lessening the amount of nuclear waste. There is no movement toward decreasing the input of radiation into Earth, so now it is time for judgment." And this might be a harsh way of looking at it, but judgment may be the tsunami; it may be the destruction of the Fukushima power plant. Then they will have to say, "Okay, that is the judgment. If you continue to use this energy, the Inner Earth, the feedback loop system, and the Spirit of Gaia are going to respond in this way."

So, in the Planetary Tree of Life and on Earth, you say, "Okay, which sphere is represented by compassion? Which sphere is represented by judgment?" Then you bring those two spheres up, you use the crystals from them, and you can also use the crystal on the top of the Planetary Tree of Life. The point that I am trying to make as clear as possible is that the way of communicating with the Inner Earth, the way of communicating with Earth's feedback loop system, has been presented to you in the Planetary Tree of Life cards and diagram. Many people do not realize this, but that is a way of communicating, because the feedback loop system is contained — metaphorically, but also in an Earth way — in these etheric crystals.

We want you to begin to more extensively understand and use the Planetary Tree of Life system and the cards. And we want you to use them as a way of communicating with the Inner Earth, with the cosmos, and with Earth's feedback loop system. This Tree of Life not only represents a way of communicating with Inner Earth; it represents a way of communicating with the cosmos, and you can use the Tree of Life system to understand what is going on now on Earth and in terms of planetary changes, for example.

First, I want to make one correction. This is a transcended ley line system, a transcended meridian system. In other words, the original meridian system is still intact, although it is blocked in many places. So perhaps it is not correct to say it is still intact, but it is there. This is not necessarily the new ley line system, but it is a transcended ley line system that can get into the whole structure. In other words, this is like a shortcut. The reason I want to use a shortcut is because there are complications in Earth's ley line system. For example, let us say that there are important ley lines in Egypt or an important part of the ley line system is in Syria or Tunisia, and those countries are going through a lot of upheaval. It might not be easy for people to travel, but these twelve systems that we have downloaded all have the ability to be easily accessed by starseeds.

Connecting the Energy of Fifth-Dimensional Planets to Earth

There is a way to achieve communication with the other fifth-dimensional planets. There is a way to travel in the Inner Earth and seek the energies of those places. But I also want to point out the complexity of this process. It is difficult to visualize the Inner Earth because of the faintness of the vibrational energy field emitted from it. To communicate telepathically with the other dimension in the Inner Earth requires a certain amplification of thoughts.

The idea that we are using to promote the connections with the Inner Earth, Era, Alano, and other cities on these other fifth-dimensional planets is to first focus on using the planetary cities of light as an energetic basis for your work. We introduced the concept, and we are recommending that planetary sister cities of light be identified. The idea is that any planetary city of light that is developed now could have a sister city of light on another fifth-dimensional planet. Because it may be difficult to get the names on the cities of the planet, you can say that such and such city of light is identified with the cities of light in the Pleiades or with the cities of light in Alano.

This is a way of connecting the inner energies of fifth-dimensional planets with the inner energies of Earth. And these inner energies are the connections to the inner energies found in the planetary cities of light. Some people have a powerful connection with the Inner Earth, and the Inner Earth has a core resonant frequency that is vibrating with the other core resonant frequencies on other higher planets.

Those other higher planetary systems are concurrently sending vibrations to Earth. The issue for Earth now is that much of its energy is being focused on stabilization. Many people do not realize how much of the whole system on Earth is destabilized and how much of the other fifth-dimensional energy and light from these other planetary systems of light — such as the Pleiades, Arcturus, and Alano — is being used for stabilization. But a good part of higher energy from other planetary systems is also going to be used to raise Earth's vibration and bring Earth into the fifth dimension.

I would say that the Native Americans such as Chief White Eagle and others used the medicine wheel as a way of communicating with the Inner Earth. And the wheel is also a glyph; it is also a paradigm for accessing fifth-dimensional energy. In essence, the center of the wheel can go to the center of Earth and the Inner Earth.

Working with Earth's Feedback Loop System

The way of communication in the feedback loop system goes something like this: The Earth feedback loop system can respond to humanity. That is the number-one point that everyone must realize. Earth's feedback loop system is seeking a new homeostasis, and it is clear that all of the different things that have happened in terms of the pollution and blockages of Earth's meridian systems, deforestation, and so forth have created a need for a new homeostasis.

The problem is that the new homeostasis may not be to the highest benefit of humanity. When you are looking at the feedback loop system, you are asking, "Well, what other information or support does the feedback loop system need in order to balance, in order to hold the current homeostasis?" But actually, you do not even want the current homeostasis, because the current homeostasis is already creating a lot of extreme patterns that are very difficult for humanity to manage.

We must investigate what type of homeostasis we want Earth's feedback loop system to create and what it should be based on. Do we want a feedback loop system based on the 1950s or based on the 1990s? I think that in terms of how you want to work with Earth's feedback loop system, you have to have a paradigm or a model of when Earth's feedback loop system was operating at an optimal level that was in a good balance for humankind.

The second thing to consider is that if you wish to influence Earth's feedback loop system, are you willing to work on it on a global level, or do you want to work on an individual area, or both? I want to recommend that you work on both levels, because actually you have to consider that any overabundance of one type of weather is counterbalancing weather in another part of Earth. So, if you maybe feel Oregon has too much rain, you would want to say, "Let us rebalance this so that Oregon does not have so much rain." But where do you want to distribute it? Do you want it distributed in a way that it is helpful to the Southwest?

The problem is that most people do not have the capacity to balance everything, even if they are using computers. You would have to use a giant computer and ask it, "Okay, if you brought this water down to Arizona, then how is that going to affect China?" When you work with Earth's feedback loop system, your input must not only say that you wish to have this one thing happen, but also that you wish for the rest of the energy on Earth to be balanced for the highest good and in the least destructive way for humanity.

In essence, you are talking to Earth using specific instructions because your mind would not be able to grasp all of the complexities. You are saying that you would like A to happen in this area, and you would like this to be balanced perhaps in the way it was in the 1960s, but you realize that there has to be some compensation, so you would like for this compensation be balanced in a way that is equally advantageous for everyone involved. And it may come back that only a lessening of the energies can be allowed. Let us say that you want all of the rain and the storms to stop, but maybe the storms will only be 50 percent of what they are now.

So I would say that the best way to communicate your wishes is through talking to Earth, and one of the best ways to do this is through the medicine wheel, because this talking represents a type of telepathic communication with Earth's feedback loop system. You are acknowledging that Earth's feedback loop system can receive your messages, that it is receptive to them, and that your messages can thus influence Earth. But you want to state those messages in the highest way and using the highest amount of arcan energy possible, because Earth is a magnificent planet, a huge planet. Maybe it is not huge in terms of comparison to other planets in the galaxy, but it is huge in terms of having so many places that are inhabitable land masses. Therefore, this only adds to the complexity of the whole situation.

It is a great honor for everyone to be involved in planetary healing, and it is a really sacred task. I think that the right approach is also important. The right approach is to look at this as a sacred task that we approach from the sacred sites. These do not necessarily have to be just the sites of the twelve etheric crystals; they could be any sacred site on the planet. We want you to ensure that Earth's energies are approached from the highest vibration that humankind can possibly bring together. We have tried to create as many planetary cities of light as possible, and we know that those cities are now sacred places and sacred areas. The sites of the twelve etheric crystals are also sacred areas now with Arcturian energy, but they are not the only sacred areas on Earth. I think that this is another important issue.

Personal Healing through the Tree of Life and Universal Energy

On the subject of personal healing, I am also recommending that we work with the Tree of Life. There are ascended masters working in each sphere of the Tree of Life to create healing in the body. At this point, I want to say that the Planetary Tree of Life is the model for planetary healing and communication with Earth's feedback loop system. The Tree of Life can also be a model for personal healing.

We have reached the point in working with these concepts where, if there were physical problems in the nervous system, in the neurogenital system, or in the heart system, there would be certain guides assigned to certain parts of the body and aspects of the Planetary Tree of Life, and they would be able to help you work on personal healing. You could work with the sphere in the Tree of Life that is designated for that particular system, and you could also work with the guide who is there to work with you and others who need the healing energy from that system. If you perform personal healing using this approach, you will increase your abilities, because this approach focuses on tapping into universal sources of energy and universal sources of light.

When you are working with universal energy, you should be aware that there are other universal planetary systems that you can connect with. That is why you might want to think, "Okay, I want to connect with the healing energy of Arcturus." When you are doing planetary healing or even when you are doing personal healing, I am very much in favor of you visualizing the star Arcturus — which is representative of the planetary fifth-dimensional energy and light — coming into your crown chakra as part of the healing energies. We have personal temple healers who are working with you, and when you connect with the star Arcturus in your mind and your crown chakra, this helps the energy from those guides and teachers to come down into your mind. Then your mind is able to transmit more powerful healing thought with more arcan power. You can also ask the person being healed to connect his or her crown chakra with the star system of Arcturus in addition to all of this. Rest assured that you are developing new groundwork, a new foundation for healing thought structures on the planet.

Working with the Subconscious of Inner Earth

The Inner Earth, because it exists on several planes, does not just exist on the physical plane, and our idea for the Inner Earth also revolves around the subconscious, the unconscious, and the universal unconscious of the planet. So the Inner Earth is metaphorically and etherically representative of a subconscious energy. And the subconscious energy from the Inner Earth needs to be shifted because of the thoughts of millions of people and the energy they have. I am referring in a general way to the energies of destruction, the energies of war, and the energies of the end times — all these types of thought structures have been deposited in the Inner Earth.

So high-level planetary healing also works with the universal Inner Earth subconscious, and that means that we have to find a way of downloading new subconscious patterns into the Inner Earth. That is a whole other lecture, but it is something that we introduced to the channel many years ago in his first book, *Connecting with the Arcturians*. If Earth is a living spirit, which it is, it does have some parallels to the mind of humanity. The mind of humanity is controlled by the subconscious. One way of accessing the feedback loop system is from the subconscious of Earth. When you want to change your own behavior, you have to change your subconscious patterns. This rule also implies to planetary change. The subconscious energy of the planet must be changed.

It is a huge step forward to bring awareness of Earth's feedback loop system to Earth itself. In one sense, I can say that Earth may not yet be aware of its feedback loop system. Earth is like you — unless you study, you do not know you have a feedback loop system, that you have a nervous system, and that 90 percent of your body is unconscious in its reactions. Once you become conscious of those things, you may then have an opportunity to shift them.

I am Juliano. We are the Arcturians. Good day.

Glossary

2012 alignment
This is a time when Earth goes into alignment with the center of the Milky Way Galaxy. This time is referred to in the Mayan calendar, and prophecies were made for this date. The Maya believed that Earth would come into alignment with the center of the galaxy on December 21, 2012. Some have interpreted the statements as marking the end of the world. Others say that this alignment represents the transformation of the world. One view is that our world will be born again on December 21, 2012. John Major Jenkins, in *Maya Cosmogenesis 2012,* interpreted the Mayan vision of this alignment in 2012 as a union of the Cosmic Mother, or the Milky Way, with the Father, represented as the Sun of the December solstice.

The Arcturian stargate
This is a multidimensional portal into other higher realms. It is very close to the Arcturus star system and is overseen by the Arcturians. This powerful passage point requires that earthlings who wish to pass through it must complete all lessons and Earth incarnations associated with the third-dimensional experience. It serves as a gateway to the fifth dimension. New soul assignments are given there, and souls can then be sent to many different higher realms throughout the galaxy and universe.

Arcturus
This is the brightest star in the constellation Boötes, also known as the Herdsman. This is one of the oldest recorded constellations. Arcturus is also the fourth-brightest star seen from Earth. It is a giant star, about twenty-five times the diameter of the Sun and 100 times as luminous. It is a relatively close neighbor of ours, approximately forty light-years from Earth. High up in the sky in the late

spring and early summer, Arcturus is the first star you see after sunset. You can find Arcturus easily if you follow the Big Dipper's handle away from the bowl.

Ascension

This is a point of transformation reached through the integration of the physical, emotional, mental, and spiritual selves. The unification of the bodies allows one to transcend the limits of the third dimension and move into a higher realm. Ascension has been compared to what is called the Rapture in Christian theology. It has also been defined as a spiritual acceleration of consciousness that allows the soul to return to the higher realms, thus freeing it from the cycle of karma and rebirth.

Biorelativity

Biorelativity focuses on group thoughts and working together telepathically to send healing energy to our planet. The practice is similar to the concept of group prayer in which people send positive thoughts to change the outcome of an event. In biorelativity exercises, groups of starseeds around the planet send healing thoughts to specific areas in the world. Storms, hurricanes, and even earthquakes can potentially be averted, deterred, or lessened in strength so that minimal damage is inflicted.

The Arcturians point out that on higher planetary systems, groups continually interact telepathically with their planet to ensure maximum harmony between planetary inhabitants and planetary forces. An example of biorelativity on Earth is Native Americans praying to Earth as a group, often asking for rain. In biorelativity exercises, we now have the powerful advantage of connecting globally with many different starseeds, uniting telepathically for the healing of Earth.

Central Sun

This is the spiritual and etheric center of our galaxy, located in the center of the Milky Way. A high spiritual energy is emitted from this area. Earth is coming into a direct alignment with the Central Sun in the year 2012. All star clusters, nebulae, and galaxies contain a nucleus at their center. Even the grand universe itself has a Great Central Sun at the center of its structure. The Great Central Sun of the Milky Way Galaxy provides life-giving energy to the entire galaxy.

Crystal temple

This is an etheric temple in the fifth dimension that has been made available for our use by the Arcturians. The crystal temple contains a lake more than one mile in diameter that houses a huge crystal half the size of the lake itself. The entire lake and surrounding area is encompassed by a huge glass dome, allowing visitors to view the stars.

Etheric crystals

These are invisible crystals containing fifth-dimensional energy that have been sent to Earth by the Arcturians. The purpose of these etheric crystals is to provide healing energies to Earth's meridians. To date, twelve etheric crystals have been downloaded. Here is a summary of the process and role each crystal plays in Earth's healing.

1. **Lago Puelo in Argentina**

    This is the home of the first crystal to be brought down to Earth. The Lago Puelo crystal holds the primordial energy for the whole planet. It is an energy of initiation and connection.

2. **Grose Valley in the Blue Mountains National Park of Australia**

    The Grose Valley crystal connects with the Rainbow Serpent, which is the feminine goddess energy of Mother Gaia and an area of great significance to the aborigines of Australia.

3. **Lake Moraine in Canada**

    This crystal contains the quantum-etheric energy-activation light that can bypass the normal laws of linear time/space and cause/effect.

4. **Lake Constance in the Bodensee in Germany**

    This crystal provides new information, new codes, new structures, and new dynamics for Earth's ley lines and allows us access to new information.

5. **Volcán Poás in Costa Rica**

    This crystal is linked to the great attractor force, that which pushes and pulls the galaxies in different directions. It also helps attract and discharge blocked energy in Earth's energy channels. One example of this is the way it has modified the Ring of Fire to create balance in that area.

6. **Mount Shasta in California in the United States**

   The combination of this crystal, the Galactic Kachina, and the imprint of the stargate means that Mount Shasta has become a powerful ascension point. It also gives us an easy connection to our souls, our soul power, and our soul mission.

7. **Lake Taupo in New Zealand**

   Number seven is a symbol of good luck and good fortune, and it brings wealth and prosperity. This crystal is representative of that wealth and prosperity and is a great attracting force of energy for those who work with it. It is also a reaffirmation of the spiritual strength and power of the native peoples on Earth and will help to reawaken them to their mission.

8. **Barrancas del Cobre in Mexico**

   The area where the eighth crystal resides is also known as Copper Canyon. This crystal gives us a new link to Arcturian energy, a link where we can connect with the moon-planet Alano and the fifth-dimensional master named Alano who resides there. This crystal also carries the special energy of shimmering, enabling us to move ourselves or objects into another dimension.

9. **Montserrat near Barcelona in Spain**

   This magnificent place is a holy site. Juliano tells us it is mostly free from wars and polarization. The ninth crystal, which was brought here recently, has a powerful, sacred, and holy energy. This crystal was downloaded to work with holy sacred light and will help the sites of the other crystals become truly sacred energy sites.

10. **Mount Fuji in Japan**

    This crystal holds the energy of life forces from Lemuria, which have now been unlocked by its arrival. It is an ancient crystal containing great secrets of light and ancient knowledge of the planet. It has a connection with the ancient grandmothers and grandfathers.

11. **Istanbul in Turkey**

    This crystal is the seat of hidden knowledge revealed.

12. Serra da Bocaina in Brazil

This crystal represents the interaction between the third and fifth dimensions.

Groups of Forty

This is a concept of group consciousness suggested by the Arcturians for our use in the ascension process. According to the Arcturians, forty is a spiritually powerful number. The Arcturians emphasize the value and power of joining together in groups. A Group of Forty consists of forty different members who focus on meditating together at a given time each month. Group interactions and yearly physical meetings are recommended. Members agree to assist each other in their spiritual development.

The Arcturians have asked us to organize forty Groups of Forty. These groups will assist in the healing of Earth and provide a foundation for the individual members' ascension. David Miller has been working with the energies of the ascension for more than fifteen years, and the Arcturians asked him to set up these Groups of Forty. These groups have been meeting for fifteen years now and have drawn members from all over the United States and Canada, as well as Australia and Germany. Because of the demand for membership, David was instructed to begin new groups. A second, third, and fourth group met. Now there are members around the world.

New groups are starting, and they will meet in meditation once a month wherever the members are located. At a specific hour during the meditation time, David channels messages from the Arcturians for all group members. A monthly newsletter is sent out with a transcription of that month's channeled lecture. A group coordinator arranges other group activities, such as healings and group meditations. Additionally, members are encouraged to meet other members — either by phone, by letter, or in person.

Meditations also include group healing, where all members of the group focus healing energy on one designated person in the group. Members who are the focus of this healing energy have reported profound healing experiences. All work is directed toward our transformation to higher consciousness through Earth healings and personal healings. As of this writing, we now have forty groups with more than 1,200 members around the world, each with a group coordinator. New groups are continuously being formed.

The Iskalia mirror

This is a fifth-dimensional mirror that is in the etheric area above Earth. The Iskalia mirror attracts and brings down higher light from the Central Sun so that greater enlightenment and healing energy can come to Earth.

Ring of ascension

This is an etheric halo of energy around Earth containing fifth-dimensional light from the ascended masters. This halo is supposed to aid Earth in her ability to ascend as a planet to the fifth dimension. Starseeds are meant to interact with this light through visualizations and meditations.

The Sacred Triangle

This is a term used by the Arcturians to denote a triangular symbol representing the unification of three powerful spiritual forces on Earth: the White Brotherhood/Sisterhood; the ascended masters, including Sananda/Jesus and the extraterrestrial higher-dimensional masters, such as the Arcturians and the Pleiadians; and the Native American ascended masters, such as Chief White Eagle. The unification of these spiritual forces will create the Sacred Triangle that will aid in the healing and ascension of Earth.

The Tree of Life

The Tree of Life is a galactic blueprint for the creation of this reality. It includes twelve energy codes placed in spheres in the shape of a tree. These codes are used for individual and planetary healing. The three spiritualities of the Sacred Triangle are included in the Tree of Life. The Tree of Life is not flat; it is multidimensional and holographic. It has twenty-two pathways of manifestation. The Tree of Life connects to the energy of the cosmos.

About the Author

David K. Miller's original spiritual study was the *Kaballah* and Jewish mysticism. He began trance channeling his Kaballistic guide and teacher, Nabur, on a camping trip at Sublime Point on the North Rim of the Grand Canyon in 1991. His focus in channeling includes ascension and integrating Jewish mysticism with soul development. He channels more than fifteen guides, including the Arcturians, Sananda, Mary, Ashtar, Archangel Michael, and Nabur, a Kaballistic rabbi.

David has published nine books and over fifty articles in both American and Australian magazines. He currently does phone readings and conducts workshops focusing on the concepts and techniques of ascension, healings, and psycho-spiritual issues while also working full time as a medical social worker. David resides with his wife, Gudrun, in Prescott, Arizona.

AUTHOR'S CONTACT INFORMATION:
David K. Miller
PO Box 4074
Prescott, AZ 86302
Email: davidmiller@groupofforty.com
Web: www.groupofforty.com

DAVID K. MILLER

Connecting with the Arcturians

Who is really out there? Where are we going? What are our choices? What has to be done to prepare for this event?

This book explains all of these questions in a way that we can easily understand. It explains what our relationships are to known extraterrestrial groups and what they are doing to help the Earth and her people in this crucial galactic moment in time.

$17⁰⁰

240 PP. SOFTCOVER
978-1891824-94-4

Teachings from the Sacred Triangle

David's second book explains how the Arcturian energy melds with that of the White Brother/Sisterhood and the Ascended Native American Masters to bring about planetary healing.

- The Sacred Triangle energy and the Sacred Codes of Ascension
- How to create a bridge to the fifth dimension
- What role you can play in the Sacred Triangle
- How sacred words from the *Kaballah* can assist you in your ascension work

$22⁰⁰

291 PP. SOFTCOVER
978-0971589-43-8

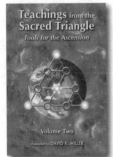

Teachings from the Sacred Triangle, Vol. 2

Good questions, intriguing answers. The teachings continue . . .

Your planet is at a dire crossroads from a physical standpoint, but from a spiritual standpoint, it is experiencing a great awakening. Never before have there been so many conscious lightworkers, awakened spiritual beings, and masters as there are on this planet now. A great sense of a spiritual harmony emanates from the many starseed groups, and there is also a new spiritual energy and force that is spreading throughout the planet.

$16⁹⁵

254 PP. SOFTCOVER
978-1891824-19-7

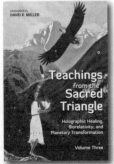

Teachings from the Sacred Triangle, Vol. 3

Chapters include:

Heart Chakra and the Energy of Love
Creating and Holding Thought Forms
The Nature of Energy Fields
Interacting with the Sacred Triangle
Multidimensional Crystal Healing Energy
Bilocating and Biorelativity

Healing Space-Time Rifts
Integration of Spirituality and Technology,
Space and Time Travel

$16⁹⁵

254 PP. SOFTCOVER
978-1891824-23-4

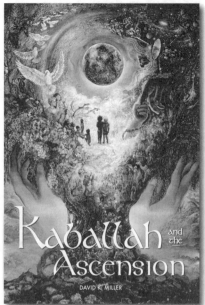

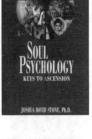

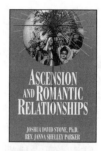
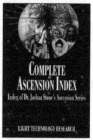

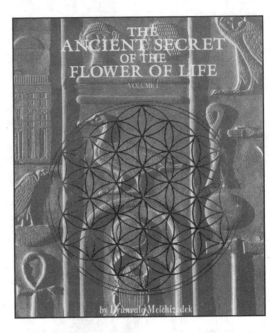

THE ANCIENT SECRET
OF THE FLOWER OF LIFE
VOLUME 2

- **The Unfolding of the Third Informational System**
- **Whispers from Our Ancient Heritage**
- **Unveiling the Mer-Ka-Ba Meditation**
- **Using Your Mer-Ka-Ba**
- **Connecting to the Levels of Self**
- **Two Cosmic Experiments**
- **What We May Expect in the Forthcoming Dimensional Shift**

$25^00 Softcover, 252 p.
ISBN 978-1-891824-21-0

The sacred Flower of Life pattern, the primary geometric generator of all physical form, is explored in even more depth in this volume, the second half of the famed Flower of Life workshop. The proportions of the human body, the nuances of human consciousness, the sizes and distances of the stars, planets, and moons, and even the creations of humankind, are all shown to reflect their origins in this beautiful and divine image. Through an intricate and detailed geometrical mapping, Drunvalo Melchizedek shows how the seemingly simple design of the Flower of Life contains the genesis of our entire third-dimensional existence.

From the pyramids and mysteries of Egypt to the new race of Indigo children, Drunvalo presents the sacred geometries of the reality and the subtle energies that shape our world. We are led through a divinely inspired labyrinth of science and stories, logic and coincidence, on a path of remembering where we come from and the wonder and magic of who we are.

Finally, for the first time in print, Drunvalo shares the instructions for the Mer-Ka-Ba meditation, step-by-step techniques for the re-creation of the energy field of the evolved human, which is the key to ascension and the next dimensional world. If done from love, this ancient process of breathing prana opens up for us a world of tantalizing possibility in this dimension, from protective powers to the healing of oneself, of others, and even of the planet.

Phone: 928-526-1345 or 1-800-450-0985 • Fax: 923-714-1132

ॐ *Light Technology* PUBLISHING

BY DRUNVALO MELCHIZEDEK

LIVING IN THE HEART

Includes a CD with Heart Meditation by Drunvalo Melchizedek

"Long ago we humans used a form of communication and sensing that did not involve the brain in any way; rather, it came from a sacred place within our hearts. What good would it do to find this place again in a world where the greatest religion is science and the logic of the mind? Don't I know this world where emotions and feelings are second-class citizens? Yes, I do. But my teachers have asked me to remind you who you really are. You are more than human being, much more. For within your heart is a place, a sacred place where the world can literally be remade through conscious cocreation. If you give me permission, I will show you what has been shown to me."

- Beginning with the mind
- Seeing in the Darkness
- Learning from indigenous Tribes
- The Sacred Space of the Heart
- The Unity of Heaven and Earth
- Leaving the Mind and Entering the Heart
- The Sacred Space of the Heart Meditation
- The Mer-Ka-Ba and the Sacred Space of the Heart
- Conscious Cocreation from the Heart Connected to the Mind

$25⁰⁰ Softcover, 120 pp.
ISBN 978-1-891824-43-2

Drunvalo Melchizedek's life experience reads like an encyclopedia of breakthroughs in human endeavor. He studied physics and art at the University of California at Berkeley, but he feels that his most important education came after college. In the past 25 years, he has studied with over 70 teachers from all belief systems and religious understandings. For some time now, he has been bringing his vision to the world through the Flower of Life program and the Mer-Ka-Ba meditation. This teaching encompasses every area of human understanding, explores the development of mankind from ancient civilizations to the present time, and offers clarity regarding the world's state of consciousness and what is needed for a smooth and easy transition into the 21st century.

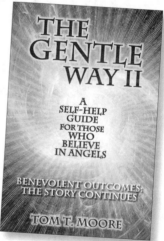